"Why do most Baptists today embrace Arminianism? In this valuable historical work, Austin Walker traces the decline of Calvinism among Baptists to the early nineteenth century, suggesting that this gradual doctrinal erosion was due, in great part, to the life, thought, and legacy of a largely forgotten minister named Robert Hall Jr., a social reformer, spellbinding orator, and preacher of questionable orthodoxy. Walker shows that Hall helped precipitate the abandonment of particular redemption as a central doctrine among the Particular Baptists by defending universal atonement and rejecting creeds, confessions, and theological systems (while inadvertently constructing his own). Walker's investigation is not only beneficial for Baptists seeking to reconnect with their Reformed roots, but it is also a sobering warning to the church against the perennial snare of separating piety from doctrinal orthodoxy."

JOEL R. BEEKE
Chancellor and Professor of Homiletics & Systematic Theology,
Puritan Reformed Theological Seminary

"Austin Walker has not hidden either his own love for and desire to promulgate the doctrines of the *Second London Confession* or his disappointment in Robert Hall Jr., for his coolness toward Calvinism and his conscientious nonconfessionalism. This posture, however, has not diminished the stringency or thoroughness of Walker's research, the objectivity of his presentation of the life and witness of Hall, or of his appreciation of Hall's infectious piety and magnetic oratory. This is an excellent example of the use of historical research in service of doctrinal argumentation. The reader will learn history, biography, doctrine, respectful polemical interaction, and be warned about lukewarm commitment to precise and coherent presentation of all the theological teachings of biblical revelation."

TOM J. NETTLES
Senior Professor of Historical Theology,
The Southern Baptist Theological Seminary

"Austin Walker's *The Theology of Robert Hall* is an important contribution to our understanding of Particular Baptist history. Relying on extensive primary sources, it demonstrates how one of the most gifted ministers of the early nineteenth century, Robert Hall, the son of a Particular Baptist stalwart, drifted away from the careful orthodoxy of his father and opened the door for loose doctrinal views in the following generations. It serves as a warning to those who treat orthodox confessional commitments as unimportant. Great gifts detached from theological faithfulness are a hindrance rather than a help to the church. Let us take heed."

JAMES M. RENIHAN
President, International Reformed Baptist Seminary

"This is a work that has long been needed. Although Robert Hall is largely forgotten his influence lives on and needs to be addressed. Austin Walker has produced a very important piece of work. Robert Hall possessed outstanding gifts as an orator as well as being a brilliant conversationist. It was claimed that he gave Baptists respectability among the literate classes of his day. A powerful advocate of causes that he chose to support, but a scathing critic of those he rejected, Hall rose to prominence at a time when English Dissenters were attracted by the preaching of experience but were isolating it from its doctrinal roots. Confessional Puritanism which had grown from the teachings of the Protestant Reformers had sought to bring congregations to an experiential knowledge of God grounded in sound doctrine. The churches served by Robert Hall identified as Particular Baptist and were the spiritual heirs of the men who published the First and Second London Baptist Confessions of Faith. Hall was dismissive of confessions of faith and of doctrinal precision. He was a significant promoter of the movement that weakened the distinction between Calvinistic and Arminian Baptists and in the end enervated Evangelical Christianity in the face of Apostacy. I welcome and strongly recommend Austin Walker's meticulously researched and powerfully written work."

ROBERT OLIVER
Retired Pastor and former History Teacher

"Austin Walker has produced a fine and much needed account of the theology of Robert Hall Jr., showing both the evangelical faithfulness and piety of the man, but also the doctrinal and homiletical emphases which, Austin cogently argues, contributed to the downgrade of Calvinistic distinctives among Baptists in the nineteenth century. Highly recommended for all interested in Baptist history and in the health and vigour of Baptist churches today."

ROBERT STRIVENS
Pastor, Bradford on Avon Baptist Church, UK

"Robert Hall Jr. is such an important figure of church history to study and know, both to learn the good to emulate as well as the warnings to heed. There is no better, more skilled guide to capture this balance than Austin Walker. *The Theology of Robert Hall Jr.* is carefully researched, pastoral in tone, and beautifully written and stands to be the definitive work on Hall's life, ministry, and impact. I commend this work to every pastor who seeks to be scripturally and pastorally faithful in such a way that will stand throughout the generations."

BRIAN CROFT
Executive Director, Practical Shepherding

"Robert Hall is a shadowy figure in the history of nonconformity in England during the late 18th century and early 19th century. He was a precociously brilliant child, the youngest of fourteen siblings. He grew in confidence and eloquence in his service of Christ. He wobbled in rejection of some basic New Testament doctrines ensuring that the Baptist churches would be confessionally a mixed group and so more vulnerable to the entry of German rationalism during the decades following his death. Three years after that decease Charles Haddon Spurgeon was born. This typically well-written and interesting book of Austin Walker gives the church all it needs to know about Hall. It is a profitable read and further advances our evaluation of the broad church of Baptist history not only in the U.K. but everywhere."

GEOFFREY THOMAS
Church Member at Amyand Park Chapel,
Twickenham, London

"Austin Walker's excellent, even compelling, study of Robert Hall Jr. is a cautionary tale for serious Christians, pastors above all, to take to heart. Reformed Christians too readily ignore the influence the intellectual and philosophical atmosphere of the times can have on orthodox Christian faith and practice. The righteous desire to preach the gospel relevantly into the times we live in, can only be too easily shaped by the times. Relevance becomes the compelling desideratum and truth becomes a casualty. Walker's careful analysis of Hall's drift from and then departure from foundational biblical truths concerning the work of Christ, truly is a cautionary tale. This is a most readable and engaging piece of historical-theological research. Most encouraging for myself, it is written by a pastor, not an academic. Walker's work exemplifies Martin Bucer's conviction (one that Calvin epitomized) that true theology is not theoretical, it is practical. The end of it is living, that is to live a godly life. I am delighted warmly and enthusiastically to commend Pastor Walker's book."

IAN HAMILTON
President and Professor of Church History,
Westminster Seminary, UK

"Few today know of the gifts and influence of the great Baptist preacher Robert Hall Jr., the man called 'the Prince of Preachers' before Charles Spurgeon was ever born. Eminent Baptist historian Austin Walker has resurrected the life and theology of Hall just as he did Keach in his *The Excellent Benjamin Keach*. Drawing heavily on Hall's personal correspondence and other primary sources, Walker has argued convincingly that Hall was one of several key influences in the decline of Calvinistic theology among Particular Baptists in England in the early nineteenth century. Surveying Hall's views on deep doctrines like justification and atonement, and practical doctrines like baptism and the Lord's supper, Walker has provided a delectable meal for anyone interested in Baptist history and theology. His work is well-researched, readable, and engaging—even gripping at points, and an impressive contribution to Baptist studies. It is also a very practical, pastoral, illustrative, and encouraging book for pastors today seeking to hold firm to the great doctrines of the 1689 *Second London Confession.*"

CODY MCNUTT
Pastor, First Baptist Church Covington, Georgia.

The Theology of Robert Hall Jr.

STUDIES IN BAPTIST HISTORY

THE THEOLOGY OF ROBERT HALL JR.

The Undermining of Calvinism among the English Particular Baptists

AUSTIN WALKER

The Theology of Robert Hall Jr.

Copyright © 2024 Austin Walker
All rights reserved. This book may not be reproduced, in whole or in part, without written permission from the publishers.

Studies in Baptist History, Volume 3

H&E Academic, West Lorne, Ontario
www.hesedandemet.com

Paperback ISBN 978-1-77484-139-6
eBook ISBN 978-1-77484-140-2

*Dedicated to
Mai, my wife,
my best friend and companion for more than fifty years*

CONTENTS

Foreword iii
   Michael A.G. Haykin
Preface v

1. Held in High Esteem 1
2. Early Theological Sentiments 11
3. Rise to Fame 33
4. Nothing Human Is Faultless 45
5. The Young Student in Bristol and Aberdeen 63
6. A Parting of the Ways 77
7. Breakdown and New Beginnings 93
8. The Erosion of Calvinistic Distinctives 113
9. Justification by Faith 133
10. Piety: The Basis for Friendship 149
10. Baptism and the Lord's Supper 167
12. Robert Hall in Perspective 177
13. Is History Being Repeated? 193
14. A Personal Testimony 201

Appendix 205
Bibliography 229
Acknowledgements 237
Index 241

Foreword

Michael A.G. Haykin

In his day, Robert Hall, Jr. was probably the second most famous Baptist in England. The most famous, of course, was William Carey the missionary pioneer. But Carey had left England for India in 1793, never to return. So, to speak literally, Hall was the most famous Baptist leader of his day who was resident in England. In fact, in today's terms he was a celebrity and renowned for his remarkable preaching abilities. He was probably also an extrovert who loved to regale audiences, large and small, with his wit and endless fund of stories. Given his family background—his father and namesake had published an influential work that provided resources for breaking the hold of High Calvinism on numerous sections of the Baptist denomination—and his circle of friends—men like Andrew Fuller, John Ryland Jr., and John Sutcliff—he was regarded widely as a trusted heir of the robust experiential Calvinism that had marked his father and his afore-mentioned friends.

But appearances can be deceiving. In certain key areas, which this monograph by Austin Walker carefully documents, Hall was not as trustworthy a guide as many of that era thought. That there was a declension during the course of the mid-nineteenth century from the theological position of men like Fuller has long been evident. But what were its roots and who were its protagonists? This careful examination by Walker reveals Hall's theology to have been a factor in this doctrinal decline. To be sure, not the only one (I think of the influence of a theological author like John Howard Hinton in this regard), but one that carried much weight because of Hall's fame. It is an examination worthy of close study and sobering to ponder. It should make all who love the theology of men like Fuller jealous for its careful transmission.

San Antonio, Texas,
November 17, 2023
(at the 75th annual meeting of the Evangelical Theological Society).

Preface

While Robert Hall Jr. (1764–1831) is today a relatively little-known figure in Baptist history, during his lifetime he was known as an eloquent orator and the "prince of preachers" during the first three decades of the nineteenth century. He was the youngest son of the manse. His father, Robert Hall Sr. (1728–1791), was pastor of Arnesby Baptist Church in Leicestershire. While the younger Hall preached from time to time in London, he never resided in the capital, but spent his ministerial life first in Bristol before moving to Cambridge and then in Leicester. Six years before his death he returned to Bristol.

He rose to fame and prominence during his days in Cambridge when he preached and published numerous sermons that caught the public's attention. While his sermons dealt largely with political issues of national interest, they nevertheless also displayed a decided religious foundation. Writing cogently and persuasively, Hall's mastery of the English language earned the admiration and esteem of his contemporaries. He was a gifted orator who could hold an audience spell bound. His fame was all the more remarkable because Robert Hall was a Dissenter and not part of the Establishment. Because Dissenters were still effectively second-class citizens during his lifetime, Hall was denied entrance into both Oxford and Cambridge University and completed his academic studies in Aberdeen. His sermons, both preached and published, helped repair and establish the reputation of Dissenters among both the Church of England and political leaders in Parliament at Westminster.

Robert Hall, Jr. grew up in Particular (that is, Calvinistic) Baptist circles. As a young man, Hall's father had studied at the

The Theology of Robert Hall Jr.

Bristol Academy, regarded as a bastion of Particular Baptist orthodoxy, under the leadership of Hugh Evans (1712–1781) and his son Caleb (1737–1791). In 1753, he was called to Arnesby Baptist Church, part of the Northamptonshire Baptist Association. As part of the that Association, Hall pastored alongside men of considerable standing like Andrew Fuller (1754–1815), John Collett Ryland (1723–1792) and his son John Ryland (1753–1825), John Sutcliff (1752–1814), Samuel Pearce (1766–1799), and William Carey (1761–1834).[1] In 1807 Hall became pastor of Carey's former congregation in Leicester.

It is often assumed that Robert Hall Jr. shared the same evangelical Calvinistic convictions as Andrew Fuller. Furthermore, it has often been suggested that the eventual merger of Particular and General Baptist churches of the New Connexion in 1891 owed more to the influence of Andrew Fuller than to any other individual. In his *History of the English Calvinistic Baptists*, Robert Oliver questions the assumptions about Hall's convictions and the significance of Fuller's influence in the merger. Oliver suggests Robert Hall as a far more likely candidate than Andrew Fuller. This book examines in detail the evidence that substantiates that claim.

The majority of studies about Robert Hall focus on his preaching and oratorical abilities. Very few have accurately traced and assessed Hall's doctrinal convictions. There is little doubt that Hall was evangelical, but was he Arminian or Calvinistic? In truth, it is a far from easy task to tease out his distinctive convictions because Hall rarely stated publicly any theological disagreements that he had with other men. Hall was, without doubt, a sober, serious-minded man who sought to walk before God with a good conscience. His life manifested a deep commitment to fervent

---

[1] See Michael A.G. Haykin, *One Heart and One Soul: John Sutcliff of Olney, His Friends and His Times* (Darlington: Evangelical Press, 1995).

Preface

prayer. In many respects, he was a committed evangelical and would satisfy David Bebbington's quadrilateral description of nineteenth-century evangelicalism.[2] Hall, however, was not a man who can be neatly fitted into any system of theology. Some of the critics of his own day pointed out that he was neither decidedly an Arminian nor clearly a Calvinist. Hall reflected the anti-confessional and anti-creedal spirit of his age and resisted the idea of adhering to any system of theology and any confession of faith. In this regard he differed from his seventeenth-century Baptist forefathers and from Bernard Foskett (1685-1758), the founder of Bristol Academy. Instead, Hall preferred to follow the paths trodden by Richard Baxter (1615-1691) and John Locke (1632-1704). While he claimed to reject all systems, he did of course develop his own system of theology and practice.

With one or two exceptions his views must be gleaned largely from his private conversations, his correspondence, and his biographers. It is often what Hall omitted to say in his sermons that proves to be important. Consequently, it is a difficult task to be definitive about some of Hall's beliefs and to decide when he first adopted or subsequently changed them. Without any doubt Hall's doctrinal convictions shifted during his lifetime. The last few months of 1804 and the early months of 1805 proved to be a major turning point in his life. At the age of forty while he was a pastor in Cambridge, Hall suffered two successive mental breakdowns. He became firmly persuaded that until that time he was an unconverted man, something many of his contemporaries and most of his biographers found very difficult to accept.

Hall was persuaded that the piety of a man was of greater significance than a man's doctrinal convictions. That outlook

---

[2] Bebbington argued that the four main characteristics of Evangelicalism are conversionism, activism, Biblicism, and crucicentrism. The accuracy of that portrayal of Evangelicalism has been questioned but insofar as it describes some of the characteristics of Hall, it is an accurate portrayal.

encouraged a denigration of the importance of biblical truth. When such an outlook is adopted, in the long term it proves disastrous for the health and well-being of the church of Christ; the nineteenth century bears eloquent testimony to this reality. To Hall's credit, however, he firmly resisted Socinianism, promoted principally by Joseph Priestley (1733–1804), hyper-Calvinism, Antinomianism, and Roman Catholicism. Regarding these matters, he and Fuller were of a similar mind.

Hall freely admitted though that he did not believe in particular redemption. Yet he still regarded himself and the churches in which he ministered as being Particular Baptist. He became a staunch advocate of open communion. As it was increasingly adopted among the Particular Baptists, the practice weakened the resolve of the churches to maintain their distinctive ecclesiology.

Hall was not alone in this undermining process among the Particular Baptists. Despite the profound influence of Andrew Fuller in the early eighteenth century, Calvinistic Baptist orthodoxy was already waning as a major force among English Baptists by the time of Hall's death in 1831, a few months short of his sixty-seventh birthday. The decline of a distinctive Calvinistic theology became widespread across the principal nonconformist denominations despite the efforts of titanic defenders of orthodoxy like Charles Haddon Spurgeon (1834–1892). Spurgeon spent much of his energy resisting that change and preached unashamedly all of the "five points" of Calvinism and republished the *Second London Baptist Confession of Faith* (1677/1689) to reassert historic Baptist orthodoxy. By the time of "the Downgrade," the issues were not simply those of Calvinism but the very fundamentals of the Christian faith. Russell S. Campbell has maintained that the decline of Calvinism was the single biggest change in theology since the days of the Reformation. Examining the ministries of three Baptists who succeeded Hall, Campbell has compellingly demonstrated the way Calvinism lost its place in many Particular Baptist

Preface

churches.³

The failure of Hall to promote a distinctive Calvinistic theology became a major factor in undermining the Calvinism of the English Particular Baptists. The principal purpose of this book is to demonstrate the ways in which Hall's influence and his sentiments significantly changed the face of English Particular Baptists, though it seems few recognised those changes at the time.

I am firmly persuaded that there are important lessons to learn from church history. This study of Hall is not written merely out of academic interest. I was a pastor in a Calvinistic Baptist Church for over forty years—a church that continues to hold to "the 1689," (*The Second London Baptist Confession of Faith*), persuaded that it states in summary fashion what we believe the Bible teaches. In writing this book, I seek to impress upon its readers, especially those who profess to be Calvinistic, the importance of maintaining Calvinistic distinctives and to outline ways in which that can and must be accomplished.

---

³ Russell S. Campbell, "The decline of Calvinism among British Baptists in the nineteenth century: a study of three ministers" (DPhil thesis, University of Oxford, 2000). Referred to and quoted from with permission of the Modern History Faculty Board, University of Oxford.

1
Held in High Esteem

When Robert Hall died in Bristol, aged sixty-six, on February 21, 1831, tributes were paid in a variety of places. Accounts of his funeral were widely reported in the weeks following his death. In addition, obituaries appeared in London and in various provincial newspapers. An extensive number of funeral sermons were preached and published and obituaries printed in numerous Christian periodicals. Typical among the obituaries was one by the Rev. William Newlands, published in *The Manchester Times*. Speaking of Hall's preaching Newlands explained:

> But for the feebleness of his voice, he would have been, as a preacher, without a rival in Europe. His discourses were premeditated, but not written before delivery. His habits of thinking being philosophical, his stores from reading and reflection being immense, his imagination active and vigorous, his conceptions rapid, and his command of the powers and graces of language astonishingly great, he delighted and instructed his audience by the continuity and logical precision of his arrangement, the magnitude of his conceptions, and the overpowering brilliancy and resistless charms of his eloquence. In the commencement of his discourse, his first efforts were scarcely perceptible, but as he proceeded he increased in splendour, scattering the darkness in his progress, till his subject was enveloped with a flame of light—his utterance at the same time becoming rapid and impassioned.[1]

---

[1] William Newlands, "Character of the Rev. Robert Hall, A.M." *The Manchester Times* (March 10, 1831): 510 (www.britishnewspaperarchive.co.uk/viewer/print/bl/0000083/18310319/013/0006).

The Theology of Robert Hall Jr.

This kind of tribute was not unusual. Since his early days as a preacher, first in Broadmead, Bristol (1785-1790) and then at St. Andrew's Street Baptist Chapel, Cambridge (1791-1806), Hall's brilliant qualities—his eloquence, in particular—had been recognised by all who knew him and especially by those who heard him. The years Hall later spent in Leicester (1807-1824) at Harvey Lane Chapel, scene of William Carey's ministry before his departure for the Indian sub-continent, and his final years in Broadmead, Bristol (1824-1831) served to enhance Hall's reputation as an evangelical preacher of rare distinction.

Preaching in the Broadmead Meeting House, two weeks after the death of Hall, Joseph Hughes (1769-1833), a hearer of Hall's preaching and one of his former pupils, referred to his mentor as "one of the phenomena of the age."[2] James Phillipo Mursell (1799-1885), Hall's successor in Leicester, preaching on the same day as Hughes, portrayed Hall as "the Colossus of the race."[3] Thomas Swann (1795-1857), pastor of Cannon Street Baptist Church in Birmingham, echoed the opinions of William Newlands and many others, when he spoke of "his princely intellect."[4] Later on during the same sermon he related:

> His voice was not powerful ... but his appearance was majestic and imposing, his eye was full of benignity and intelligence, his pronunciation was distinct and clear, and when absorbed in his subject, his eloquence was mellifluous and

---

[2] Joseph Hughes, *The Believer's Prospect and Preparation described in a discourse delivered In Broadmead Meeting House, Bristol on Sunday morning, March 6, 1831, on the occasion of the death of Robert Hall, A.M.* (London: Holdsworth and Ball, 1831), 46.

[3] J.P. Mursell, *A sermon occasioned by the death of the Rev. Robert Hall, A.M., preached at Harvey Lane, Leicester, March 6, 1831 by J. P. Mursell* (London: Hamilton, Adam and Co., n.d.), 38.

[4] Thomas Swann, *A sermon occasioned by the death of the Rev. Robert Hall, A.M. of Bristol. Preached In Birmingham, on the Lord's Day, March 6, 1831, by Thomas Swann, Pastor of the Baptist Church, Cannon Street* (London: Hamilton, Adam and Co., 1831), 5.

fascinating. Its power was irresistible. It made its way directly to the heart, filling the hearer with alternate emotions of penitence and hope, of humility and admiration. One rare excellence strikingly appeared in him. He possessed the happy art, so difficult of attainment, of losing sight of himself in his subject. ... On every attentive hearer he produced a deep impression; but it was the impression of truth in the forms of the purest eloquence.[5]

The author of the obituary in *The Evangelical Magazine and Missionary Herald* also extolled the virtues of Hall, but perhaps more judiciously than other writers, identified the source of his genius and eloquence. In his opinion it was not a matter of mere human giftedness and ability but the result of God's work of grace and power evident in Hall's life. The obituary concluded, "But his piety, his ardent piety, which led him to walk with God and which baptised his ministry in the Spirit of Christ, was his noblest, his highest distinction."[6]

Robert Hall was a Baptist, a Particular or Calvinistic Baptist, but he was held in great esteem by the Christian world of his day. General Baptists, Anglicans, Congregationalists, indeed anyone with evangelical sympathies held him in high regard. William Newlands regarded him as equal to any preacher in America. The majority of Hall's contemporaries agreed that he was the prince of evangelical preachers in the first three decades of the nineteenth century.

Hall's works and biographies

Immediately following Hall's death, his sermons, letters, book reviews, published works, and various other pieces were collected and published under the oversight of Olinthus Gregory (1774–

---

[5] Swann, *Death of the Rev. Robert Hall*, 21.
[6] Anonymous, "Obituary for Robert Hall," *The Evangelical Magazine and Missionary Chronicle* 9 (1831): 159.

1841). Gregory, a fellow Baptist and professor of Mathematics at the Royal Military Academy, had first met Hall in Cambridge in 1797, and the two had maintained a close friendship for over thirty years. At the request of Hall's widow, Eliza, and the family, a few friends undertook to superintend a complete edition of his works. On Saturday, May 2, 1831, a notice appeared in the *Leicester Chronicle* for the "most interesting letters and tolerably full notes of sermons" of Hall to be sent to either John Foster or Dr. Olinthus Gregory, together with an assurance that they would be returned.[7]

In 1831, Gregory published the first volume. Once completed, twelve editions of these works followed in the ensuing 35 years. With the editorial help of Joseph Belcher (1794-1859), an English Baptist who had emigrated to the United States in the 1840s, Hall's works were also published in New York. The American edition contained several works that were not found in the British edition, including Hall's *Expository Discourses on the Epistle of Paul to the Philippians*. Both in America and Britain these volumes were entitled *The Works of Robert Hall, A.M.*[8]

While the collected works contain several memoirs of Hall, including one by Gregory, the most valuable portrait was drawn by Baptist minister and author, John Webster Morris (1763-1836).[9] Morris had known Hall for forty-eight years and regarded him as

---

[7] *Leicester Chronicle* (Saturday 2 May, 1831) (www.britishnewspaperarchive.co.uk/viewer/print/bl/0000172/18310402/018/0001).

[8] Gregory, ed., *Works*, 6 vols., will be referred to as Gregory, *Works*, with volume and page number in subsequent references. Gregory and Belcher, eds., *Works*, 4 vols., will be referred to as Gregory and Belcher, *Works*, in subsequent references. These volumes form the principal sources used in this book to assess the life and ministry of Robert Hall, together with other sermonic material and letters that have only come to light in more recent years.

[9] J.W. Morris, *Biographical Recollections of the Rev. Robert Hall, A.M.* (First published 1833, reprinted in India, New Delhi: Isha Books, 2013).

Held in High Esteem

a man of "extraordinary talents and piety."[10] Since Hall left no diaries and consistently refused to provide information about himself while he was alive, Morris believed that "my own memoranda and recollections might furnish a variety of facts and circumstances that could not well be known to others."[11] Hall himself had not been happy at the prospect of a memoir of his life being written but conceded that if such a memoir was ever produced then Morris would be his preferred author.[12] The American edition of Hall's works also included the personal reflections of John Greene, who first became acquainted with Hall in 1795 and kept in contact with him all his life.[13]

The publication of Hall's works certainly enhanced his reputation during the middle years of the nineteenth century. Causes that Hall advocated, like open communion, continued to be debated among Particular Baptist churches throughout this era. Largely through Hall's influence, open communion became increasingly the practice of English Baptists. The memories of his preaching proved to be indelible in the minds of those who heard him. Writing some fifty years later, Frederick Trestrail (1803-1890), Secretary of the Baptist Missionary Society, recalled the profound impression made on him as a student at the Bristol Academy the first time he heard Hall preach:

> But what most struck me was the *style* of the discourse. I had never before heard such *spoken* English. The remarkable combination of elegance and vigour, the perfect mastery of the most felicitous language, the exquisite blending of argument with metaphor, the marvellous rapidity of utterance, yet withal distinct and clear, gradually acquiring greater

---

[10] Morris, *Biographical Recollections*, viii.
[11] Morris, *Biographical Recollections*, iv.
[12] Morris, *Biographical Recollections*, v.
[13] John Greene, "Reminiscences of the Rev. Robert Hall" in Gregory and Belcher, *Works*, 4:11.

depth of tone, ultimately glowing into intense fervour and vehemence, pervaded too, by a pathos that "ought to have been irresistible," produced an excitement which I had never known before. The subject of the sermon was, "The Ministry of the Gospel, a Divine Appointment," producing an indelible impression that it was to the noblest end to which the human faculties, however lofty, could be devoted.[14]

Something of the respect that he was still garnering late in the nineteenth century can be seen in the fact that on November 2, 1871 a magnificent statue of Robert Hall was unveiled in De Montfort Square, Leicester. Carved from Sicilian marble and placed on a Cornish granite pedestal, it was the work of the sculptor John Binnie Philip (1824–1875). It depicts Hall preaching "in full flow" with his right hand raised, his face animated and alive, and his left hand holding down by his side a Bible with one finger inserted in its pages. *The Leicester Chronicle and Leicestershire Mercury United*, reported that the statue had been "raised in honour of one of the greatest men ever identified with this town," where Hall had ministered from 1807 until 1824.[15] At the time of the statue's unveiling, J.P. Mursell, Hall's successor in the church in Leicester, was then in his early seventies. He delivered a short speech to the assembled crowd that included the mayor, local members of political parties, and representatives from various denominations including Churchmen and Dissenters, together with surviving family members and others, who like Mursell could still recall Hall's ministry. Mursell spoke warmly of his predecessor as a remarkable man, unrivalled, who "stood alone in unassumed but solitary

---

[14] Frederick Trestrail, *Reminiscences of College Life in Bristol during the ministry of Rev. Robert Hall, A.M.* (London: E. Marlborough and Co., 1879), 32.

[15] *The Leicester Chronicle and Leicestershire Mercury United* (November 4, 1871).

grandeur."[16] Quoting Samuel Parr (1747-1825), the vicar of Warwick, Mursell said that Hall, "like Bishop Taylor, had the eloquence of an orator, the fancy of a poet, the acuteness of a schoolman, the profundity of a philosopher, and the piety of a saint."[17] He also recalled William Jay (1769-1853) of Bath laying a wreath on Hall's coffin and quoting Zechariah 11:2: "Howl, fir tree, the cedar has fallen."

Mursell's tribute also heralded Hall's concern for the poor. While in Leicester he had taken up the cause of Leicester textile workers who had become destitute due to frequent unemployment. He then briefly commended his catholic spirit and his lack of bigotry. He cited Hall's friendship with the Rev. Thomas Robinson (1774-1813), the evangelical vicar of St. Mary's, Leicester, as a prime example in this regard. Mursell concluded his tribute to Hall by saying that Hall was unashamedly a Nonconformist and part of that distinguished group of men in the Midlands that included Andrew Fuller and Thomas Toller, both of Kettering.

How was Hall being remembered forty years or so after his death? Both Mursell and Trestrail place great emphasis on his elegant and animated eloquence. In his address Hall's successor pointed out that many went out of their way to hear Hall preach in Leicester, among them peers, jurists, and men of the highest distinction. Mursell also stressed the popularity of his published discourses such as *Modern Infidelity*, *The Duties Proper to the Present Crisis*, *The Death of Princess Charlotte*, and his funeral oration for John Ryland. He also predicted that Hall's writings would be read and studied long after monuments of marble and granite had turned to dust. Mursell praised his critical writings for their judgment, their imagination, which were often laced with wit and

---

[16] *The Leicester Chronicle and Leicestershire Mercury United* (November 4, 1871).
[17] *The Leicester Chronicle and Leicestershire Mercury United* (November 4, 1871).

sarcasm.

However, Mursell's assessment has proven to be too optimistic. While the statue of Hall remains, "now Hall's sermons lie unopened on library shelves."[18] This is in marked contrast to the sermons of Charles Haddon Spurgeon, whose sermons were read by thousands during his lifetime and continue to be published and read to the present day. Nearly two hundred years after his death, very few have any idea who Robert Hall was. People who pass by his statue in Leicester know little or nothing about him, and his writings lie forgotten.

The impact of Robert Hall, his preaching, his writings and not least his life, lasted certainly to the end of the nineteenth century. Gregory argued that once Hall was settled in Leicester and until his death in Bristol in 1831, "Hall became much more known and revered as the correct and eloquent interpreter of the Christian faith, the intrepid asserter of the infinite superiority to all human systems of philosophy and morals."[19] Yet, despite his influence, Hall's fundamental convictions escaped rigorous examination. In 1947, Baptist historian A.C. Underwood noted that while there were a number of small biographies and memoirs which had appeared during the last one hundred and fifty years dealing with his published works, nearly all of them focused on Hall the preacher. Few dealt with his doctrine, his convictions, and practice.[20] Only in the last half century have Hall's beliefs and practices been more

---

[18] A.C. Underwood, *A History of the English Baptists* (London: The Baptist Union, 1947), 169.

[19] Gregory, *Works*, 1:102.

[20] The main biographies besides that of J.W. Morris are Gregory, "A brief memoir of the Rev. Robert Hall, A.M." Gregory, *Works*, 1:1-157; John Greene, *Reminiscences*, 1832 (also in Gregory and Belcher, *Works*, 4:11-100); E. Paxton Hood, *Robert Hall*, 1881; Graham W. Hughes, *Robert Hall* (London: The Carey Press, 1943). A briefer version by Hughes subsequently appeared by the same author, *Robert Hall 1764-1831* (London: Independent Press, 1961).

thoroughly examined.[21]

No true estimate of Robert Hall's legacy can be made until his "sentiments" (used in Hall's day to describe a man's beliefs) are identified and assessed. Hall's convictions, especially in the early years of his public ministry in Bristol and Cambridge, were not those of the evangelical Calvinism expressed by his father, Robert Hall, Sr., nor that of Andrew Fuller and the other men who were key players in the Northamptonshire Association of Particular Baptist Churches. By examining Hall's sentiments it will be possible to assess how he changed the face of English Particular Baptists, though it seems few recognised those changes at the time.

---

[21] Angus Hamilton MacLeod, "The Life and Teaching of Robert Hall, 1764-1831" (Master of Letters thesis, University of Durham, 1957); Cody Heath McNutt, "The Ministry of Robert Hall Jr.: The Preacher as Theological Exemplar and Cultural Celebrity" (PhD Dissertation, Southern Baptist Theological Seminary, 2012).

2
Early Theological Sentiments

Robert Hall was born in Arnesby, Leicestershire in 1764, the fourteenth child of the Particular Baptist preacher Robert Hall, Sr., and his wife Jane. Only six children survived, and young Robert barely. He was a precocious child who, with the help of his nurse, learned to read from the graveyard inscriptions behind his father's chapel. Once at school in nearby Wigston, he proved to be too bright for his teacher. He composed hymns, and had his brothers and sisters hear him preach. He knew Latin and Greek, and was reading Bishop Butler and Jonathan Edwards before he was ten years old. As part of his education he was sent to Northampton, to the school of John Collett Ryland.

He professed faith in Christ and was baptised at the age of fourteen and then when he was sixteen he was set aside by the church to preach, studying at the Bristol Baptist Academy. He went to university in Aberdeen where he graduated MA in 1785. He was not fond of Aberdeen and in a letter to his father spoke against "frosty spirited Calvinists" he heard preach there.[1]

Having graduated from Aberdeen he returned to Bristol Baptist Academy to assist the principal, Caleb Evans. Hall became the classics tutor and remained there until the middle of 1791. In the Broadmead church (the Academy was attached to the church) he was at first popular as a preacher but then suspicions arose as to his orthodoxy, which will be considered later. His friendship with Evans crumbled and a spirit of alienation set in. Hall resigned, writing a letter to the church to explain his views.

At some point prior to his Cambridge ministry it is reasonable

---

[1] W[arren], R.[obert] H.[all], *The Hall Family* (Bristol: J.W. Arrowsmith, 1910), 48.

to assume that Hall's sentiments with regard to the extent of the atonement underwent a change. When, and to what extent he changed, is difficult to discover. Morris was of the opinion that during the early part of his ministry (he was referring to the period 1781-1787), Hall was strongly inclined to Arminianism because he was attracted by its practical tendency. This included his years at Aberdeen. His experience of Calvinistic ministers there may well have led to his becoming disenchanted with Calvinism, something we shall examine in a later chapter. Morris went on to note: "the Arminianism of Mr. Hall however was never complete: it was chiefly confined to two or three points, confessedly of some importance, but did not extend to an entire adoption of the system."[2] Morris does not identify those two or three points but it is possible that he was referring to Hall's rejection of the eternal electing love of God and particular redemption. However, Morris did go on to describe some of Hall's struggles with other Calvinistic doctrines. He was reluctant to affirm his agreement to them:

> He demurred to the doctrine of original sin, and invincible depravity; to the final perseverance of all the regenerate, while with Baxter he admitted the perseverance of all the elect. Though not an advocate of universal grace, he maintained the influence of the Holy Spirit was indefinitely promised, and might be obtained in answer to the prayers of the unregenerate, if offered up with fervour and sincerity. At the same time, he more than doubted the distinct personality of the Holy Spirit, and rather maintained the duality of the divine nature, than cordially embraced the trinitarian hypothesis.[3]

---

[2] J.W. Morris, *Biographical Recollections of the Rev. Robert Hall, A.M.* (1833 reprint; India, New Delhi: Isha Books, 2013), 57.

[3] Morris, *Biographical Recollections*, 57-58. By referring to the doctrine of the Trinity as a hypothesis perhaps raises questions about the strength of Morris' doctrinal convictions.

Early Theological Sentiments

Such observations as these raise serious questions about his orthodoxy, issues that were to be raised again before he left Bristol for Cambridge. They also force us to ask again whether at this point Hall was genuinely converted to Christ. What is clear is that Hall was struggling to determine what he really did believe. It is reasonable to conclude that his sentiments became more settled after 1804. He expressed them when he dedicated himself to God.

Concerns for Hall by those closest to him
During these earlier years his father, Andrew Fuller, and John Ryland expressed concerns over his apparent theological trajectory. Fuller seems not to have conveyed his thoughts to Hall but Ryland and his father certainly did.

On one occasion Fuller heard the twenty-year old Hall preach from "He that increaseth knowledge, increaseth sorrow" (Ecc. 1:18). He heard him with some apprehension, judging by his comments in his diary for May 7, 1784: "Felt very solemn in hearing some parts! The Lord keep that young man!"[4] The same prayerful concern was evident just over a year later, on June 14, 1785, Fuller recorded in his diary, "Taken up with the company of Mr. Robert Hall, jun.: feel much pain for his churches in this country, keep him in the path of truth and righteousness."[5] Fuller was ten years older than Hall and seemed acutely aware of the danger of pride for such a young man, thinking that he could easily wander into the serious errors of Socinianism and thus cease to be useful to the church of Christ. In a similar vein John Ryland had been moved to admiration for many things in Hall's preaching, but there were other things "that made me fear for him. O that the

---

[4] Andrew Fuller, *The Complete Works of the Rev. Andrew Fuller*, 3 vols. (Harrisonburg, VA: Sprinkle Publications, 1988), 1:35.
[5] Fuller, *Complete Works*, 1:48.

The Theology of Robert Hall Jr.

Lord may keep him humble, and make him prudent."[6] Hughes suggests that Fuller and others had identified a missing evangelical note in Hall's preaching. He was too preoccupied with the intellectual side of the gospel and was thus in danger of falling away into error.[7]

Hall's father had also spoken openly to his son on several occasions about his concerns. In March 1791 his father died, and that led Hall to earnestly investigate "the truth as well as the value of those high and sacred principles, from which his eminent piety and admirable consistency flowed.[8] Gregory recorded: "he [Hall] called to mind, too, several occasions on which his father, partly by the force of reason, partly by that of tender expostulation, had exhorted him to abandon the vague and dangerous speculations to which he was prone."[9]

These concerns were not groundless. One of the vague and dangerous speculations that concerned Fuller, for example, was Hall's materialism: "that the nature of man is simple and uniform; that the thinking powers and faculties are the result of a certain organization of matter; and that after death he ceases to be conscious until the resurrection."[10] Such a view was far from biblical orthodoxy and in 1790 he told the church in Broadmead that he had held this view for a long time but never made it the subject of his preaching. It was a "mere metaphysical speculation."[11] In his youth he was inclined to indulge free and daring speculations, but only expressed them in private conversation. Gregory

---

[6] Gregory, *Works*, 1:23.
[7] Graham W. Hughes, *Robert Hall* (London: The Carey Press, 1943), 37.
[8] Gregory, *Works*, 1:36.
[9] Gregory, *Works*, 1:36.
[10] Hughes, *Robert Hall*, 39. Hall's materialism was also a factor in his departure from Bristol, following his disagreement with Caleb Evans and the Broadmead church in 1790.
[11] Gregory, *Works*, 1:32.

Early Theological Sentiments

affirmed Hall's testimony, "he never promulgated direct and positive error from the pulpit."[12] Hall was struggling with a number of key theological issues but on the occasion of his father's death those urgent exhortations eventually bore fruit. Hall renounced his materialism, often declaring that he had "buried [it] in his father's grave."[13]

John Ryland wrote to Hall with both urgency and tenderness in 1785 and again in 1786. He was very distressed and expressed both his fears and his grief to his younger friend. Hall had been in Birmingham and had made some unwise statements in speaking about Joseph Priestley, the leading Socinian preacher of his day. Hall had upset his former friends in the city by apparently saying he could not condemn Priestley. Ryland was under no illusions about the dangers of Priestley's errors and was persuaded there was not enough genuine Christianity in Priestley, or any Socinian, to carry him to heaven. He did not want his friend to follow the same dangerous track. Hall replied graciously, thankful that Ryland had taken the time to write to him about so important a matter. He explained himself to Ryland, denying the use of the precise language that had been imputed to him, admitting at the same time he had not been wise in what he said, and went on to tell Ryland that he utterly rejected the suggestion that he had any sympathies for Socinian doctrines. He wrote,

> You seem to suspect, I am far gone in Socinianism; but in this, my dear friend, give me leave to say, you are utterly mistaken. Since I first began to reflect, I do not recollect a time when I was less inclined to Socinianism than at present. I can truly say, it would remove from me all my salvation and all my desire.[14]

---

[12] Gregory, *Works*, 1:22.
[13] Gregory, *Works*, 1:36.
[14] Gregory, *Works*, 1:25. The correspondence between Ryland and Hall and some of Ryland's comments on hearing Hall preach are found in Gregory, *Works*, 1:22-26.

The Theology of Robert Hall Jr.

The suspicions that he was still sympathetic to Socinianism lingered, however, and questions were raised by some in the church in Broadmead prior to his departure from Bristol. Hall rejected the Socinian heresies associated with the person and work of Christ, which asserted that there was no such thing as a substitutionary sacrifice made by Christ, the Son of God. However, until his first occasion of intense soul-searching in 1799 when he was brought close to death by a dangerous fever, he was not a Trinitarian. Morris had already identified his doubts as to the personality of the Holy Spirit.

Gregory's *Memoir* contains a reference by an unnamed, elderly gentleman who in the late 1790s came to know Hall well enough to be able to say that during this period, "his creed was imperfect, wanting the personality of the Holy Spirit, and wavering between the terrors of Calvin and the plausibilities of Baxter."[15] How long had he doubted the personality of the Holy Spirit? Did anyone else know about it sufficiently for them to do something about it? It was not a part of Christian orthodoxy at all. Hall had been solemnly set apart to the Christian ministry and now he was a pastor, preaching and living among the Particular Baptists. At some key points he displayed serious shortcomings in his orthodoxy. Apart from his father and John Ryland did those who knew about his speculations made in private, and his denial of the personality of the Spirit say and do nothing because he never made his views public? We do not know the answer to that question.

Hall faced a crisis in 1799. The threat of dying drove him to draw support from the doctrine of the cross. Feeling very uncertain about some matters he began to investigate them more carefully. Up to that point he had believed in the necessity of divine

---

[15] Gregory, *Works*, 1:45. Foster also has a footnote regarding Hall's rejection of the personality of the Holy Spirit. See Gregory and Belcher, *Works*, 3:110

Early Theological Sentiments

power in order to change a person's character and to enable them to continue to live in that way. Yet, as we have seen, he doubted the doctrine of the distinct personality of the Holy Spirit. He spoke only of "the influence of the Spirit of God."[16] He thought of the Spirit as an impersonal force issuing from God, rather than being really and truly God. Gregory records that when Hall withdrew privately in prayer he found himself in a deeply devotional state of mind. At such times he wanted to adopt a full Trinitarian theology. By 1800 it appears he was affirming the personality of the Holy Spirit in his public doctrinal statements.

Hall's emerging sentiments
Some speculations he had embraced were a temporary feature. Once he had reflected carefully on them he was prepared to renounce such views as his materialism. However, there were some doctrinal sentiments that were to become fixed points in Hall's theology. He was losing some key Calvinistic distinctives. From the ground that produced the sturdy kind of Calvinists like his father and Andrew Fuller a different plant was growing. It had all the marks of a hybrid. Hall was seeking to combine two different theologies. It had many characteristics that were evangelical, but it was not fully Calvinistic.

It is strange that some of Hall's biographers appear to have completely overlooked the clear evidence concerning the doctrinal differences between father and son. Morris and Gregory, the older biographers, had recognized them. More recently, Graham Hughes, for example, explicitly states that Hall's doctrines were those of his father and of Andrew Fuller—that is moderate Calvinism.[17] However, Hall set out in a different direction, trying to steer a middle course between what he regarded as the rigidity of

---

[16] Gregory, *Works*, 1:62.
[17] Hughes, *Robert Hall*, 144.

The Theology of Robert Hall Jr.

Calvinism and the laxity of Arminianism, but avoiding at all costs hyper-Calvinism. Both his father and Fuller had been caught up in the latter but firmly rejected it when they came to see that it was a serious and pernicious error. However, to identify Hall's theology at this point in his life as being the same as that of his father and Fuller overlooks Gregory's and Morris' portrayal of his convictions and also Hall's own assertions elsewhere. In fact he made significant changes and reached some very different conclusions.

Hall's Calvinistic background

As a son Robert Hall had a high regard for his father. Whatever differences might exist between them theologically, Hall would have thought himself to be very deficient in Christian duty if he dishonoured his father. He wrote in the preface to his father's *Help to Zion's Travellers*,

> I shall ever esteem it one of the greatest favours an indulgent Providence has conferred upon me, to have possessed such a father, whom in all the essential features of character it will be my humble ambition to imitate, though conscious it must ever be—*Haud passibus aequis*.[18]

Attention has already been drawn to the fact that Hall regarded his father as being more doctrinal in his preaching and more attached to Calvinism than he was. He had sat under his father's teaching both in public and in private. A very capable child, he had read Jonathan Edwards's *Freedom of the Will* and *The Religious Affections* by the time he was nine, books he had borrowed from his father's library. Following five years as a day scholar in Wigston his father arranged for his son to be educated in the school of John

---

[18] "An Introductory Preface by the Late Robert Hall, A.M. of Bristol, Eng.," in Robert Hall [Senior], *Help to Zion's Travellers* (London: 1814), xxiv. Hall originally wrote this preface for the third edition in 1824. The Latin phrase at the end of the quotation may be translated "not with equal steps."

Early Theological Sentiments

Collett Ryland in Northampton from 1775 until 1777. Ryland was also a member of the Northamptonshire Association and the pastor of the Particular Baptist Church in Northampton from 1759 until 1781. Under Ryland the young student would have been exposed to similar theological convictions that he had experienced in his home.

In 1789 Carey became pastor of the Harvey Lane Baptist Church in Leicester. Robert Hall became pastor at the same church in 1807, fifteen years after Carey had left for India. Carey's congregation in Harvey Lane maintained a clear Calvinistic summary of what they believed as a church. The Church Book for Harvey Lane contains two versions of this confessional summary, one dated 1760 and the second, in a slightly different format dated 1791.[19]

Harvey Lane was a Particular Baptist church. The doctrinal statement affirmed the fundamentals of the Christian faith such as the Scriptures as the only rule of faith and practice, the doctrine of the Trinity, an orthodox statement concerning the person and work of Christ. It also made explicit their Calvinistic distinctives: God's eternal election; the fall of the human race in Adam, including the imputation of Adam's sin and the corruption of Adam's offspring; eternal redemption was special and particular, for the elect alone; justification was only by the imputed righteousness of Christ; regeneration, conversion, sanctification and faith was the result of the efficacious and irresistible grace of God; and, the perseverance of the saints. Those same doctrines, expressed in almost identical language, were also the basis of faith for the Northamptonshire Association. They had been drawn up at the first meeting in Kettering in May, 1765.[20]

---

[19] Church Book for Harvey Lane Particular Baptist Church, Leicester, Leicester Records Office, Wigston, Leicester, I, 1760-1794. Catalogued as 24D71.

[20] T.S.H. Elwyn, *The Northamptonshire Baptist Association: A Short History* (London: The Carey Kingsgate Press Limited, 1964), 12.

The Theology of Robert Hall Jr.

Hall's sentiments also differed from older Particular Baptists like Abraham Booth (1734-1806), as expressed in his famous book, *The Reign of Grace*, for instance. Booth had come to Calvinistic convictions and parted company with his former Arminian sympathies. Seventeenth-century Particular Baptists like Hanserd Knollys (1599-1691), William Kiffen (1616-1701) and Benjamin Keach (1660-1704) would not have agreed with all of the sentiments of Robert Hall, nor would John Bunyan (1628-1688) have been of the same mind. Evangelical Calvinism had marked those who became known as Particular Baptists ever since they emerged out of Separatist Independency in the late 1630s and 1640s. They traced their heritage back to the Reformation of the sixteenth century, persuaded that they were continuing the work begun by men like Martin Luther and John Calvin.

Distinctive evangelical Calvinism also characterised Bristol Academy where Hall went first, as a student (1778-1781), and then, following his graduation from Aberdeen, he assumed responsibilities as a tutor in classics (1785-1790). Caleb Evans, and his father Hugh Evans were firm Calvinists, as was the man originally responsible for the Academy, Bernard Foskett. In 1734 Foskett, together with his associate Hugh Evans, affirmed the doctrinal position of the re-established Western Association, by adopting the third edition (1699) of *The Second London Confession of Faith* as their standard. It had followed over a decade of dispute, but the effect was the exclusion of anyone who was a General Baptist, or who had Antinomian, hyper-Calvinistic or Arian sympathies.[21] In 1720 Foskett had assumed two responsibilities in Bristol. He became an assistant in the Broadmead church and also a tutor in the Academy. The Academy was stamped with the same commitment to evangelical Calvinism.

---

[21] Roger Hayden, *Continuity and Change: Evangelical Calvinism among eighteenth-century Baptist ministers trained at Bristol Academy, 1690-1771* (Chipping Norton, Oxfordshire: Nigel Lynn Publishing and Marketing Ltd., 2006), 30-36.

Early Theological Sentiments

Benjamin Beddome (1718-1795) had been a student at Bristol for a short while, under the tutelage of Foskett. In 1752 Beddome published *A Scriptural Exposition of the Baptist Catechism by Way of Question and Answer*. He had taken *Keach's Catechism* and made additions to it from *A Scripture-catechism* by Matthew Henry (1662-1714). A second edition was published in 1776 which was widely used at the Bristol Baptist Academy. Beddome was a man of Calvinistic convictions firmly in the school of his Puritan and Particular Baptist forefathers. Haykin notes, "Due to its use at this seminary one can expect that it would have had a significant influence on many of the congregations that graduates of this seminary went on to pastor."[22]

Sadly, it would appear that Hall was at least one exception to that expectation. John Ryland, who succeeded Caleb Evans at Bristol in 1791, was also known for his commitment to evangelical Calvinism. Hall was to succeed Ryland in Bristol on his death in 1824. However, as shall be seen, Hall did not share all of the Calvinistic convictions of these men associated with Bristol Baptist Academy.

Robert Hall Sr. and *Help to Zion's Travellers*

If we are to properly understand Hall's departures from the Calvinism of his father and appreciate their significance it is necessary to consider his father's Calvinism more fully.

Robert Hall Sr. was the pastor of a church in Arnesby, a few miles south of Leicester, from 1753 until his death in 1791. He was a key figure in the Northamptonshire Association of Particular Baptist Churches.[23] The first meeting was held in Kettering on

---

[22] Michael A. G. Haykin, "Glory to the Three Eternal," in Haykin, Paul, and Yoo, eds., *Glory to the Three* Eternal (Eugene, OR: Pickwick Publications, 2019), 43.

[23] The Association was not confined to churches in the county of Northamptonshire but included churches from Leicestershire, Nottinghamshire, Buckinghamshire and even Hertfordshire.

The Theology of Robert Hall Jr.

May 14–15, 1765 and the older Hall was present with eleven others who signed the circular letter that was sent out to the churches. The association was decidedly Calvinistic in its theology as expressed in the opening paragraph of the first and subsequent circular Letters.

> The ministers and messengers of the several Baptist churches met in an Association at Kettering, May 14 and 15, 1765, maintaining the great doctrines of three equal persons in the Godhead, eternal and personal election, the original guilt and universal depravity of mankind, particular redemption, free justification by the imputed righteousness of Christ, efficacious grace in regeneration, and the final perseverance of the saints to glory; professing also Independency respecting Church government.[24]

Hall remained a member of the Association all his life, a period covering two and half decades. He died the year before the Particular Baptist Missionary Society for the Propagation of the Gospel among the Heathen was formed in 1792. He made significant contributions to the life of the Association and emerged as a father figure among the younger members. Olin C. Robison concluded that "Hall's greatest contribution was as much his personality as in his writings, for he was held in high esteem by the rising generation of young men who were to spread from the Midlands throughout the country as Baptist leaders."[25] These younger men included Andrew Fuller, John Sutcliff, John Ryland, Jr., and in particular William Carey. Both Robison and Nathan Finn also speak of the beneficial influence that the father Robert Hall had

---

[24] Elwyn, *Northamptonshire Baptist Association*, 12.
[25] Olin C. Robison, "The Particular Baptists in England, 1760–1820," (PhD dissertation, Oxford University, 1963), 59.

Early Theological Sentiments

on his son.[26] However, neither of them explains that the younger Hall did not share all his father's Calvinistic convictions, nor those of Fuller, Sutcliff, Ryland, and Carey. Clearly many aspects of Hall's own convictions he heard first-hand from his father's lips. He reached his own conclusions at certain points and rejected, for example, both his father's understanding of election and the doctrine of particular redemption. At what point he did this is very difficult to determine and we will need to return to this matter to consider Hall's conclusions in more detail.

The older Hall's most significant contribution to the Association was the publication in 1781 of *Help to Zion's Travellers*. Originating as a sermon at the 1779 meeting of the Association, and based on Isaiah 57:14, "And shall say, Cast ye up, cast ye up, prepare the way, take up the stumblingblock out of the way of my people," it was then expanded following the encouragement of Fuller, Sutcliff and Ryland. Hall had originally accepted hyper-Calvinistic views but had changed his mind once he had read *Freedom of the Will* by Jonathan Edwards and two sermons by another New England divine, John Smalley, lent to him by Ryland.[27] Hall became persuaded that the free offer of the gospel was not inconsistent with either personal election or particular redemption. These new convictions were clearly stated in *Help to Zion's Travellers* which became the expression of the evangelical Calvinism that characterised Fuller, Sutcliff, Carey and the churches in the Northamptonshire Association. Those convictions also were the foundation for the subsequent concert of prayer for revival, and the sending out of Carey and others to the foreign mission field.

The elder Hall's theology was decidedly Calvinistic in its

---

[26] Robison, "The Particular Baptists in England," 59, and Nathan Finn, *Help to Zion's Travellers* (Dallas, TX/Memphis, TN: Borderstone Press LLC., 2011), xxxix.

[27] In *Freedom of the Will* Edwards distinguished between a person's moral ability and natural ability to respond to the gospel by believing on Christ. This same distinction was to be crucial in Fuller's *magnum opus*, *The Gospel Worthy of all Acceptation*.

understanding of divine election, human sinfulness, particular redemption, regeneration by the Holy Spirit, union with Christ and adoption. However, it should be pointed out that by writing *Help to Zion's Travellers* Hall's aim was not so much to fully state and explain these doctrines as to remove stumbling blocks to Christian understanding and growth, whether they were doctrinal, experimental or practical difficulties. He had come to reject hyper-Calvinism (as had Andrew Fuller) that denied the duty of repentance and faith. He believed that the inability of the unregenerate was of a moral nature, which was due to the corruption of the will, and therefore provided no basis for excuse. In his son's opinion, his father's book and Fuller's treatise, *The Gospel Worthy of All Acceptation*, had a decided effect on the sentiments of the denomination to which he belonged. Hall was positive in stating the benefits of both books: they aided in

> emancipating them [the denomination] from the fetters of prejudice, and giving free scope to the publication of the gospel ... the excresences of Calvinism have been cut off; — the points of defence have been diminished in number, and better fortified; — truth has shone forth with brighter lustre; — and the ministry of the gospel has been rendered more simple, more practical and more efficacious.[28]

His father's work dealt with some of the hot issues of the day such as Socinianism, Antinomianism and the "modern question."[29] Hall had embraced a warm and systematic evangelical Calvinism. He firmly resisted hyper-Calvinistic arguments that sinners are not obliged to do the very thing which they were

---

[28] "An Introductory Preface by the Late Robert Hall," xxii.

[29] "The modern question" concerned whether it was the duty of all men who heard the gospel of Christ to repent and believe in Christ. This duty was denied by hyper-Calvinism. Both Hall and Fuller affirmed that it was the duty of all who heard the gospel to repent and believe.

Early Theological Sentiments

unable to do, namely to repent of their sins and to trust in Christ for their salvation. He argued that the call to repent of sin is universal, even if the divine call to repent and believe is only effectual in the elect. It was here that he made use of the distinction of Edwards between the natural and moral ability of man. In Hall's view, it was not inconsistent for God to decree that salvation was for the elect and yet for God to command the gospel to be preached and Christ offered to everyone because every man has the responsibility and natural ability to believe. However, moral inability, overcome only by the powerful working of the Spirit of God in regeneration, means that the non-elect do not believe. Haykin has concluded that "Hall clearly intends that the preaching of the gospel should not be restricted in any way, but that men everywhere and in every condition be exhorted to repent and believe on Christ for salvation."[30]

Hall's adoption of universal atonement

What impact did Hall's book and the Calvinistic convictions it set out have on his son? He came to understand the message of the gospel in a different way. He re-shaped the Calvinism of his father. Perhaps consciously following the path of Richard Baxter whom he greatly admired, he became persuaded of universal atonement. He made it the basis for the free offer of the gospel and suggested that election was something which took place after the atonement, at the point of the application of the work of Christ in a person's life. Precisely when he reached this conclusion remains unknown but it must have been early on in his life.

In 1810, after he had left Cambridge for Leicester, he wrote to a Rev. W. Bennett. He expressly rejected particular redemption and affirmed that he believed Christ died for all men:

---

[30] Michael A.G. Haykin, "The Elder Robert Hall and his *Help to Zion's Travellers*," *The Banner of Truth*, No. 343, (April 1992): 19.

I am fully persuaded it is a doctrine of scripture, and that it forms the only consistent basis of unlimited invitations. I think the most enlightened Calvinists are too reserved on this head; and that their refusal to declare, with the concurrent testimony of Scripture, that Christ died for all men, tends to confirm the prejudices of methodists, and others, against election and special grace.[31]

He continued to hold these convictions about universal atonement throughout his life. In three or four conversations with Robert Balmer (1787-1844) of Berwick-on-Tweed between 1819 and 1823 Hall affirmed to Balmer: "I believe firmly in 'general redemption:' and I often preach it ... I consider the fact that 'Christ died for all men' as the only basis that can support the universal offer of the Gospel."[32] Balmer asked for further clarification and for advice on what he should read. Hall directed him to Joseph Bellamy's (1719-1790) *True Religion Delineated*.[33] This was first published in America in 1750 and then in England in 1803. Following the lead given by Bellamy, Hall spoke to Balmer at considerable length on those passages which speak of "the world," "all," and "every man" and showed the absurdity of some of the arguments advocated by those who held to particular redemption.

---

[31] Gregory, *Works*, 4:394.

[32] Gregory, *Works*, 1:160. Robert Balmer (1787-1844) was a member of the United Secession Church and had become the minister in Berwick-upon-Tweed in 1814. He was in correspondence with Hall and also visited him in Leicester when he travelled to London.

See www.electricscotland.com/history/other/balmer_robert.htm. It would appear that he was questioning the extent of the atonement and wrote to Hall for counsel. Balmer was to play a significant role in the atonement controversy in Scotland that erupted in the years 1841-1845, a decade after Hall's death. Balmer was one of two professors (the other was John Brown) who believed that there was a divinely-intended universal reference to Christ's atonement, "teaching which went beyond the traditional Lombardian sufficiency-efficiency commonplace," Ian Hamilton, *The Erosion of Calvinistic Orthodoxy* (Fearn, Ross-shire: Mentor Imprint, 2010), 45. Balmer reached conclusions that appear very similar to those held by Hall.

[33] Gregory, *Works*, 1:161.

Early Theological Sentiments

He was especially vigorous against those who maintained that "the world" in John 3:16 meant the elect. He also underlined that, in his view, general redemption fitted in with other parts of the Christian system especially, the universal offers and invitations of the gospel.

By adopting general redemption Hall was taking a significant step away from his Particular Baptist heritage and identifying with similar convictions held by the New Connexion Baptists associated with Dan Taylor (1738-1816). Taylor, in turn, had been influenced by Wesley. He had joined the Methodists in 1761 but, reacting to Wesley's authoritarianism he became a General Baptist, while maintaining some of Wesley's Arminian sentiments.[34]

Abandoning particular redemption Hall adopted a truncated Calvinism. By actively promoting general atonement Hall was inadvertently making the eventual union of the Particular Baptists with the General Baptists much easier. Thus we have one clear indication that it was not so much Andrew Fuller, but rather Robert Hall, who paved the way for that union. Hall did not mention Fuller, but he had reached a different conclusion from that of Fuller.

Andrew Fuller consistently defended particular redemption. In the late 1780s he was opposing the arguments for universal atonement maintained by Dan Taylor. Fuller explained seven reasons why he was persuaded that the Scriptures taught particular redemption. For example, he pointed out that "in proportion as he extends the objects for whom Christ died beyond those who are actually saved, he diminishes the *efficacy* of his death, and renders

---

[34] See Richard T. Pollard, *Dan Taylor (1738-1816), Baptist Leader and Pioneering Evangelical*, Monographs in Baptist History, vol. 9 (Eugene, OR: Pickwick Publications, 2018), especially 105-140, where Pollard details Taylor's novel advocacy of general redemption.

all the promises concerning it of no account."[35] He went on also to reason that "if the doctrine of eternal, personal, and unconditional *election* be a truth, that of a special design in the death of Christ must necessarily follow." He followed his argument with a number of scripture passages that "appeared to him to be conclusive."[36] In Fuller's second edition of *The Gospel Worthy of All Acceptation* (1801) he argued that there was no contradiction between particular redemption and the universal obligation on those who hear the gospel to believe, or in a universal invitation being addressed to them. For Hall this was a contradiction he was not able to accept. Fuller was firmly persuaded that:

> If God, through the death of his Son, have promised salvation to all who comply with the gospel; and if there be no natural impossibility as to a compliance, nor any obstruction but that which arises from aversion of heart; exhortations and invitations to believe and be saved are consistent; and our duty as preachers of the gospel, is to administer them, without any more regard to particular redemption than to election; both being secret things, which belong to the Lord our God, and which, however they be a rule to him, are none to us.[37]

There was nothing new about the doctrine of universal atonement. It had been considered by the famous Synod of Dort in 1617–1618 and found by them to be wanting. Rejecting the teaching of Arminius and the Remonstrant party the Synod had come down firmly on the side of particular redemption. A century before Hall, Richard Baxter had promoted the doctrine of universal atonement. In the eighteenth century John Wesley also became a firm advocate.

---

[35] Fuller, *Complete Works*, 2:490.
[36] Fuller, *Complete Works*, 2:493.
[37] Fuller, *Complete Works*, 2:374.

Early Theological Sentiments

The convictions of Fuller regarding particular redemption were in keeping with the Particular Baptist confessions of faith published in 1644, in 1646, as well as in 1689. By adopting the notion that Christ died for all men Hall was also making a crucial departure from the Calvinism of his father, the Northamptonshire Association group of churches and also from the Calvinism of the two veteran Particular Baptist pastors in London, Samuel Stennett (1728-1795) and Abraham Booth. In 1791, in connection with the Particular Baptist Fund, the latter two pastors had clearly defined the boundaries of the Particular Baptist denomination for a new edition of the rules and orders of the Fund. They affirmed that:

> Particular Baptists are those ... solemnly immersed by water upon a personal confession of faith ... who profess the doctrines of three persons in the Godhead—eternal and personal election—original sin—particular redemption ... and the final perseverance of the Saints according to The Confession of Faith that was published in London by the Calvinistic Baptists in ... 1689.[38]

A statement like this, with its reference to the 1689 *Second London Baptist Confession of Faith*, was actually quite rare in the late eighteenth century even though particular redemption remained one of the hallmarks of the denomination. However, universal atonement had taken root in Hall's thinking and became a key point in his preaching of the gospel. During his years in Cambridge, prior to his breakdown, Hall read widely. According to Gregory, much as he loved classical literature, he gave himself to reading:

---

[38] Particular Baptist Fund Minutes, vol. 5, 1774-1802, entry for March 1, 1791. Held in the Angus Library, Regent's Park College, Oxford.

The Theology of Robert Hall Jr.

the early Christian fathers, the fathers of the Reformation, the theological writers, both puritan and Episcopalian, of the seventeenth century, the most valuable authors on all similar topics down to the present time, including the most esteemed French preachers, were perused with his characteristic avidity: what was most valuable in them became fixed in his unusually retentive memory.[39]

Such reading demonstrates that Hall did not develop his own theological convictions out of ignorance. He was very well-acquainted with theological matters, both Calvinistic and Arminian. His theology was the result of wide reading and of informed reasoning. Nevertheless, his conclusions proved to be a significant departure from some of the fundamentals of evangelical Calvinism.

The overall picture now becomes clearer. The ten years between 1799 and 1809 proved to be something of a watershed in his life. In 1799, at the age of thirty-five he had been in danger of dying as a result of a serious fever. In 1809, when he was forty-five, he re-dedicated himself to God. He was newly settled in Leicester, having escaped what he regarded as the depressing and monotonous countryside around Cambridge. Two mental breakdowns in 1804 and 1805 (the significance of which will be covered in a later chapter) were to prove pivotal in his spiritual development as a man and a minister of the gospel.

In the opinion of John Webster Morris the impact of the events of 1804 and 1805 on Hall's life were considerable. He described the effects thus:

> A deeper tone of piety was diffused into his devotional exercises, increasing zeal and fervour marked his pulpit

---

[39] Gregory, *Works*, 1:52.

Early Theological Sentiments

addresses, while a growing attachment to the distinguishing doctrines of the gospel, and a more vivid sense of their importance, were becoming more and more evident.[40]

By the time he re-dedicated himself to God in 1809 it appears he had finally resolved many of his theological doubts and had reached more settled doctrinal convictions. It had taken a long time. The fact remains, however, that some of the conclusions he reached were largely those formulated by him prior to what he regarded as a profound spiritual experience that permanently changed him.

---

[40] Morris, *Biographical Reflections*, 180.

3
Rise to Fame

Any evaluation of Hall must also take into consideration the fact that he became something of an evangelical celebrity. Hall was first thrust into the public arena of political debate by the issue of the slave trade. He had returned to Bristol in 1785 as a pastor and as a tutor in classics at the Baptist Academy. A port city, second only to London in importance in the eighteenth century, Bristol had been involved in slave trading since 1698. Between 1698 and 1807, over two thousand ships left Bristol for Africa to exchange goods for enslaved Africans and take them to the Caribbean.[1] Bristol had thus grown very wealthy as a result of the transatlantic slave trade.

In 1787–1788 the issue became a matter of intense debate among the citizens of Bristol. Angered by the glaring inhumanity and injustice of the slave trade, Hall wrote to the *Bristol Gazette* in February of 1788 to express moral outrage over Bristol's participation in the slave trade.[2] Timothy Whelan remarks that Hall's letters "reveal much about the emergent rhetorical precision of Hall's discourse and his affinity with political issues that would mark him as one of the most powerful voices of Dissent in England for the next forty years."[3] Whelan continues,

> Even in these brief letters we see his biting satiric wit, his keen insight into the heart of the issue, and his brilliant rhetorical skills honed so carefully in those endless debates

---

[1] Bristol City Council, Port Cities, Bristol, http://discoveringbristol.org.uk/slavery/routes/bristol-to-africa/bristol-trading-port/slave-trade-entry.

[2] Timothy Whelan, "Robert Hall and the Bristol Slave-Trade Debate of 1787-1788," *The Baptist Quarterly* 38, No. 5 (2000): 212–224.

[3] Whelan, "Robert Hall," 217.

with James Mackintosh at Aberdeen. The writer who would shine so brightly in two of the most pointed political pamphlets of the 1790s, *Christianity Consistent with a Love of Freedom* (1791) and *An Apology for the Freedom of the Press and for General Liberty* (1793), is evident in these early attempts to mould public opinion about the inhumanity and inconsistency of the slave trade. Any attempt at defending the practice of "turning the human species into a commodity, and trafficking in blood" was to Hall "an insult on the use of language and the art of reasoning," for "the principles of humanity are immutably the same" for all people in all times and places, and the most basic of those principles is the right to liberty.[4]

While Hall was fundamentally a humble man who had no pretensions to grandeur, these letters mark the beginning of Hall's rise to public prominence. Everyone in Bristol was agreed that Robert Hall was a powerful preacher, whose rhetorical, oratorical and conversational brilliance outshone anyone else they knew. Hall began to emerge as a "cultural celebrity."[5]

He came face to face with controversy in Cambridge after his very first sermon. The Baptist Church meeting in St. Andrew's Street was known for its radical political views as well as for showing sympathy for heterodox Socinian views. Hall provoked a strong reaction from some members of the congregation. Having accepted the call to go to Cambridge, he preached a sermon from Hebrews 9:13 on the atonement which was evangelical in its thrust. Immediately after the sermon a man approached him in

---

[4] Whelan, "Robert Hall," 217–218.

[5] Cody Heath McNutt, "The Ministry of Robert Hall Jr.: The Preacher as Theological Exemplar and Cultural Celebrity," (PhD Dissertation, Southern Baptist Theological Seminary, 2012), 185. Gregory used similar language in his memoir, noting this period of Hall's as one in which he "acquired a signal extension of celebrity." Hall, *Works*, 1:73.

Rise to Fame

protest, "Mr. Hall, this preaching won't do for us: it will only suit a congregation of old women."[6] Hall ably rebuffed the comment. Subsequently, the man, with three or four other men of influence, together with about twenty others from the congregation, withdrew themselves from the church and secured Rev. William Frend, an "avowed Socinian," as their pastor.[7]

It would have been very difficult for Hall to maintain silence in Cambridge. As a university town noted for its contending parties, controversy was part of the culture. Published sermons and pamphlets expressing different opinions about the issues of the day were all too frequent. Thus, it is no surprise that Hall entered into the fray with the publication of two sermons. *Christianity Consistent with a Love of Freedom*, published in 1791, followed in 1793 by *Apology for the Freedom of the Press and for General Liberty*, drew wider public attention. Hall was dealing with matters that were not only being avidly discussed in Cambridge intellectual circles but also with matters of national interest.

Gregory was persuaded that there was some evidence to suggest that Hall had been pressured into publishing his opinions and that he was acting against his better judgment.[8] He was not yet thirty years of age.

He was an advocate of freedom and the natural rights of man. Hall was persuaded that good government should promote the happiness of those who were governed. He abhorred those European governments which were based on oppression and trampled on the natural rights of man. He also vigorously opposed those who objected to Dissenters being engaged in politics and he was impatient with those who promoted passive obedience and non-resistance to such governments. He believed in freedom of religion. At first he had supported the French Revolution of 1789 and

---

[6] Gregory, *Works*, 1:37.
[7] Gregory, *Works*, 1:37.
[8] Gregory, *Works*, 1:40.

the principles of liberty held in the early days of the Revolution. However, the situation in France turned increasingly sour. Instead of religious freedom, there was renewed oppression and increasing atheism, and Hall abandoned the path of liberty at all costs. This, however, was not before he had published his *Apology* in which he set out the fundamental principles of liberty and dissent, and concluded with a call for Parliamentary reform in England.

He had written in haste and he thought the publications to be of little value. The public thought otherwise. Three editions of the *Apology* were published in six months, and other editions appeared without the author's knowledge and consent. He was quoted in periodicals and his arguments were held by many to be conclusive. His views were also circulated widely in the thirteen former colonies of America, where political freedom from Great Britain had been declared on July 4, 1776. Hall had expressed his opinions as a reformer and as a dissenter and now his name became well-known. He regretted his decision to advocate his views in public but the damage had been done. He did not draw back from his principles but realising that the controversy threatened to damage his ministry he decided that he would not publicly pursue the issues.

However, hopes that the French Revolution would promote religious freedom and moral virtue were dashed. Hall was not alone in concluding that far from promoting the good he so much desired there was an increasing tendency towards atheism which he dreaded. Neither was it limited to France. In the years 1795-1799 debating rooms opened in London where atheism was actively being promoted. By 1800 Hall felt compelled to speak out against this trend. This time his sermon, *Modern Infidelity Considered*, was much more carefully prepared. It was the deliberate result of seven weeks of intermittent considered reflection on the dangerous links between radical politics and atheism. Hall was

Rise to Fame

moving away from the pursuit of liberty at all costs. This would bring him into conflict with some key individuals in Cambridge, including Benjamin Flower (1755-1829), a member of his congregation and editor of the *Cambridge Intelligencer*, and Henry Crabb Robinson (1775-1867).[9]

Hall's sermon was based on Ephesians 2:12, "Without God in the World" and it was preached first in October 1800 in Bristol and then later in Cambridge. It is not necessary for us to consider the details of the sermon but rather to assess its effects on Hall's fame. Its key theme was the destructive power and influence of atheism and its inevitable propensity to promote a life without standards of truth and morality. It was arguably one of Hall's greatest sermons. He left his hearers and readers in no doubt as to the effects of atheism,

> Settle it therefore in your minds, as a maxim never to be effaced nor forgotten, that atheism is an inhuman, bloody, ferocious system, equally hostile to every useful restraint and to every virtuous affection; that leaving nothing above us to excite aware, nor round us to awaken tenderness, it wages war with heaven and with earth: its first object to dethrone God, its next to destroy man.[10]

He certainly did not anticipate its success and the resulting increase of his reputation as a profound thinker and as an elegant writer. Not everyone agreed with Hall and he was widely criticised. Nevertheless, the overall response was positive. Many members of Cambridge University agreed with Hall and his congregation grew as a consequence. Sir James Mackintosh (1765-

---

[9] For more details of this conflict see the following: McNutt, "The Ministry of Robert Hall," 206-208, and Timothy Whelan, "'I have confessed myself a devil': Crabb Robinson's Confrontation with Robert Hall 1798-1800," *Charles Lamb Bulletin*, New Series 121 (2003): 2-25.

[10] Gregory, *Works*, 2:37.

1832), who had been a close friend of Hall since the time they were students in Aberdeen, praised his sermon in *The Monthly Review*, a significant literary journal. Similar approval was expressed in *The Quarterly Review*, which had been very critical of Hall's *Apology*, and in the *Edinburgh Review*, which had been very dismissive of William Carey's labours. It was subsequently published both in America in 1801 and even in France in 1836, five years after Hall's death.

Hall's fame had now spread far beyond Baptist circles. What he had to say was of interest to the public at large. He had expressed the mood of the nation following disillusionment with the French Revolution. Bearing in mind that Hall was a Baptist Dissenter and that much of the academic world of Cambridge, in particular, was wedded to the Church of England, his acceptance and his rise to fame was a remarkable event. Prejudice, suspicion, and discrimination against Dissenters were still widespread at the turn of the century.[11] Hall had won many of them over by his elegant language and his carefully argued sermon. Men like the bishop of London, Beilby Porteous, and politicians such as Henry Brougham, William Pitt, and Lord Hardwicke joined in the praise.[12]

Hall's national reputation was enhanced even further by two sermons he preached in successive years in response to the threat of a Napoleonic invasion. From 1793 the French had repeatedly triumphed in Europe, such that England became isolated and seemingly faced imminent defeat. It was only navy commanders,

---

[11] Hall had gained his A.M. degree from the University of Aberdeen and had been schooled in Bristol, one of the Dissenting Academies. Admission of non-Anglicans to Cambridge and Oxford was only granted in the 1850s. For details see David L. Wykes, www.qmulreligionandliterature.co.uk/research/the-dissenting-academies-project/legislation.

[12] MacLeod gives an extensive review of the sermon and includes a list of those who were positive in their response. See Angus Hamilton MacLeod, "The Life and Teaching of Robert Hall, (1764-1831)" (Master of Letters thesis, University of Durham, 1957), 53–156.

Rise to Fame

like Horatio Nelson who inflicted a decisive defeat on the French navy at the battle of the Nile in 1798, who kept Napoleon at bay. The war dragged on until a temporary lull in hostilities was secured by the Peace of Amiens in March 1802.

A national day of thanksgiving was appointed for June 1, 1802. On that same day Hall preached the annual sermon for the Benevolent Society in Cambridge, entitled *Reflections on War*. His text was Psalm 46:8-9, "Come, behold the works of the Lord, what desolations he hath made in the earth. He maketh wars to cease unto the end of the earth; he breaketh the bow, and cutteth the spear in sunder; he burneth the chariot in the fire." In his sermon he echoed the spirit of national thankfulness and joy in having been delivered from the horrors of war. The published sermon was well received, not least because of its patriotic fervour. MacLeod is of the opinion that *Reflections on War* was "a clear example of Hall's genius for saying the right thing at the right time and in the right way, and was justly applauded."[13]

However, in less than twelve months the national crisis returned. In May 1803 there was a dispute over one of the articles of the peace treaty and the threat of a Napoleonic invasion became very real. The patriotic spirit of Hall was kindled once again. On October 19, 1803, a national day of prayer and fasting, Hall was visiting Bristol and preached from Jeremiah 8:6, "I hearkened and heard, but they spake not aright: no man repented him of his wickedness, saying, What have I done? every one turned to his course, as the horse rusheth into the battle."

The sermon was entitled *The Sentiments Proper to the Present Crisis*. Hall called on his congregation to adopt a different response from that of Israel who had excluded God from their considerations. Rather he called for conduct that God would approve, namely repentance for failing to acknowledge the hand of God; for

---

[13] MacLeod, "The Life and Teaching," 162.

placing false confidence in human ability to secure safety; for unwarranted criticism of government measures; for the false assumption that victory would be granted to England because of supposed superior virtues; and finally for simply blaming the crisis on the corruptions of the age. Instead Hall was specific, detailing the signs of what he termed "national degeneracy." He was persuaded that there was a departure from Christian truth, especially in receiving the doctrines of the fall and redemption, a decline in personal Christian piety, and a neglect of the Lord's Day and public worship. He called for repentance and a return to God.

Once preached, the printed sermon was widely circulated and was published in various periodicals. It met with widespread approval. Few criticised it, Benjamin Flower being the most notable exception. In a time of real crisis it caught the imagination of the nation and served to reinforce Hall's growing reputation as a preacher who had the capacities to speak with dignity, clarity, power and feeling appropriate to the occasion. Gregory, who by this time knew Hall well, was of the opinion that:

> This sermon, perhaps, excited more general admiration that any of the author's former productions; on account of its masterly exposure of prevailing errors, its original and philosophical defence of some momentous truths, and its remarkable appropriateness to the exigencies of the crisis. The last ten pages were thought by many (and by Mr. Pitt, among the number) to be fully equal in genuine eloquence to any passage of the same length that can be selected from either ancient or modern orators.[14]

Gregory had also found evidence of careful thought regarding the contents of *The Sentiments Proper to the Present Crisis*. He

---

[14] Gregory, *Works*, 1:83.

Rise to Fame

discovered a manuscript of Hall's containing outline notes of sermons preached between 1801 and 1803. There he also discovered "the first rude sketch of this valuable sermon."[15] Hall had clearly learned from his earlier mistakes of rushing into print. As a result of his experiences in connection with the publication of *Christianity Consistent with a Love of Freedom* and *Apology for the Freedom of the Press and for General Liberty*, he seemingly developed an aversion to public controversy. This may partly explain Hall's reluctance to speak publicly about the ways in which some of his own doctrinal views differed from those of his Particular Baptist forefathers.

Hall was now in his late thirties and during his time in Cambridge he had emerged as a recognized spokesman on issues of national interest and concern. When he left Bristol he was relatively unknown but by moving to Cambridge and addressing the issues of freedom, the dangers of atheism in the aftermath of the French Revolution, and then facing the crises presented by the threat of Napoleon, Hall became well-known and respected in many quarters outside Baptist circles. His name was now found on the lips of politicians and in the pages of key literary periodicals of the day. His opinions and convictions had been aired among a very wide audience, something that Hall scarcely conceived possible.

He did not seek that fame. However, what was unusual about Hall's fame was the fact that he was a Christian minister, *and* a dissenting minister, rather than a politician or a literary figure. He had risen to prominence in the academic town of Cambridge, a bastion of the establishment and in particular of Anglicanism. McNutt suggests that "the rise of Romanticism created an environment that catered to the rise of celebrities. Literary figures and politicians rose to fame, but it was a relatively new phenomenon

---

[15] Gregory, *Works*, 1:83–84.

for such a cult of celebrity to surround religious figures."[16] He cites George Whitefield as the first of such celebrities followed by men like Rowland Hill, Thomas Chalmers and Edward Irving. He claims that Hall became for "the Baptists their first true cultural celebrity."[17]

However, any rise to further fame was rudely interrupted. His voice was silenced and his pen laid to one side. His health deteriorated so much so that he suffered a period of depression and a mental breakdown between 1804 and 1806. On his recovery he was able to resume his labour but it would no longer be in Cambridge. On March 4, 1806, Hall ended his fourteen years in Cambridge. Giving himself time to recover, he gradually began to preach again. In 1807 he accepted the invitation of Carey's former congregation and moved to Leicester.

While there he was thrust into the public eye once again in 1817. His status as a "celebrity" was further cemented by a published sermon on Jeremiah 15:9 which he preached in Leicester, following the death of Princess Charlotte. The sudden death of the young princess had a direct bearing on the succession to the throne and immediately became a matter of national interest and concern. Gregory described it as a "stately, ornate, and solemn," sermon that "strikingly accords with the event which called it forth."[18] He also drew attention to the fact that Hall's sermon, "by universal acknowledgement, bore the palm above all the numerous valuable sermons that were then published."[19] It went through a number of editions during his lifetime because of its popularity. Gregory opined that the very nature of Hall's sermon was "calculated to make a permanent and salutary impression,"

---

[16] McNutt, "The Ministry of Robert Hall," 253.
[17] McNutt, "The Ministry of Robert Hall," 253.
[18] Gregory, *Works*, 1:106.
[19] Gregory, *Works*, 1:106.

and as such "this sermon probably stands unrivalled."[20]

The previous year, 1816, Hall had suffered from spasms in the chest and his life was in danger once again. Having reached the age of fifty-two he reflected on his previous ministerial labours. Thinking of the manner in which he had fulfilled his ministry he confessed a sense of shame and confusion of face because of his sins, and took refuge and comfort from the atonement of Christ Jesus his Lord and Saviour, and exclaimed, "I never in all my life saw so fully into the necessity of justification by faith alone, as I do at this moment. I should perish without it —utterly perish."[21] As to the subject matter of his ministry he had this to say,

> So far as I know I have not shunned to declare the whole counsel of God; no preconceived system, no fear of man, no influence of example, has biased my judgment, or fettered me in any respect; my aim has been to include the whole system of revelation, and to exclude from it everything extraneous.[22]

There can be no question about Hall's Christian sincerity. His fame was a far-distant concern. His reflections expressed his thought-out convictions. Like any good man he was persuaded they were right. But there were some significant changes. Those changes represented a departure from evangelical Calvinism and what most of his contemporary Particular Baptists, particularly those among whom he had been nurtured, believed was the content of the whole counsel of God.

Once in Leicester it became clear that all kinds of people had acquired a very definite perception of Robert Hall. As a result of

---

[20] Gregory, *Works*, 1:107.
[21] J.W. Morris, *Biographical Reflections of the Rev. Robert Hall, A.M.* (1833 reprint; India, New Delhi: Isha Books, 2013), 311.
[22] Morris, *Biographical Reflections*, 311.

some widely circulated sermons that had attracted national attention and his reputation as an exceptionally gifted preacher he was popular and famous. He gained the ear of many people and became the revered, "correct and eloquent interpreter of the Christian faith."[23]

When he died in 1831 there were an unusual number of funeral sermons preached and published. He was widely admired as a distinguished minister of Christ, not only by those with whom he was more intimately connected but also by the church of Christ at large. The foundations of that admiration were in place by the time Hall was in his early forties. In this regard his fourteen years in Cambridge proved to be crucial.

---

[23] Gregory, *Works*, 1:102.

4
Nothing Human Is Faultless

Historians of English Dissent have recorded the remarkable expansion of evangelicalism during the late eighteenth and nineteenth centuries.[1] Baptists, Methodists, and Congregationalists especially mushroomed in growth. For example, one such historian indicates that "in the Baptist communion as a whole the numbers of churches grew from 652 in 1801 to 2,789 fifty years later."[2] Much of the impetus for this growth had come from the Great Awakening and the Methodist movement.

That growth was also reflected in Particular Baptist circles by the formation of the Northamptonshire Association, first planned in 1764, the year in which Robert Hall was born. Two circular letters for the association from his pen were to be published in 1809 and again in 1813.[3] The Association was characterised by evangelical Calvinism and was led by a remarkable group of like-minded leaders. Robert Hall's father was the elder statesman, together with John Ryland, Andrew Fuller, John Sutcliff, and William Carey. This expansion was not limited to England. William Carey left home for India in 1792. He was sent by The Particular Baptist Society for the Propagation of the Gospel among the Heathen, which had emerged out of the Association. This Society and the Baptist Home Mission, formed in 1797, owed much to the Association and its leaders.

---

[1] Ian Sellers, *Nineteenth-Century Nonconformity* (London: Edward Arnold Ltd., 1977); D.W. Bebbington, *Evangelicalism in Modern Britain: A History from the 1730s to the 1980s* (London: Unwin Hyman Ltd., 1989); Michael R. Watts, *The Dissenters, II: The expansion of evangelical nonconformity, 1791-1859* (Oxford: Clarendon Press, 1995).

[2] Sellers, *Nineteenth-Century Nonconformity*, 2.

[3] Gregory, *Works*, 1:397-436. These are entitled, "On the Work of the Holy Spirit" and "On Hearing the Word."

The Theology of Robert Hall Jr.

In his mid-fifties the younger Robert Hall, an enthusiastic supporter of Carey and his initiatives in taking the gospel to the nations, was preaching in Bristol in 1820 and he observed, "During the latter part of the last century, and down to the present time, there has been a manifest increase and improvement of Christian instruction. Evangelical truth has been administered in a purity and abundance to which preceding ages bear no proportion."[4] The growth of evangelicalism during this period is beyond dispute. However, there was a significant theological transformation taking place at the same time. That change, which was not confined to Particular Baptists, has sometimes been overlooked. Hall spoke of "the purity" of evangelical truth. However, the "evangelical truth" that he believed and preached was not the same as the evangelical Calvinism of his father or that of Andrew Fuller. Significant differences in Hall's theology were emerging. Furthermore, it was not the same Calvinism that was expressed in the Puritan era in the *Second London Baptist Confession of Faith*, and prior to that in *The Westminster Confession of Faith* of the Presbyterians and *The Savoy Declaration* of the Congregationalists.

The decline of Calvinism

In a fairly recent Oxford University thesis Russell Campbell maintains that the decline of Calvinism in the nineteenth century was the most significant theological change since the Reformation. He traced some of those changes in the lives of three Baptists who succeeded Robert Hall—men who moved further away from historic biblical Christianity than Hall did.[5] He also maintained, at

---

[4] "The Signs of the Times," Gregory, *Works*, 4:188.

[5] Russell S. Campbell, "The decline of Calvinism among British Baptists in the nineteenth century: a study of three ministers" (D.Phil. thesis, University of Oxford, 2000). Campbell says very little about Robert Hall and concentrates on William Brock (1807-1875), Charles Stanford (1823-1886), and William Landels (1823-1899).

the time of writing in 2000, that no one has traced out the decline of Calvinism in the nineteenth century.[6]

Some interpreters of the early nineteenth-century Baptist history suggest that Robert Hall and Andrew Fuller were exponents of a similar evangelical Calvinistic theology. Ernest Payne intimated that "Fullerism" should be seen as the bridge between Particular Baptists and the New Connexion of General Baptists.[7] On that basis Fuller would be the man who set the eventual merger in motion, a process that culminated in the formal union of General and Particular Baptists in 1891, a few years after the Downgrade Controversy which had erupted in 1887. Robert Oliver suggests that among the Particular Baptists Robert Hall has a better claim to be seen as this catalyst, given his rejection of particular redemption and his close associations with the General Baptists. The latter was an indication of his hope for a union between them and the Particular Baptists.[8] There is no doubt that Hall's theology was not identical to that of his Particular Baptist forefathers. Rather, he made a significant contribution towards what Frank Rinaldi has called an "erosion of distinctives" between General (the New Connexion) and Particular Baptists.[9]

That erosion began long before the formal union of those two groups in 1891. When the first Baptist Union was set up in 1813 some sixty men favoured the proposed plan for union. It was essentially a union of Particular Baptists with a Calvinistic doctrinal basis. Robert Hall was absent from the inaugural London meeting,

---

[6] Campbell, "The decline of Calvinism," 1.

[7] Ernest A. Payne, *The Baptist Union: A Short History* (London: The Carey Kingsgate Press Limited 1959), 61.

[8] Robert W. Oliver, *History of the English Calvinistic Baptists 1771-1892: From John Gill to C. H. Spurgeon* (Edinburgh: Banner of Truth Trust, 2006), 329-30. For part of his evidence Oliver refers to MacLeod, "The Life and Teaching of Robert Hall."

[9] Frank W. Rinaldi, *The Tribe of Dan: The New Connexion of General Baptists 1770-1891: A study In the transition from revival movement to established denomination*, Studies In Baptist History and Thought, Vol. 10 (Milton Keynes: Paternoster Press, 2008), 20.

yet he was invited to preach at the next meeting to be held the following year.[10] That union never prospered.

Twenty years or so after that first meeting in London a new union of churches was created (in 1832, a year after the death of Hall). This time the "erosion of distinctives" was much easier to see. The constitution was extremely vague, stating as its first aim the extension of "brotherly love and union among Baptist ministers and churches who agree in the sentiments usually denominated evangelical."[11] John Howard Hinton (1791–1873), himself no strong advocate of evangelical Calvinism, many years later described the constitution as a "poverty stricken resolution."[12] Hinton was secretary of the Baptist Union for twenty-five years, from 1841 until 1866. Ernest Payne, however, saw the omission of the familiar Calvinistic doctrinal statement, present in the 1813 declaration, as a decided advantage, paving the way for the eventual merger of the two groups of Baptists sixty years later.[13]

Hall's lack of distinctiveness

It would be misleading to suggest that Robert Hall was the only catalyst for theological change in the early nineteenth century but he did play a significant part in the changes taking place among the Particular Baptists. His own theological views and practice reflected the declining impact of Calvinism not only in his thinking and ministry but also in that of other Baptists. There were those who were in full sympathy with Hall's approach. In his tribute to Hall William Newlands commented:

> enlightened and pious men before, and especially since the appearance of the works of Mason and Hall, have felt it their

---

[10] Payne, *The Baptist Union*, 21.
[11] Payne, *The Baptist* Union, 61.
[12] Payne, *The Baptist* Union, 61.
[13] Payne, *The Baptist* Union, 61.

duty to merge, not only points of church government, but even points of doctrine; the differences, for example between Arminians and Calvinists, which Mr. Hall did not rank among the essentials of Christianity, as these are separable from a full participation in all the blessings of the new covenant. A catholic spirit, we have uniformly observed, is the fruit of a deep piety, or of an extraordinary mental enlargement; in Mr. Hall it was connected with both these principles.[14]

Not everyone shared that evaluation of Hall. Rather they looked on his assessment of the differences between Arminianism and Calvinism as one of his weaknesses. An anonymous correspondent for the periodical *The Pulpit*, writing at much the same time as Newlands, provided a critical analysis of Hall's writings.

The Pulpit was first published on April 23, 1823 in London. In that edition readers were informed that the periodical was "designed to be the vehicle, not of any class of religious opinions, but of such real information and practical instruction, as may be acceptable to all who acknowledge one common Redeemer."[15] The substance of the periodical was to be "a Report of Sermons delivered in London during each week, accompanied occasionally with critical remarks."[16] Readers of the March 24, 1831, edition would not have been surprised to read an analysis and an assessment of Robert Hall's writings. They were already familiar with Robert Hall, for in previous editions Hall's sermons, especially those

---

[14] William Newlands, "Character of the Rev. Robert Hall, A.M." *The Manchester Times* (March 10, 1831): 510 (www.britishnewspaperarchive.co.uk/viewer/print/bl/0 000083/18310319/013/00006).

[15] Anonymous, "A Critical Analysis of the Writings of the late Rev. Robert Hall, A.M.," *The Pulpit* (April 23, 1823): 1, quoted by McNutt, "The Ministry of Robert Hall," 190. I am indebted to Cody McNutt for drawing my attention towards these editions of *The Pulpit*.

[16] *The Pulpit* 1 (April 23, 1823): 1, quoted by McNutt, "The Ministry of Robert Hall," 190.

preached in or near London, had appeared in its pages. Invariably those sermons were printed together with appreciative comments. Some of them drew attention to his great popularity and his extraordinary powers as a preacher.

The anonymous correspondent was aware of the danger of becoming "intoxicated with the general delirium" that followed the death of Robert Hall, and of forgetting that he was human and had his faults.[17] The author had many positive things to say about Hall and highlighted his religious sentiments as being of first importance. Hall, he explained, believed in the Trinity, the incarnation of the Lord Jesus Christ, the divinity and personality of the Holy Spirit, the atonement, justification by faith, regeneration, the obligation of the moral law on believers, personal holiness, the resurrection of the Lord Jesus Christ, the judgment of God, and the future state of rewards and punishments, which were of eternal duration. He affirmed that every sentiment Hall held was infused with "the views of a philosopher, the energy of a champion, the learning of a scholar, the eloquence of an orator, and the affection of a friend."[18]

As for his pamphlets and tracts, the anonymous critic asserted they were well known and highly commended. His controversial works, such as those on the communion question, were also familiar to many and held in high esteem by numerous people. Commending his sermons he told his readers that Hall "gives gold in the block, rather than in the leaf," and with his purely English style there is a "happy combination of the dignity of history, and the elegance of poetry, with the flow of oratory, and the purity of Scripture."[19]

However, towards the end of his assessment he affirmed:

---

[17] Anonymous, *The Pulpit* 430 (March 24, 1831): 285.
[18] Anonymous, *The Pulpit* 430 (March 24, 1831): 285.
[19] Anonymous, *The Pulpit* 430 (March 24, 1831): 287.

Nothing Human Is Faultless

But nothing human is faultless; every human production is a legitimate subject of criticism: the sun has spots in him. In Mr. Hall's discourses there is too little theology, and the Scriptures are too sparingly quoted. Neither does he present the truth in any decisive character, of Calvinistic or Arminian; so that his sentiments on these points cannot be known from his works; while truth compels us to add, there is sometimes too much sharpness and acrimony discovered for a minister, whom the apostle has said is "to be gentle towards all men."[20]

Leaving aside the fourth and last criticism, the first three, and especially the third, introduce us to the heart of the matter. Here was candid criticism in a periodical that had no particular doctrinal axe to grind. Some, like William Newlands, thought that this lack of decisiveness was one of Hall's strengths. However, a reading of Hall's sermons bears out the correctness of the observations made by Hall's critic. Reading his sermons two hundred years or so after they were preached it is still virtually impossible to discern whether Hall was a decided Calvinist or had Arminian sympathies. There are a few exceptions perhaps in sermons he preached in his later life. However, even in these his particular sentiments are not always clearly identified or boldly and decisively declared as biblical truth over against error. To discover what he believed requires a reading of his sermons and asking not only what he does say but what he omits. His letters that have survived are sometimes helpful, together with records of his biographers who have remembered his private conversations and comments. Hall was a great conversationalist and his biographers have recorded many of his comments made in such circumstances. These records are more revealing than his sermons. One difficulty arises however, because it soon becomes apparent that Hall modified some of the

---

[20] Anonymous, *The Pulpit* 430 (March 24, 1831): 287.

sentiments he expressed during the earlier part of his life. The task of making an accurate and fair assessment becomes more demanding because we are confronted with what is, in effect, a moving target.

What then were Hall's doctrinal sentiments? By asking that question I am not calling into question the genuineness of Hall's Christian faith any more than did the reviewer in *The Pulpit*. Hall was unquestionably a real Christian, a man of prayer and true piety, and a man who held firmly to the fundamentals of the Christian faith. He was an evangelical, who believed in the inspiration and authority of the Bible and the atoning sacrifice of the Lord Jesus Christ. He was a preacher with rare gifts.

Yet without question Robert Hall was not distinctively Calvinistic in his theology. That set him apart from his father, and from the men of the Northamptonshire Association of Particular Baptists. His father had written *Help to Zion's Travellers* in which he had expressed a distinctive evangelical Calvinism. The same was true of Andrew Fuller in *The Gospel Worthy of all Acceptation*.[21]

William Carey had been greatly helped by Hall's *Help to Zion's Travellers*. John Ryland had commented that Carey had been "perplexed between the statements of the Arminians, and the crudest representations of Calvinism, [and] by persons bordering closely on Antinomianism." Ryland was able to affirm that Carey searched the Scriptures attentively for himself and discovered that Hall's *Help to Zion's Travellers* was "the first summary of evangelical truth, which appeared to him fully to accord with the sacred standard."[22] It was a defining moment in Carey's life and the book never left his side. He took it to India and it was found,

---

[21] See Michael A.G. Haykin, "Particular Redemption in the Writings of Andrew Fuller (1754–1815)" in *David Bebbington, ed., The Gospel in the World: International Baptist Studies*, Studies In Baptist History and Thought, vol. 1 (Carlisle, PA/Waynesboro, GA: Paternoster Press, 2002), 107–128.

[22] John Ryland, "Preface" to Robert Hall [Senior], *Help to Zion's Travellers* (London: 1814), x.

Nothing Human Is Faultless

with his personal annotations in the margins, among his personal possessions after his death. He testified of its value to him:

> I found all that arranged and illustrated which I had been so long picking up as scraps. I do not remember ever to have read any book with such raptures as I did that. If it was poison, as some then said, it was so sweet to me that I drank it greedily to the bottom of the cup; and I rejoice to say, that those doctrines are the choice of my heart to this day.[23]

However, his father's book did not have the same impact on the son as it had on William Carey.

Sadly, Hall was to undermine the distinctives of Particular Baptists by his failure "to present the truth in any decisive character." He was well aware that he did not share his father's theology. In 1814, when he was approaching fifty years of age and in his prime at Leicester, he wrote a preface for a third edition of his father's book in which he stated that his father's views were "decidedly Calvinistic."[24] In that same preface Hall expressed his own convictions that the differences between Calvinists and Arminians were not differences about essentials. He was fully satisfied that upon either system, "the foundations of human hope remain unshaken, and that there is nothing in the contrariety of views entertained on these subjects, which ought to obstruct the most cordial affection and harmony among Christians."[25] Commenting on his father's theology to John Greene in 1825, only six

---

[23] Eustace Carey, *Memoir of William Carey, D.D., late missionary to Bengal: Professor of Oriental Languages In the College of Fort William, Calcutta* (London: Jackson and Walford, 1836), 16–17. Carey's own annotated copy of Hall's book is now in the possession of Bristol Baptist College.

Hall, *Help to Zion's Travellers*, xvi. Hall's "Recommendatory Preface" to his father's work was first published in the Second London Edition, and dated September, 1824.

[25] Hall, *Help to Zion's Travellers*, xvi.

years before his own death, Hall told him, "my father, sir, was very doctrinal in his preaching, and more attached to Calvinism than I am. If there are any sentiments to which I could subscribe, they are Baxter's."[26] Baxter's piety is undisputed but he did not believe in particular redemption nor did he maintain the biblical doctrine of justification by faith. He also had little sympathy for creeds and confessions of faith, a sympathy echoed by Hall.

Earlier in his life while at Cambridge, Hall was asked whether he was an Arminian or a Calvinist. His reply was, "Neither, Sir: but I believe I recede farther from Arminianism than from Calvinism. If a man profess himself a decided Arminian, I infer from it that he is not a good logician; but, Sir, it does not interfere with his personal piety ... I regard the question more as metaphysical than religious."[27]

When Hall was a young man of twenty-five, he left Bristol and became a pastor in Cambridge. When he parted company with Caleb Evans and the Academy he wrote to Evans. In a letter dated December 4, 1790, a ruffled and irritated Hall made his views plainly known, "You profess yourself a Calvinist. I do not."[28] It was a word spoken in anger, but it did contain a large element of truth. In his latter years Hall made comments in two or three of his sermons that seem to indicate a softening in his attitude towards Calvinism.

Enough evidence has been provided at this point to show that Hall held some views that diverged from the Calvinism of his father and others among whom he had grown up, including those who had been his teachers. Subsequent chapters will consider these divergent views in more detail. But there is no disputing that

---

[26] John Greene, *Reminiscences of the Rev Robert Hall*, Gregory and Belcher, *Works*, 4:74.

[27] Gregory, *Works*, 1:60.

[28] J.W. Morris, *Biographical Reflections of the Rev. Robert Hall, A.M.* (India, New Delhi: Isha Books, 2013), 79.

Hall's sentiments were part of that "erosion of distinctives." He was inclined to be ambivalent, declaring himself more a Calvinist than an Arminian, but not a decided Calvinist like his father, though he still regarded himself as a Particular Baptist. Early in his life he reached the conclusion that the differences between Calvinism and Arminianism were not differences about essentials. That conclusion appeared to remain a life-long conviction. The anonymous critic writing in *The Pulpit* was correct. Hall did not "present the truth in any decisive character." For him, it was not a matter of primary importance.

Hall's tendency not to connect with his hearers

The same anonymous writer in *The Pulpit* also thought that Hall's publications were "not poor man's book ... but chiefly to be found in the hands of ministers and scholars, and literary and scientific men. They are capable of doing great good in their own particular walk."[29] William Steadman (1764-1837), a prominent Particular Baptist who admired Hall and greatly mourned his death in 1831, agreed, but also commented:

> His preaching was doubtless, useful; not only in forming and improving real Christians, but in the conversion of sinners, though, in the latter department I am inclined to think many, greatly his inferiors, have been more successful. If I were to speak freely, I should say, the effect of his preaching was that of admiration and applause, rather than of permanent utility. In this, however, I speak with hesitation; and admitting it, I impute it not so much to any intention of him, as to the folly of his admirers.[30]

John Foster (1770-1843) was an English Baptist pastor and

---

[29] Anonymous, *The Pulpit* 430 (March 24, 1831): 287.
[30] Thomas Steadman, *Memoir of the Rev. William Steadman, D.D.* (London: Thomas Ward and Co., 1838), 423.

essayist. He had trained at the Bristol Academy but had only become a regular hearer of Hall during the last few years of his life. He believed he had identified the reasons why Hall's sermons had the effect that Steadman pinpointed. He addressed what was, in his opinion, a serious deficiency in Hall's preaching, namely his failure to consistently address the different conditions and the consciences of his hearers.

He was asked to provide an essay for the American edition of Hall's works, "Observations on Mr Hall's Character as a Preacher."[31] He regarded Hall as the first preacher of the age and although he felt that Hall has lost some of his fire in his latter days in Bristol there was no diminishing of his intellectual powers, his powerful reasoning abilities, and his mastery of the English language. He drew attention to the unpretentious character of Hall, the absence of any self-promotion or vanity, and the seriousness of his spirit and manner when preaching. He regarded Hall as being "strictly orthodox" in his sentiments "on the model of what has come to be denominated moderate Calvinism"[32] It is not clear what Foster understood by "moderate Calvinism." He may have been saying that Hall's theology was the same as that of Andrew Fuller. Given that he only came to hear Hall in his later years in Bristol he may not have been fully aware of the differences that existed between Hall and Fuller in the last decade of the eighteenth century and the first decades of the nineteenth century.

Foster did not comment on Hall's lack of theological distinctiveness. Rather, he observed that he was too general and theoretical in his preaching. John Ryland had expressed the same opinion as Foster: "Mr Hall's preaching had, with an excellence in some respects unrivalled, the fault of being *too general*; and he

---

[31] Gregory and Belcher, *Works*, 3:95–124.
[32] Gregory and Belcher, *Works*, 3:110.

contrasted it with that of Mr. Hall's father, who had erred, he thought, on the side of too minute particularity."[33] Foster pointed out a tendency in Hall which he considered to be a serious defect. He qualified that by saying that his observation was a general fact and that there were exceptions, but:

> his preaching did not bring and keep the people under a *disciplinary* process. It allowed them too much of the privilege of the spectators of a fine and well-ordered series of representation, of such a nature, that they can look on at ease from any similar disturbance to that of the king in Hamlet, at sight of the acted garden-scene.[34]

His explanation focussed on Hall's "cast of mind and his addiction to prolonged speculative studies" such that he became pre-occupied with his subject and not the particular needs and varied conditions of his hearers.[35]

In Foster's opinion there was therefore, too often a "disconnect" between Hall the preacher and his congregation. A distance existed between "the theoretic speculation and high-pitched rhetoric to which he was addicted, and, on the other, that recognition of what men actually are in situation and character, to which his mind did not easily descend."[36] Foster had in mind the realities of everyday life which he maintained should be a focal point of application in preaching, and worthy of the preacher's best exertions. He listed them at some length:

> There is the sad catalogue of the perversities and deceits of the heart; there are the distortions and presumptions of prejudice; the principles, which in disguised form perhaps,

---

[33] Gregory and Belcher, *Works*, 3:123.
[34] Gregory and Belcher, *Works*, 3:114.
[35] Gregory and Belcher, *Works*, 3:115.
[36] Gregory and Belcher, *Works*, 3:122-123.

and afraid of audacious avowal, but of malignant essence, react against the Divine authority; the subterfuges of insincerity, the various ways in which men evade conviction, falsify in effect the truth to which they assent in terms, or delude themselves in their estimates of their own spirit and conduct. There is the estrangement from reflection, the extreme reluctance to honest self-examination. There is also in the majority of any large congregation, many of those who make a direct profession of personal religion, not excepted, an indistinct apprehension, and lax application, of the principles and rules of Christian morality.[37]

This meant that Hall's hearers tended to become more spectators than hearers and doers of the word. Their spiritual needs and situations had not been addressed and more importantly their consciences had not been pricked with the truth about themselves. They could leave the congregation, comment to others about how wonderful the sermon was, yet be unchanged in their hearts and character.

Foster also gave an example of the impact of Hall's preaching on Christians. Taking the subject of Christian happiness, Hall described it in glowing and exalted tones, speaking of enjoying confidence in God's favour, and the superiority of this happiness to the cares and distractions of life. Yet it left some of his hearers "high and dry," in distress, or even dismissive and contemptuous of such happiness because it was not their experience. Again, Hall tended not to address the realities of life in his sermons. Foster reasoned:

> Some of them are harassed, without the possibility of escape, by the state of their worldly affairs; perhaps suffering or dreading disasters beyond the reach of prudence to prevent; anxiously awaiting a critical turn of events; vexed

---

[37] Gregory and Belcher, *Works*, 3:114.

Nothing Human Is Faultless

beyond the patience of Job by the untowardness, selfishness, or dishonesty encountered in their transactions. Some are enduring the cares and hardships of poverty. Some are distressed by the bad dispositions among their nearest kindred; perhaps by anticipations, grievous in proportion to their piety, of the conduct and ultimate destiny of their children.[38]

He continued by mentioning those facing the loss of loved ones, those battling with the presence of good and evil in their lives, those who had backslidden, those inclined to depression, those depressed by moral evil around them. Foster explained how much more helpful it would be if the preacher dealt with these kinds of issues and showed how Christian happiness could be found and enjoyed in the midst of these realities.

It is not clear what Foster thought about Hall's lack of distinctiveness. He himself did not seem to have much personal sympathy for creeds but chose rather to speak of a "system of theological tenets," adding immediately, "*creed* is an ill-favoured term."[39] The particular defect in Hall's preaching identified by Foster concerned the character of his preaching and its impact on his hearers rather than its theological content.

However, this does provide a note of caution, preventing anyone from uncritically placing Hall on a pedestal even though he was regarded as the prince of preachers by many of his contemporaries. Of first importance was the lack of distinctiveness in his preaching. Whatever his convictions were at the end of his life, there is no evidence that he ever changed his conviction that the differences between Calvinism and Arminianism were not of primary importance because they were not about essentials.

The implications of that stance for Particular Baptists was to

---

[38] Gregory and Belcher, *Works*, 3:120.
[39] Gregory and Belcher, *Works*, 3:110.

prove crucial as many of them, together with other Dissenters, drifted away from their Calvinistic roots. Hall was not the only Particular Baptist to lean in that direction. John Howard Hinton is another example, but he went much further than Hall. Hinton became the pastor of the historic Particular Baptist church in Devonshire Square, London. He thought he had discovered a new synthesis between Arminianism and Calvinism. He went on to freely admit that were predestination and election abandoned and Arminianism to triumph, "I confess it would not be to me the heavy calamity which some people perceive it to be."[40]

In contrast, some twenty-five years after Hall's death, Spurgeon had founded the Pastors' College in London. Reflecting on his reasons for doing so he expressed his doubts about the doctrines being taught in other institutions of theological learning, including Baptists. He did not think it was genuine Calvinism. He frankly admitted:

> my views of the gospel and of the mode of training preachers were and are somewhat different from those which I believed to sway the then existing Dissenting colleges. I may have been uncharitable in my judgment, but I thought the Calvinism of the theology then taught to be very doubtful, and the fervour of the generality of students to be far behind their literary attainments.[41]

Towards the end of the nineteenth century Dr. John Clifford (1836–1923), the prominent London Baptist, who opposed Spurgeon during "the Downgrade," defended his own "scriptural, broad, and anti-Calvinistic creed." He believed that "by the

---

[40] J.H.Y. Briggs, *English Baptists of the Nineteenth Century (1689-1815)* (Didcot: Baptist Historical Society, 1994), 163.

[41] Spurgeon, "Concerning the College," *The Sword and Trowel* (1 April, 1870), 146.

Nothing Human Is Faultless

1880s the hand of Calvin had become an extinct force in living theology."[42] That was just two generations or so after the death of Robert Hall. Clifford's claim would eventually prove to be a premature judgment but it reflected what he saw in Baptist Union circles towards the end of the nineteenth century. The drift away from Calvinism in the earlier part of the century led to its disappearance in many dissenting churches. There were some notable exceptions though. Charles Spurgeon at the Metropolitan Tabernacle and Archibald Brown at the East London Tabernacle were two of them.

---

[42] Briggs, *English Baptists*, 117–118.

5
The Young Student in Bristol and Aberdeen

At this point we need to retrace our steps and consider in more detail what precisely led to the dispute between Hall and Caleb Evans and the effects that had on Hall's mental breakdown. The latter was to result in what he believed was his conversion to Christ.

August 1780 was a momentous day for the sixteen year old Robert Hall, for his father, and for the Particular Baptist church in Arnesby. On that day the church set him apart for the work of the ministry. The account of his call is found in the church's minute book.

> The said Robert Hall was born at Arnesby May 2 1764 and was seen from his childhood not only serious and given to secret prayer before he could speak plain[ly] but was always intensely inclined to the work of the ministry. He began to compose hymns before he was quite seven years old and therein discovered marks of piety, thought and genius. Between 8 and 9 years old he made several hymns which were much admired by many, one of which was printed in the Gospel Magazine. About that time he wrote his thoughts on various religious subjects and select portions of Scripture. He was likewise possessed of an intense inclination for learning and made such progress that the Country Master under whom he was could not instruct him any further. He was then sent to Northampton Boarding School under the care of the Revd Mr. John Ryland [John Collett Ryland] where he continued about a year and a half and made great progress in Latin and Greek—In October 1778 he went to the Academy at Bristol under the care of the Revd Mr Evans

and on August 12 1780 was sent out to the ministry of this church being sixteen years and three months old—The manner the church obtained satisfaction with his abilities for the great work was, his speaking in his turn at Conference meetings from various portions of Scripture; in which and in prayer he had borne a part for upwards of four years before and having when at home at their request frequently preached on Lord's day mornings, to their great satisfaction; they therefore consequently and unanimously requested his being in a solemn manner set apart to public employ.

Accordingly on the day aforesaid he was examined by his father before the church respecting his inclination, motives and end on reference to the Ministry and was likewise disposed to make a declaration of his religious sentiments. All which being done to the entire satisfaction of the church, they therefore set him apart by lifting up their right hands, and solemn prayer.

The father then delivered a discourse on him from 2 Tim. 2.1 Thou, therefore my son, be strong in the grace that is in Christ Jesus. Being thus sent forth as before said he preached that afternoon from 2 Thes. 1:7–8. May the Lord bless and grant him great success.[1]

At this point in his life there appeared to be nothing in his stated religious sentiments that prevented Robert Hall from being ordained. The church knew the young man well. He had grown up in the congregation. Two years before he had given "a very distinct account of his being the subject of special grace." He was subsequently baptised with another young man, John Noon, on 6 September and added to the church.[2] His father had examined him and both he and the church were entirely satisfied with what they had heard. It therefore seems reasonable to assume that his

---

[1] Arnesby Baptist Church, Minute Book, 1752–1819, Leicester Records Office, N/B/7/3, 32.

[2] Arnesby Baptist Church, Minute Book, 31.

The Young Student

sentiments at this point were in keeping with those of his father and the church, otherwise they would have not accepted him. It is not until 1790, after he had returned to Bristol to teach classics at the Academy and be the assistant minister to Caleb Evans at the Broadmead church, that he publicly expressed different sentiments, contrary to those of his father and his home church.

The wisdom of setting apart a young sixteen-year old man to the Christian ministry may be called into question. However, it should be remembered that Hall was a man of exceptional talents. His recognition at that age was not a unique event. In 1771 John Ryland had been set apart at the age of eighteen. Like Hall, he showed exceptional gifts, as did Charles Spurgeon who took up the ministry in Waterbeach, Cambridgeshire, when he was only seventeen years of age. Even though Robert Hall was formally recognised as a minister of the gospel he did not immediately become a pastor of a settled congregation. He became a student at Bristol and was to continue his studies in Aberdeen before becoming an assistant to Caleb Evans in 1785

It seems that at some point during the period 1781–1787 Hall began to speculate about certain doctrines. We have already referred to his materialism and denial of the intermediate state. Morris records a highly animated dispute between father and son on these subjects that left the pair of them deeply affected and very distressed.[3] What led Hall to begin questioning what was regarded as accepted orthodoxy? It seems he was more vulnerable to speculative notions in his youth. He was more inclined to adopt Arminian ideas in the earlier part of his ministry but he never imbibed them completely. These inclinations to Arminianism may have been a reaction against the hyper-Calvinism which had long plagued some Particular Baptists.

---

[3] J.W. Morris, *Biographical Reflections of the Rev. Robert Hall, A.M.* (India, New Delhi: Isha Books, 2013), 54–55.

The Theology of Robert Hall Jr.

Confessions of faith and systems of theology

When Hall entered the Academy in 1778 he entered an institution which was marked by a robust evangelical Calvinism. Some notable ministers attended the Academy before and after Hall, including Andrew Gifford, John Ash, Benjamin Beddome, Benjamin Francis, Isaiah Birt, Samuel Pearce, John Sutcliff, Joshua Thomas, Joseph Kinghorn, William Steadman, and John Rippon. Caleb Evans had been exercising his ministry in Broadmead for just over a decade. He was to play a key role in the early life of Robert Hall, especially when Hall returned to Bristol as a teacher and pastor. Evans had been ordained in 1767 and on that occasion had made a decisive public confession of his own faith. It was customary at that time for a pastor to make his own confession of faith at his ordination. That confession would have reflected the Calvinism expressed in *The Second London Confession of Faith*, as well as that expressed in the articles of the church.

Evans was very aware of the significance of his confession of faith. He was persuaded it was his responsibility to tell those to whom he would preach what he believed, especially at a time when many others were expressing contrary views. In a determined mood he stated, "I am very sensible that many of these doctrines are quite opposite to the fashionable tenets of the present day," and declared he was ready to be branded, "with the odium of a weak superficial head, and sometimes with much greater reproach of a dishonest, bad heart."[4] His confession of faith was marked by evangelical Calvinistic orthodoxy that had characterised both his father Hugh Evans, and Bernard Foskett. Evans noted the spirit of the age in which he was living. Different currents of opinion were in full flow, many of them rejecting any

---

[4] Hugh and Caleb Evans, *A charge and a sermon together with an introductory discourse and confession of faith delivered at the ordination of Rev. Mr. Caleb Evans, August 18, 1767 in Broadmead, Bristol* (Bristol: 1767), 34.

The Young Student

kind of creed or systematic confessions of faith. But he was not to be moved by those whom he called "specious declaimers" and deny the value of creeds and confessions of faith. He was conscious that he and others like him stood on the same ground as the earlier sixteenth century reformers:

> I am very sensible it is become now quite fashionable, zealously and indiscriminately to decry all creeds and systematic confessions of faith, and vehemently to inveigh against them, so invading the liberty wherewith Christ has made us free. But it is very easy to see the grand rock of offence with the specious declaimers is not any creed or system, for they all have some creed or system of their own, and are not a little sanguine in defence of it; but it is that particular system of faith which has long been and still is the bulwark and glory of the reformation, which is the object of their eversion, and to destroy which they seem determined to leave no artifice untry'd. But great is the truth and it will prevail.[5]

The influence of John Locke

The English philosopher John Locke (1632-1704) exercised a significant influence on eighteenth-century thinkers and his ideas were studied both by Anglicans and Dissenters. He was not regarded as a skeptic for he was a professing Christian. Instead he was considered by many both as an ally against rationalists and as a champion of toleration and liberty. His works became staple diet in many dissenting academies, often supplemented by Isaac Watts' (1674-1748) and Philip Doddridge's (1702-1751) works on logic and philosophy. Bristol was no exception to this pattern.[6]

---

[5] Hugh and Caleb Evans, *A charge and a sermon*, 16-7.

[6] Roger Hayden, *Continuity and Change: Evangelical Calvinism among eighteenth century Baptist ministers trained at Bristol Academy, 1690-1791* (Chipping Norton: Nigel Lynn Publishing and Marketing Ltd., 2003), 67, 74-75. Caleb Evans was familiar with Locke. Hayden, *Continuity and Change*, 137.

The Theology of Robert Hall Jr.

Alan Sell has evaluated Locke's influence on eighteenth-century divines.[7] He drew attention to Locke's sustained plea for an indispensable minimum of belief, a view that can also be found in the writings of Richard Baxter and John Howe, which would have been met with a sympathetic response from Hall. All three were persuaded that creeds and confessions of faith created schism and disunity among Christians. That plea was ultimately driven by Locke's own theory of knowledge in which he maintained it was not possible to be certain about doctrinal matters. However, he also hated schism and sectarianism, believing that toleration meant tolerating differences in doctrine. Howe and Baxter argued that to make large creeds and confessions of faith was to go beyond the conditions for Christian fellowship that Christ, the head of the church, had laid down.[8]

Hall also hated sectarianism and schism. This explains why he championed the cause of open communion. The extent to which Hall was directly influenced by John Locke is very difficult to determine but he appeared to reflect Locke-like ideas in his attitudes to confessions of faith and systems of theology, whether they be Arminian or Calvinistic.

Reacting to John Gill and John Owen

A similar attitude also lies behind Hall's biting criticism of John Gill (1697-1771). Gill was a Particular Baptist scholar of the first order and one of his principal aims as a theologian had been to provide a single and biblically coherent system of truth.

In conversation about the Welsh language with Christmas Evans (1766-1838), Evans expressed the wish that Gill's works had been written in Welsh. Hall's retort was immediate, "I wish they

---

[7] Alan P. F. Sell *John Locke and the Eighteenth-Century Divines* (Cardiff: University of Wales Press, 1997).

[8] Sell, *John Locke and the Eighteenth-Century Divines*, 186-187.

The Young Student

had, Sir; I wish they had with all my heart: for then I should never had read them. They are a continent of mud, Sir."[9] Hall also dismissed John Owen (1616-1683) in similar language. "I never read a page of Owen ... without finding some confusion in his thoughts, either a truism, or a contradiction in terms ... he is a double-Dutchman, floundering in a continent of mud."[10]

Hall was critical of Gill in particular because he was persuaded that by concentrating on the systematizing of doctrine he tended to produce little practical instruction, failing to sufficiently emphasise the precepts of Christ and the duties of Christian morality. Hall feared Antinomianism and anything that had a tendency in that direction and vigorously opposed it during his lifetime. He was not alone in his fears. It was an issue "which absorbed the attention of the Calvinistic Baptist community in England from the 1770s to the 1820s." [11] Caleb Evans would probably not have felt the tensions that Hall appeared to recognize. It was never a matter of upholding evangelical Calvinistic sentiments or of upholding piety and practical godliness. Hall always emphasised the importance of piety and in so doing downplayed the importance of doctrine. Later, in 1821, Hall made a keen observation on the difference between Andrew Fuller and Thomas Toller, both pastors in Kettering.

> The secretary of the Baptist Mission attached, in my opinion, too much importance to a speculative accuracy of sentiment; while the subject of this Memoir [Toller] leaned to

---

[9] Gregory, *Works*, 1:175. Gill was read by hundreds in the eighteenth-century and his writings gave men confidence in Calvinistic theology at a time when rationalism was gaining the upper hand. This dismissal and forgetting of Gill by Hall was both unfair and unwarranted.

[10] Greene, *Reminiscences of the Rev Robert Hall*, in Gregory and Belcher, *Works*, 4:37-38.

[11] Michael A.G. Haykin, "'The Sum of All Good': John Ryland, Jr. and the Doctrine of the Holy Spirit." *Churchman* 103/104 (1989): 337.

the more contrary extreme. Mr. Fuller was too prone to infer the character of men from their creed; Mr Toller to lose sight of their creed in their character.[12]

For Hall character was paramount, a man's creed invariably took second place whether he was writing a memoir, providing biographical details, or giving a public tribute to someone following their death. He based his sympathies for Baxter and Howe on that principle.

Hall developed his own "system" of doctrine. While there is no evidence that Hall was directly influenced by Locke he would have been familiar with the man and his writings, from his own reading and certainly from his days as a student in Bristol. Olin Robison astutely observed, "If Gill had moved in a theological world which owed more than it realized to the medieval scholastics, Hall and his like owed more than perhaps they cared to concede to John Locke."[13]

Tensions at Bristol

Given Hall's attitude towards creeds, confessions, and systems of theology, it is not difficult to see how tensions arose between Hall and Caleb Evans. To determine exactly when those tensions rose to the surface is difficult to discern. There is no evidence that this happened while Hall was a student at Bristol. Evans had taken Hall under his wing, recognising the calibre and potential of the young man. Hall had come to the Academy in 1778, at the age of fourteen. Evans prepared him for further studies at King's College, Aberdeen, where Hall graduated with a master's degree. Had Oxford or Cambridge been an option for Hall he would have gained entry without any difficulty. Hall was not an Anglican and

---

[12] Greene, *Reminiscences of the Rev Robert Hall*, in Gregory, *Works*, 4:313–314.

[13] Olin C. Robison, "The Particular Baptists in England, 1760-1820" (PhD dissertation, Oxford University, 1963), 36.

The Young Student

therefore those doors were firmly closed.

He began his studies in Aberdeen in November 1781 but maintained very close links with the Broadmead church and with Evans in particular. In October 1783 at a church meeting Hall was invited to become co-pastor with Caleb Evans on concluding his studies in Scotland. James Newton was the classics tutor in Bristol but his health was failing. Hall was the obvious choice to replace him. In 1785 as part of his responsibilities in Bristol he became the pastor of the Independent paedobaptist congregation which had been part of the Broadmead church since 1757. They celebrated the Lord's Supper separately from the baptised believers in Broadmead.

In 1785, Hall was twenty-one and Caleb Evans forty-eight. The next five years saw tensions reach a climax that would lead to Hall's resignation in November 1790. There were significant changes in Hall's theology which perhaps were in embryo while he was a student in Bristol and then began to grow while he was in Aberdeen, but reached maturity in the crucial five years between 1785 and 1790.

Aberdeen
On completion of his student days in Bristol Hall began at King's College, Aberdeen in November 1781. He was seventeen years of age. He immersed himself in fresh studies in Greek grammar and literature, in Latin, Natural History, Mathematics, Natural Philosophy, and Moral Philosophy. He also studied theology at Marischal College under Dr. Campbell. The brief time Hall spent in Aberdeen can easily be overlooked and its significance discounted. Neither Gregory nor Morris appeared to appreciate Hall's growing discontent with Calvinism during these four years.

While a student Hall formed a close friendship with James Mackintosh (1765-1832), who was to make his name in the realms of law and politics. Together they read Greek literature, and vigorously debated morals, metaphysics, the doctrines of and evidences for Christianity, as well as Jonathan Edwards on the will. It has been said of Mackintosh that he became interested in "speculation" inspired by the writings of Joseph Priestley, William Warburton, and James Beattie; the latter being the professor of moral philosophy at Marischal College.[14] Hall and Mackintosh would not necessarily have been in agreement, the attraction and foundation of their friendship rather was their "mental greatness."[15] Discussion and debate with his friend may have served to loosen any hold Calvinism had on the young Hall, and accelerating his tendencies to speculation in the realm of Christianity.

Calvinism was deeply rooted in the national Presbyterian Church of Scotland. Commitment to the doctrinal standards of *The Westminster Confession of Faith* was prevalent but not universal. In the earlier part of the eighteenth century there had been a secession led by Ebenezer and Ralph Erskine. One of their concerns had been the apparent half-hearted adherence to the standards of the Reformed faith not only among church leaders but also in the universities.[16] When Hall came to Aberdeen in late 1781 Presbyterianism and Calvinism appeared to hold sway.

There is clear evidence of a growing disenchantment with Calvinism from two letters Hall wrote in the first few months of 1782. Shortly after settling in the town he had written letters to his father and to John Ryland. There are many similar passages in these letters and they both contain expressions of disillusionment. Hall sat under the shared ministries of Mr. Abercrombie and Mr.

---

[14] Christopher J. Finlay, "Mackintosh, Sir James, of Kyllachy, (1765-1832)," *Oxford Dictionary of National Biography* (Oxford: Oxford University Press, 2004), 35:675–679.

[15] Morris, *Biographical Reflections*, 47.

[16] Stewart J. Brown, "Protestant Dissent in Scotland" in Andrew C Thompson, ed., *The Oxford History of Protestant Dissenting Traditions, Volume II: The Long Eighteenth Century c.1689-c.1828* (Oxford: Oxford University Press, 2018), 145.

The Young Student

Peters at New Aberdeen. Gregory states that these men were "regarded as holding correct sentiments."[17] Hall assessed them otherwise. Writing to his father on January 26, 1782 he protested:

> They profess themselves Calvinists, but they never preach any of the distinguishing parts of Calvinism, and it is a settled principle with the Calvinists here that their distinguished tenets are not proper to be preached. Our advantage therefore is no more than if we were to attend Arminians. Better not to know than shun to declare the whole counsel of God. Deliver me from such frosty spirited Calvinists. I go to the house of God empty, seldom profiting any under their preaching ... how glad should I be to hear some good savoury preacher. The meanest who preached Jesus Christ and him crucified would be sweeter than the honey or the honeycomb.[18]

In similar vein he writes to John Ryland on March 25, 1782:

> Our situation affords us few religious advantages. The students are profane & profligate the professors formal the preachers dead. We attend the church at the New Aberdeen where Mr. Abercromny and Peters preach who call themselves Calvinists what for I do not know since they make a point of concealing from their hearers the distinguishing doctrines of Calvinism. Mr. Abercromny is a remarkably dry unaffecting preacher & and the latter though he seems rather more affectionate and evangelical ... [bottom corner of page 1 is torn] gives into an unmeaning declamatory manner.[19]

---

[17] Gregory, *Works*, 20.

[18] W[arren]., R[obert] H[all], *The Hall Family* (Bristol: J. W. Arrowsmith, 1910), 48.

[19] Gregory, *Works*, 1:15–20. Gregory was aware of both letters and quotes from parts of them. The full text of the letter to Dr. Ryland, dated 25 March 1792 is to be found in the archives of Bristol Baptist College and also in *The Baptist Record, and*

At that point he had also been to hear Dr. George Campbell once in Marischal College, but had come away disappointed, "I have been once to hear Dr. Campbell who expounds once a fortnight but I take him not to be Calvinistical."[20]

Later in the same letter he gives his opinion of what he had observed during his few months in Aberdeen, including his strictures against the Scottish system of patronage:

> I am afraid real religion is scarcely to be met with amongst the Presbyterians at least in any abundance. Much of the form but little of the power which seems to adhere to the very nature of great establishments for as the people have no hand in the choice of the minister they have consequently no sphere in which they can exert their influence & it is surely an easy transition from an incapability of action to an indifference whether they act or no, which gradually introduces formality, lukewarmness & hypocrisy the counterfeit and bane of true piety. Another obvious abuse in establishment is patronage by which the appointment of the minister & consequently the spiritual nourishment of souls depends upon the whim, the folly or the caprice of a landed (or lorded) Rascal who is corrupt in his principles and profligate in his practice and therefore one is [illegible script] & ill-qualified to direct in such an affair. Another thing which I am sorry to see abound so much in Scotland is the timid cowardice among the Calvinists which prevents them from an open adherence to their principles and inclines them to equivocation & concealment, as an instance of which I would just observe, that I have since I have been here talked with ministers and others who tho' they profess to believe the doctrine of election yet maintain that is not proper to be preached before a congregation and in this they are consistent for one may safely sit for 40 years under their

---

Biblical Repository 1 (1844): 133–136.

[20] Hall, Letter to Dr. John Ryland, 25 March, 1792. Held in Bristol Baptist College.

The Young Student

ministry without once suspecting them of that heresy. But my Dear Sir is this not shocking? What meaneth the making known the whole counsel of God?[21]

Given that these are the observations of a young man (he was not yet eighteen), and that he had been in Aberdeen less than six months it might be thought they can be easily dismissed. Whether Hall was correct in his assessments or not, these comments he made to his father and to Ryland seemed to have become lasting impressions. His experiences in Aberdeen did nothing to encourage him to remain thoroughly Calvinistic. The Hall family biographer (displaying his own sympathies) recorded that Robert Hall, "had shaken himself free from the dismal chains of Calvinism."[22] Aberdeen had contributed to that new-found "freedom." Furthermore, in the same letter to Ryland, Hall was questioning the distinction made by Edwards between natural and moral ability, and seeking for an opportunity to discuss the matter with Ryland. That distinction was foundational, both in his father's *Help to Zion's Travellers* and in Fuller's *The Gospel Worthy of all Acceptation*. Hall came to reject that distinction. Gregory records a conversation with him some years later in which Hall blamed John Owen for the distinction, claiming it was not original with Edwards.[23]

Perhaps it is not possible to be conclusive about the impact Aberdeen had on Hall. However, the fact remains that within a few years, when he left Bristol under a cloud, Robert Hall had declared publicly that he was not a Calvinist in the strictest sense of that term.

---

[21] Letter to Dr. John Ryland
[22] W. [Warren], *The Hall Family*, 56.
[23] Gregory, *Works*, 1:164-165.

6
A Parting of the Ways

The few years Robert Hall spent in Bristol as an assistant to Caleb Evans and as the classics tutor in the Academy proved to be a very significant time in his life. For the first time he expressed in some detail his doctrinal convictions. Although there is evidence that he changed some of these convictions, many of them he maintained for a period of at least twenty years. The parting of their ways in 1790 was painful for both Evans and Hall. The sad experience seemed to overwhelm Evans, and it may have contributed to his death the following year.

Hall's reservations about his own preaching

On returning to Bristol, Hall began to preach. He was well-received and drew crowds from among the distinguished men of Bristol, including several Anglican clergymen. Based on comments made later by Hall, Gregory recorded that it was Hall's own conviction "that at this time he was very inadequately qualified for the duties of a minister of the gospel."[1] Gregory allowed for the fact that Hall may have been putting himself down, but at the same time he admitted that there was a serious defect in his ministry which Hall himself later deplored. The evidence came from notes of Hall's sermons taken down by one of the members of the Bristol congregation. Furthermore, it was at this point, 1784–1786, that Fuller and Ryland were expressing their concerns about the young Robert Hall. While Hall never expressed his "free and daring speculations" in the pulpit he was doing so privately, to the "grief of his more wise and judicious friends."[2]

---

[1] Gregory, *Works*, 1:20.
[2] Gregory, *Works*, 1:22.

Gregory explained the serious defects in Hall's ministry as follows:

1. He had embraced the fundamental truths about God and though he often preached on the divine attributes and constantly exhorted his hearers to follow carefully the path of duty, he did so without much reference to evangelical, gospel motives.
2. His knowledge of Christianity as a way of restoration and reconciliation was somewhat defective and obscure and Hall acknowledged he was not aware of or alive to the peculiarities of the new gospel dispensation.
3. His preaching was too general and though his subject matter may have elevated the minds of his hearers his chosen topics did not flow immediately from the great scheme of redemption in Jesus Christ. As a preacher that should have been his principal work.[3]

Comparing his Bristol days with his later ministry Gregory, not unlike Steadman, focused on some of the features missing from Hall's preaching:

> The extent of God's matchless love and mercy—the depth and mystery of his designs—the inexhaustible treasury of his blessings and graces—the wonderful benefits flowing from the incarnation, humiliation and sacrifice of the Son of God—the delightful privileges of the saints,—were themes to which he recurred far less frequently than in latter days; and he persuaded himself that this was not *very* wrong, because his colleague, Dr. Evans, who had "the care of the church," adverted so incessantly to the doctrines of our Lord's divinity and atonement, of spiritual influence and regeneration, as to leave room for *him* to explore other regions of instruction and interest.[4]

---

[3] Gregory, *Works*, 1:20-21.
[4] Gregory, *Works*, 1:21.

A Parting of the Ways

Given the unsettled nature of his mind and the fact that he was still working out what he actually believed it is possible that he decided it would be better to leave the fundamentals to Evans and concentrate on those subjects that he felt he could preach with certainty. Gregory, and Hall by his comments to his friend, seemed to suggest that his preaching was defective in evangelical truth and evangelical motives. If Hall was not at this time in his life a converted man, as he came to believe, then this defect will be better understood.

Firm as to foundational truth

In 1787 Hall was asked to write the annual circular letter from the ministers and messengers of the Baptist churches which formed the Western Association. The subject was *The Excellence of the Christian Dispensation*. He did so reluctantly and left the composition to the very last moment. Morris maintained that the letter displayed, "how comprehensive and energetic were the views he entertained of the great scheme of human redemption, and how unfounded the suspicions of his holding a latitudinarian creed."[5] Morris was writing to defend the subject of his memoirs. In the letter Hall acknowledged the necessity of divine revelation. Without it, he said, we are left with vague and uncertain conjectures. He related how sin and disorder had entered into the world and that men were no longer what they once were, nor what they ought to be. Referring to the dark backdrop of human sinfulness portrayed in Romans 1, he then described the supreme excellence of the Christian dispensation. That excellence resided in the incarnate Christ, who is both God and man, in his humiliation and his death on the cross. The cross, Hall affirmed, demonstrated both the compassion and justice of God. Forgiveness of sins is

---

[5] J.W. Morris, *Biographical Reflections of the Rev. Robert Hall, A.M.* (India, New Delhi: Isha Books, 2013), 63.

secured by the sacrifice of Christ and God's righteousness is declared in the pardoning of sin. This sacrifice alone, declared Hall, provides consolation of the highest order because only in this way can we be assured of pardon, of answers to our prayers, be sure that afflictions will be turned into blessings, and be confident that our existence will be prolonged to endless duration.[6] He affirmed that Christianity is not the religion of one age or of one nation. It is universal and the risen Christ will return as the judge and the redeemer.

As he drew his conclusions he spoke in tones which seemingly contradict the comments made by Gregory. There was a clear note of certainty about the gospel of Jesus Christ and its impact on the person who has believed it:

> If your religion is genuine, it will often be the source of the warmest and most interesting feelings. It will be a spring of consolation within, which will often be full and pour itself forth. If the gospel has not taken a share in the feelings of our hearts, if it has not moved the great springs of our hopes and fears, we may be assured we have never experienced its force. It is filled with such views as cannot fail to interest and transport us. Besides, if we do not feel the gospel as well as believe it, how can it support against the overwhelming influence of what we *do* feel? The world steals upon us, and engages our affections on all sides. Its prospects enrapture, and its pleasures are seducing us. Will a religion which rests only on opinion, and a conviction, at times extorted from us, keep us firm against those assaults, and stem the force of a torrent which never ceases to flow?[7]

It is not sufficient to explain this seeming anomaly by drawing the distinction between what Hall was prepared to say publicly, on

---

[6] Gregory, *Works*, 1:391.
[7] Gregory, *Works*, 1:393.

A Parting of the Ways

the one hand, and what he was prepared to disclose privately, on the other. Neither is it adequate to explain this discrepancy by suggesting that Hall was something of a hypocrite.

Morris was quite right to affirm that Hall had embraced the fundamentals of the faith, focusing on the divine revelation of the gospel in the Scriptures, the incarnation of the Son of God, the death, burial, resurrection and return of the Lord Jesus Christ. Hall was never a Socinian, despite some of his unwise remarks in defence of Joseph Priestley, which had aroused the concerns of Fuller and Ryland. Further evidence of his convictions regarding the person of Christ have come to light more recently. Among his Bristol congregation on Sunday November 5, 1786 there was a discerning lady by the name of Jane Attwater. In her diary for that day she recorded:

> Mr. Hall preach from ye 63^d of Isaiah part of ye first verse viz "Mighty to save"—wch he applied to our Saviour as God spoke exceedingly clear of his belief in Christ as God as well as man & I was quite satisfied with his sentiments in this discourse & can with sincerity vindicate him from those things wch some who misunderstood him accused him of I greatly admire him & desire to bless God for gifting & qualifying such an able minister to stand up for ye truth &c.[8]

There is no evidence to suggest that Hall ever questioned the fundamentals of the Christian faith. Perhaps the simplest explanation of the question is that Hall covered the fundamentals of the faith, which he firmly believed, in the 1787 circular letter. Yet in his ministry in Bristol he tended to leave these subjects to Caleb Evans. In so doing he had been unwise and left himself open to the suspicion that he held defective views of the gospel and perhaps

---

[8] Timothy Whelan, *Nonconformist Women Writers 1720-1840*, 8 vols. (London: Pickering and Chatto, 2011), 8:243.

had begun to embrace Socinianism in particular. Yet at the same time, Morris, eager to protect Hall from unjustified criticism, was overlooking the fact that during his time in Bristol, Hall was not a thoroughly convinced Trinitarian. He still doubted the personality of the Holy Spirit, and he was still a materialist, denying the intermediate state, and he was in all probability still working out the sentiments he was later to express in his resignation letter to the church in Bristol.

Growing tensions

An atmosphere of uneasiness developed in the Bristol congregation. The "honeymoon" was over and by 1788 the personal friendship between Evans and his younger assistant came under increasing pressures. Questions were being asked about Hall's integrity. A crisis was looming. The possibility of Hall going to Cambridge to replace Robert Robinson (1735-1790) arose following Robinson's death. Hall went there and preached for a brief period and then received a further invitation to return. Such were the tensions in Bristol that the prospect of Hall's removal to Cambridge seemed an ideal way to resolve the issue and restore unity and peace to the church in Broadmead. Caleb Evans advised him to take up the invitation and after consulting with his friends Hall decided he would move to Cambridge.

After Hall had resigned his position in Bristol, the Broadmead church wanted to know Hall's doctrinal convictions in more detail. He gave them a "frank expression of his opinions" in a letter read to the Broadmead church on December 9, 1790.[9] The contents of this letter are important because it was one of the few occasions on which Robert Hall publicly made known his theological

---

[9] Gregory, *Works*, 1:31. The complete letter, dated Thursday, 9 December 1790 is to be found in Gregory, *Works*, 1:31–33. The original is to be found in the archives of Bristol Baptist College.

A Parting of the Ways

views. A few days before the church meeting of December 9, Hall told Evans, "You are a Calvinist. I am not."[10] Hall further explained himself in his letter read to the church. He qualified what he had said to Evans telling them, "I am not a Calvinist, in the strict and proper sense of that term."[11]

It is not possible to separate Hall's doctrinal views from the events which led up to his departure from Bristol. However, they do not appear to have been the principal reason for his decision to resign. He was persuaded that in Cambridge he would find sentiments more in agreement with his own views. It is true that some of his opinions were not well-received by the entire congregation in Broadmead. Some were persuaded that holding to all the five points of Calvinism was essential. Hall, for his part, was seeking a middle path between Calvinism and Arminianism. He was seeking to find a solution that he was persuaded was consistent with the free offers and invitations of the gospel and the predestinating purposes of God. He was to resolve it to his own satisfaction by believing that the Lord Jesus Christ died for all men and not just for the elect. However, no one in the church ever accused him of heresy. Morris declared that his views were "speculative singularities ... and had no perceptible influence on his religious and devotional feelings."[12]

Was it for that reason that Caleb Evans consistently maintained that Hall was orthodox in his views? Did he do this publicly in order to prevent the opposition in the church from gaining the upper hand and thus protect his younger colleague? If Caleb Evans knew what Hall's sentiments were, why did he insist on saying that they were orthodox? If he was well-acquainted with Hall's views why did he not take some further action? Hall recognised the differences between them, by stating that he did not entertain

---

[10] Morris, *Biographical Recollections*, 79.
[11] Gregory, *Works*, 1:32.
[12] Morris, *Biographical Recollections*, 61.

the same Calvinistic views as Evans.

As far as can be determined Hall left Bristol for Cambridge not only because he no longer held consistently to Calvinism but principally because of his falling out with Caleb Evans and the suspicions that he entertained about Evans' conduct towards him. The consequences of the manner of his leaving Bristol were far-reaching. Key doctrinal issues, which were a significant departure from Particular Baptist, or Calvinistic orthodoxy were allowed to go unchallenged by the church in Broadmead and, it appears, also by Caleb Evans. In Hall's opinion his convictions would not be an issue in Cambridge. A letter of invitation to Hall from the St. Andrew's Street Baptist Church in Cambridge, asking him to come and preach for six months, confirmed his opinion. Dated October 16, 1790, it included the following statement:

> The church has no doctrinal covenant or any other bond of union than Christian love and virtue, and having been well instructed by their late excellent pastor [Robert Robinson] in freedom of enquiry and (as they think) the true principles of Christian liberty they mean not to be brought under a yoke of bondage to any man. This liberty which they claim for themselves they cheerfully allow to others and especially to their pastor.[13]

The opposition he experienced in Bristol because of his convictions was only one reason why he decided to leave. All the circumstances and reasons for his departure need to be clarified before we are able to assess his stated theological views.

---

[13] Roger Hayden, ed. *Church Book: St Andrew's Street Baptist Church Cambridge, 1720-1832*, English Baptist Records 2 (Baptist Historical Society, 1991),75. The *Church Book* contains very little information about Hall's ministry in Cambridge apart from a letter of invitation to Hall and his letter of resignation.

A Parting of the Ways

The parting of the ways

Hall wrote a letter of explanation to the church at Broadmead on November 11, 1790. He spoke in general terms about the differences between them. He told them candidly that he held

> opinions on some points of religious and moral speculation ... different from those professed by this society, and that I wish to be connected with a congregation in which I shall meet with sentiments more congenial with my own, and where I shall not be in danger of falling into the arts of collision, or of incurring the vexations of honesty.[14]

Feelings ran high in the Broadmead congregation. Some wished him to remain and called for a re-invitation to be issued to Hall. Others were more cautious and more inclined to raise questions about his opinions. The church decided that before any such re-invitation could be issued they ought to know the precise content of the differences between them and Hall. For a church meeting held on December 9, Hall produced a written letter which was then read to them. He also informed them that he was no longer in a position to accept any re-invitation as he was now committed to fulfil his undertaking to serve as a probationer for six months in Cambridge. The church accepted Hall's explanation without any reference to his opinions and informed him that, in keeping with his original letter of resignation, he was no longer under any obligations to the church at Broadmead and that they were therefore free to look for another minister to succeed Hall.[15]

---

[14] Morris, *Biographical Recollections*, 70.

[15] John Harris and Arthur Tozer, a pamphlet issued by them referring to the details of the disagreement of Robert Hall and Caleb Evans noted at length in the Church Meeting book, between November 1790 and January 1791, Bristol, Jan. 31 1791, 11. Page numbers used here refer to the document produced by Roger Hayden and not to those in Appendix 1, where the full text appears. It is held in Bristol Baptist College (G99A, 19428) and is used with their permission. The dilapidated document was copied by Roger Hayden, 5-6 June 2002. The original is to be found in Bristol Archives, 30251, *Records of Broadmead Baptist Church—1644-2009*.

That might have been the end of the matter had not Hall written to Evans two days before the church meeting requesting a meeting between the two of them. Hall said:

> I earnestly wish for some friendly conversation and amicable discussion. Certain considerations have presented themselves to my mind, as if there were something like a premediated scheme, and perhaps foreign influence exerted in my intended removal from Bristol. I have long resisted such impressions, but they force themselves upon me to a degree I cannot altogether resist. I should be happy to see you, either by yourself, or in company with any other common friend, when I can explain the nature and causes of my apprehensions more at large, and meet I hope with the satisfaction I so earnestly desire.[16]

The letter triggered a response that led to an ever-increasing distance between the two men. In his reply to Hall the very same evening Evans responded positively saying he would gladly meet Hall the following day, and:

> As to the premeditated scheme, and foreign influence you speak of, I know nothing at all. I am willing to be examined on that or any subject you may think proper to discuss, I was as open as the day with you from first to last, till you thought proper, for so it appeared to me, to desert me and enlist with those you style your friends against me.
>
> Since then I have withdrawn from the business, and it has been out of my power, as well as inclination to interfere any further.
>
> Much pains have been taken to alienate your mind from me. I regret the success with which their efforts have in too greater measure been followed, but hope still to continue,

---

[16] Harris and Tozer, Letter of Hall to Evans, 2.

A Parting of the Ways

what I have always been,
 Your faithful, upright and zealous friend ...[17]

These letters indicate some of the tensions that existed between the two men. On the one hand Hall was suspicious. On the other hand Evans seems aware of some who had attempted, with some success, to drive a wedge between the two of them. It may be that he believed that these men were the source of Hall's suspicions. Over the next few days letters continued to be exchanged but there was no agreement on the place or the time of meeting and questions remained about who would accompany them to such a meeting. Finally, it was agreed that they would meet at the Mansion House on Monday, December 13. John Harris and Arthur Tozer would come with Evans and Mr. Protheroe and Mr. James with Hall.

It is clear from the reports published later by Harris and Tozer that serious disagreements emerged almost immediately during the four-hour meeting. The letters that had passed between them were then read before Hall produced a letter which he had intended to send to Evans but had not done. Instead he read it at the meeting. In the opinion of Harris and Tozer "the letter contained ... many gross insults and bitter invectiveness against Dr. Evans as well as misrepresentations of his character."[18] Furthermore it appears Hall accused Evans of dictating the resolution proposed by the chairman at the church meeting of December 5. The "disagreeable controversy" continued, sadly, into the new year.[19] Protheroe and James entered the fray and defended Hall, rejecting the notion that he had used insulting language and indulged in bitter invective. They were not convinced that Evans gave adequate

---

[17] Harris and Tozer, Letter of Evans to Hall, 3.
[18] Harris and Tozer, No. I, 8. Despite requests by Harris and Tozer that Hall publish this paper it never seems to have appeared in print, leaving us unable to draw definitive final conclusions.
[19] Harris and Tozer, No.II, 12.

answers to Hall.

> There was not one charge of importance advanced by Mr. Hall, to which Dr. Evans gave a satisfactory answer. The charge of most consequence, which stated, that the resolutions of the last church meeting were occasioned by the personal influence of Dr. Evans, appeared to us to be established upon the most indubitable evidence; for one of the Gentlemen (either Harris or Tozer) acknowledged, that he had written letters and personally requested the attendance of members to vote against Mr. Hall, and Dr. Evans himself confessed he had come to a resolution to resign if Mr. Hall should be re-chosen.[20]

Finally, Harris and Tozer stood their ground, "in vindication of the injured character of Dr. Evans."[21] They gave a lengthy reply declaring that Hall's original suspicions were founded on misconceptions and misrepresentations. Hall, it appears, simply would not believe what Evans had said about the matter despite his protestations of innocence. Evans denied that there was "any foundation for what you have advanced," and then added, "I mean to deny it, Root and Branch."[22]

It appears the matter was left unresolved. Harris and Tozer had published the letters and the reports of the meeting on December 13 to defend the character and the integrity of Evans. They affirmed that the fault lay on the shoulders of the younger man, Robert Hall. Based on their record of events Hall does not emerge from the episode in a favourable light.[23] The published pamphlet makes sad reading. The tensions escalated over a period of six weeks. The longer the controversy continued the more entrenched became the convictions of the two sides. The issues were

---

[20] Harris and Tozer, No. II, 11.
[21] Harris and Tozer, No. III, 13.
[22] Harris and Tozer, No. III, 19.
[23] See Appendix 1 for further comments on this unpleasant business.

A Parting of the Ways

not over matters of doctrine. There were significant differences of doctrine between the Caleb Evans and Robert Hall but it does not appear that they were ever discussed. Instead they ended up in dispute with Hall entertaining, what appeared to Harris and Tozer, to be unfounded accusations, which called into question the integrity of Hall's senior colleague.

Hall became very critical of the manner in which Evans had handled the matter of his departure before the church, and concluded that Evans' conduct in the entire matter meant they could no longer work "together as colleagues with unanimity and confidence."[24] He ended his letter of December 4 with words that would have stung the heart and conscience of Caleb Evans.

> Under the strongest professions of personal attachment, in which you are certainly sincere, induced by reasons I cannot penetrate, you have thrown your whole weight into the scale of the disaffected, have crushed every hope of my continuance, and in my ministerial capacity have stood out as my last and almost only oppose. In all these transactions a plain path lay open before you; but seduced by the inveterate love of rule, you chose rather to purchase lasting resentments by doing every thing, that secure your repose by doing nothing.[25]

Included in the letter there was the following critical statement of Evans by Hall: "You profess yourself a Calvinist. I do not. But this difference of sentiment is of no importance in your opinion. It might be thought strange that a Calvinist should hold his religious system as nothing, whilst a philosophical subtilty [referring to his sentiments on materialism] swelled to such importance."[26]

The situation that developed in Bristol meant Hall was

---

[24] Morris, *Biographical Recollections*, 80.
[25] Morris, *Biographical Recollections*, 80.
[26] Morris, *Biographical Recollections*, 79.

virtually compelled to declare his hand, something he was extremely reluctant to do. He did not consider himself to be a Calvinist, or at least a Calvinist like Caleb Evans.

A further ground for suspicion

Caleb Evans was a friend and frequent visitor to the Steele family in Broughton, Hampshire. In particular he was an admirer of the hymns of Anne Steele (1717–1778). He collected her hymns together and published them in three volumes.

Apart from Morris none of his biographers mention the following matter, perhaps to avoid embarrassment to either the Hall or the Steele family. However, there is no doubt that having fallen "prey to all the miseries of unrequited love," Hall experienced deep grief and bitterness of soul.[27] Morris knew that the lady in question was a relation of Anne Steele but he did not mention her name.

Mary Steele was a niece of Anne Steele, the hymn writer. Evans wrote to Mary several times in 1778 and 1779 following the death of her aunt. A few years later in a letter dated June 15, 1784, he spoke highly of Robert Hall, who had recently returned from Aberdeen:

> Mr. Hall is once more with us, improv'd in his person and address, and if possible in his conversation and Sermons. He is no small [letter torn] to my domestic felicity, & sh.^{d} I live to [letter torn]... as much the man of business for purposes of practical life as he is ye Man of Genius, Taste and Sublimity of Soul, I shall die in peace & be happy to withdraw & leave the church to be illuminated warm'd and cheer'd by his rising beams.[28]

---

[27] Morris, *Biographical Recollections*, 82.
[28] Whelan, *Nonconformist Women Writers*, 3:305–306.

A Parting of the Ways

Other letters from this period reveal the same admiration and love that Evans felt personally for Hall, speaking of him almost as if he was his son. He also expressed a deep appreciation of his preaching.

It was Mary's half-sister Anne, who became the object of Robert Hall's romantic interest in 1786-1787. Hall was in his mid-twenties, a rising star in Bristol, and a very eligible bachelor. However, Anne rejected him, perhaps because of his eccentricities. In 1791, she married Joseph Tomkins. According to Morris this rejection left Hall devastated. He became restless and it had a profound effect on his writing, his preaching, and even his reputation. Some newspapers in Bristol rubbed salt into his wounds by publishing a variety of anecdotes which tended to ridicule Hall. But what also caused him grief was the strong suspicion that Evans had cast a dark shadow over the whole affair, "the same agency which had been employed in effecting his removal from Bristol had likewise been exerted in endeavouring to alienate the object of his affections, and had contributed in procuring to him the severest of all human disappointments."[29]

Morris was not sure whether Hall was mistaken in his suspicions of Evans. Whelan thinks Hall had good grounds for his suspicions given the closeness of Evans to the Steele family and the knowledge he had of Hall himself. The evidence is inconclusive but if Evans did interfere in the affair he probably did so because he thought he was acting in the best interests of both parties. It appears that Hall only discovered the role Evans probably played three years after he had been rebuffed by Anne. If so it would greatly increase the tensions that led to the parting of the ways in 1790.

What is more certain is the lasting effect Anne's rejection had on Hall. It was a contributory factor to his breakdown in 1804

---

[29] Morris, *Biographical Recollections*, 84-85.

while in Cambridge. Morris records that there were pointed allusions to his intense sorrows in his letters for upwards of twelve years after the events. Barbed sarcastic comments hardly soothed the troubled spirit of the young Hall. On one occasion, he visited a lady whom he knew in Hertfordshire, but he seemed detached and uninterested in any conversation. Wearied by his seeming indifference she told him, "I suppose sir, if I had been polished 'Steel' I might have expected some of your attention." Aroused by such a comment Hall replied, "Madam, you make yourself quite easy: if you are not polished Steel, you are polished Brass!"[30] His sarcastic wit was equal to hers but no one could measure the pain that such a comment brought to increasing his sorrows. He poured out his feelings in a prose piece "Reverie" under the signature of "Leptos." It was subsequently published in the *Salisbury Journal* in 1787, and was clearly the work of a distraught mind, bitter about the miseries of spurned love.[31]

Tranquility and stability of soul deserted Hall in the late 1780s and into the 1790s. The growing distance between him and his pastor Caleb Evans, those in Broadmead who had questioning his orthodoxy, the ill-fated pursuit of Anne Steele, all were made worse by the suspicions that Hall entertained regarding the conduct of Evans. It must have been with some relief that he went to Cambridge. However, none of these events, important as they are, should be allowed to distract us from the theological issues that Hall himself raised when asked to do so by the Broadmead congregation. There was also a theological parting of the ways and these matters have for too long been overlooked or disregarded.

---

[30] Morris, *Biographical Recollections*, 86–87.
[31] Gregory, *Works*, 6:410–420.

7
Breakdown and New Beginnings

In his *Memoir of Robert Hall*, Gregory records his first impressions of him:

> I was struck with his well-proportioned athletic figure, the unassuming dignity of his deportment, the winning frankness which marked all that he uttered, and the peculiarities of the most speaking countenance I ever contemplated, animated by eyes radiating with the brilliancy imparted to them by benevolence, wit and intellectual energy.[1]

Such a figure was completely unrecognisable for several months, first in late 1804 and again in November 1805, when Hall suffered two mental breakdowns.

Declining health 1799-1805

Robert Hall was born into a family which had known such affliction. His mother Jane had undergone a period of insanity from which she partially recovered, but not before she had made several attempts to commit suicide. Her sufferings were almost certainly responsible for her premature death in 1776 when her youngest son was only twelve years old.[2] Those sufferings and her death left a deep impression on him. As a result of the encouragement of friends, his father published a detailed account of her

---

[1] Gregory, *Works*, 1:47. C.f. Gregory's estimate of Hall with Foster, in Hall, *Works*, 1:204-205.

[2] At least one writer has suggested that the Calvinism of his upbringing was responsible for his doubts, his depression and breakdown but they do not take into account the family history. See Angus Hamilton MacLeod, "The Life and Teaching of Robert Hall, 1764-1831"(Master of Letters thesis, University of Durham. 1957), 197.

experiences.³

Writing thirty years after the events of 1804 and 1805, neither Gregory nor Greene gave their readers a full account of events surrounding Hall's two periods of intense suffering. At the time the church in Cambridge described his severe afflictions as "mental derangement."⁴ More recently, drawing on an unknown eyewitness's account of events between October 31 and November 11, 1804, discovered in the Angus Library, Oxford, Timothy Whelan has provided a fuller and very helpful picture of what actually happened.⁵ Whelan suggests that his early biographers did not reveal all the details of what took place because they wished to preserve Hall's reputation.

Hall's condition may have been triggered by a bout of fever. In 1799 that fever nearly cost him his life and left him physically weakened. His usual cheerful spirit was now being disturbed by fits of depression, which increased in frequency and duration. To his friends he seemed to be more and more absorbed with morbid feelings about his own state before God and increasingly depressed by the monotony of the flat Cambridgeshire countryside. Gregory, Greene, and Morris all commented on his increasing and seemingly incurable dislike of his surroundings. Hall remarked to Gregory, "shocking place for the spirits, Sir; I wish you may not find it so; it must be the very focus of suicides."⁶ Writing became an intolerable burden, not only because of his mood but also because of acute back pain caused by renal calculi (kidney stones). He even reached the point where he considered resigning from his public ministry altogether. Recovering a little in the summer of

---

[3] Robert Hall [Senior], *Mercy manifested: a letter to a friend, relating the dying consolations of Mrs. Jane Hall* (London: 1777).

[4] Roger Hayden, ed., *Church Book: St Andrew's Street Baptist Church, Cambridge, 1720-1832*, English Baptist Records 2 (Baptist Historical Society, 1991), 78.

[5] Timothy Whelan, "I am the greatest of the prophets": A New Look at Robert Hall's Mental Breakdown, November 1804," *Baptist Quarterly* 42 (2007): 114-126.

[6] Gregory, *Works*, 1:51.

Breakdown and New Beginnings

1802 he was able to preach his sermon *Reflections on War*, and prepare it for publication. By the autumn though, his physical pain and depression of spirit returned.

Hall increasingly confined himself to his rooms. The solitude and excessive hours of reading, invariably a minimum of twelve hours a day, increased his suffering. Hall felt this amount of reading was necessary to redeem time and also to keep ahead of the reading men in Cambridge. But such intense labour unhinged him. He became even more severely depressed, displaying manic feelings, together with expressions indicating a great sense of personal unworthiness and sinfulness.

By the autumn of 1804 his condition reached crisis point and on November 11 he was placed under the care of Dr. Thomas Arnold in Leicester. Prior to that, while still in Cambridge, Hall experienced delusions of grandeur. In one evening of intense derangement he "deliver'd a kind of prophecy, and declared his commission which was that he was the Greatest Prophet the world ever saw."[7] When William Hollick, the senior deacon from the church in Cambridge, arrived to see Hall, "he was no sooner seated than in the utmost grandeur of voice he said, "*I am the son of God*," talked about his supernatural birth, said he was born with only half a head, which was always too small for his brains, but that he had a new head given him."[8]

When Hollick dared to disagree, an enraged Hall drove him out, "leaping out of bed, ran after him downstairs, through the passage & round the garden ... declaring he would send him to Hell &c—"[9] Hall was restrained by a straitjacket but he broke free and refused all medication. Some days later in a calmer spirit he asked that Psalm 51 be read to him. This was done and the

---
[7] Whelan, "A New Look at Robert Hall's Mental Breakdown," 118.
[8] Whelan, "A New Look at Robert Hall's Mental Breakdown," 118.
[9] Whelan, "A New Look at Robert Hall's Mental Breakdown," 118.

eyewitness recorded that Hall "turned every verse into prayer applying it to his own case in a most sublime manner the most sublime language as he thinks was ever uttered by mortal ... After this he became happy & comfortable."[10] Hall spent some time recovering in a private asylum in Leicester under the care of Dr. Arnold. Hall later commented to John Greene that the severity of the cure was almost as bad as the condition and asked that if further treatment was needed in the future that he would not be sent back to that asylum.

By April 1805 he was able to return to Cambridge and his ministry, only to suffer a second breakdown in the following November. The same distressing signs returned. He forgot the Sunday services, made no preparation for preaching, and was sometimes discovered wandering in the streets. One Sunday he did not turn up for the morning service but arrived ten minutes late for the afternoon meeting. Half-way through he began to speak incoherently. Having complained of a bad head he managed to complete his sermon. Following the communion service, which Hall conducted, he called out wildly,

> Stop! stop!, my friends; I have something very important to communicate to you. I have to inform you that the Millennium is come, that period which we have been waiting for, hoping for and praying for so long, is come. Let us kneel down and bless God that we have lived to see this day.[11]

Eventually, Hall was taken to Fishponds in Bristol where he was placed in the care of Dr. Cox. Here he received "mild and kind treatment" and later praised the superior treatment he

---

[10] Whelan, "A New Look at Robert Hall's Mental Breakdown," 119.

[11] Greene, *Reminiscences of the Rev. Robert Hall* in Gregory and Belcher, *Works*, 4:33.

Breakdown and New Beginnings

received at Cox's hands. The proof, he affirmed, was simple; he never had a relapse.[12] Cox gave him three directions to prevent any return of his condition. Firstly, he must leave Cambridge. Secondly, he should take up smoking as "a composing habit." Thirdly, he was advised to marry, to relieve the solitude of single life. On his recovery he returned to relatives and friends in Leicestershire, and included visits to his former home in Arnesby. At first he avoided all preaching engagements, allowing his body and his mind to recover from the severe trauma of his mental breakdowns. With returning strength came significant changes in his life.

Permanent health problems

One health issue though was never resolved. While he never experienced any further mental breakdowns he was increasingly plagued with acute back pains, the result of renal calculi. The pain he endured and the sleepless nights it caused were certainly a contributory factor to his breakdown. In order to alleviate this pain he was in the habit of taking large doses of laudanum, the prescribed painkiller of the day. This habit was life-long as it was with other well-known figures among his friends such as William Wilberforce and Sir James Mackintosh.[13] The medicine prescribed was a tincture of alcohol and opium. As well as relieving pain it invariably had a powerful narcotic effect capable of producing hallucinations and deep sleep. Several drops were the recommended dose. Hall was taking very large doses of laudanum together with an additional half glass of brandy! Greene records how one day he found Hall, then in his late fifties, in intense pain and highly dependent on laudanum (which he was now taking in the form of opium tablets). On taking a further dose Hall said he had now taken the

---

[12] Gregory and Belcher, *Works*, 4:34–35.
[13] Gregory gives an account of their friendship, Hall, *Works*, 1:17–19.

equivalent of 1500 drops that day and was resolved to take another 250 if he got no relief. Greene managed to restrain him, urging a cup of warm tea instead to aid diffusion of the opium. When a medical friend joined them Hall remarked to him,

> What a merciful provision laudanum is, sir! I could not exist without it. It seems as if Providence has designed it as a specific for me. Most persons complain that it affects the head, and stupefies them; I always feel more lively after taking it. How do you account for this, sir?

The gentleman confessed his inability to account for it, and stated that Mr. Hall's was a solitary instance.[14]

It is hard to imagine that the amounts of opium had no detrimental effects on Hall. It seems extremely likely that he was addicted to the opium even if he did not realise it. However, he did not die a premature death as a consequence. He lived until he was sixty-six years old. Furthermore, there is no evidence from Hall himself, his congregations, or his close friends, that he suffered any debilitating effects despite the huge amounts that he took in order to ease his intense pain. John Foster was of the opinion that Hall only experienced diminished energy in the last few years of his life, "the period when an increased, but reluctant use of opiates became absolutely necessary, to enable him to endure the pain which he suffered throughout his life," and when the heart disease that led to his death set in.[15] One witness recorded in a letter to Gregory "the only instance in which I have ever seen him at all overcome by the soporific quality of the medicine.[16] That occasion was a few days before his death when Hall took no less than 125 grains of solid opium, which was more than 3000 drops, and

---

[14] Greene, *Reminiscences of the Rev Robert Hall*, in Gregory and Belcher, *Works*, 4:90–91.
[15] Gregory, *Works*, 1:204.
[16] Gregory, *Works*, 1:150–151.

Breakdown and New Beginnings

equivalent to four ounces of laudanum!

There is no evidence that he wrote and preached under the stimulating but potentially wild effects of laudanum. Samuel Taylor Coleridge (1772-1834) wrote the well-known poem *Kubla Khan* as a result of the hallucinatory effects of the drug. He was one of several contemporary poets and authors, especially among the Romantics, who used laudanum to stimulate creativity in their writing. Although Hall said he felt "more lively after taking it," it would be reading too much into that statement to suggest that he was deliberately using it in order to provide himself with a stimulant. However, that statement may reflect the unintended effects of such doses that he imbibed.

New beginnings

There were significant changes during the three years after what Hall referred to as "a succession of afflictive dispensations," which led to his resignation as pastor in Cambridge.[17] Hall was now in his early forties. He had left Bristol under a cloud and became the pastor of St. Andrew's Street Baptist Church, Cambridge. Apart from falling out with Caleb Evans, there were sore open wounds, the result of the failed love affair. Following the counsel of his doctor to leave Cambridge, he resigned from his pastoral office in March 1806.

Three significant changes took place in Hall's life. First, he became pastor to Carey's former congregation in Leicester; second, in 1808 he married Eliza Smith; and third, following on from his illness, and in particular his experiences in late 1804 and early 1805, he drew up a solemn dedication of himself to God. This was in 1809 by which time he had been in pastor in Leicester for eighteenth months.

---

[17] Hayden, ed., *Church Book*, 78.

Harvey Lane Baptist Church, Leicester

A year or so after his illness he began to preach in a number of villages in and around Leicester, and was soon preaching every Sunday. Hall hoped the church in Clipstone would invite him to be their pastor, but no invitation was forthcoming. The church in Arnesby invited him, but instead he accepted the call to Harvey Lane, believing this was God's will. He began his ministry in October 1807. William Carey had been pastor from 1789 until 1793. The church had prospered for a few years but by the time Hall came it was half empty and reduced to seventy-six members.[18]

He would be pastor in Harvey Lane for almost twenty years and during his time there the mature Robert Hall emerged further into the limelight. He became the most prominent figure in Baptist circles—especially after 1815 when Andrew Fuller died—and the leading voice in English nonconformity. Leicester was situated in the heart of the Midlands, and was a centre for the manufacture of textiles. It had a population of just over 23,000 according to the 1811 Census. Wherever he preached, overflowing congregations heard him. Gregory reported that he preached to all kinds of people. They included Churchmen and Dissenters, men of rank and influence, men of simple piety, others who had a deep theological knowledge, some who admired Christianity as a beautiful system, some who received it into their hearts by faith, others full of doubts and unbelief.[19]

Within two years the building had to be extended, bringing the seating capacity to eight hundred. Even this was not enough and the building was full to overflowing again. Hall delighted to preach largely to plain people, often plunged into poverty, many of whom were Leicester framework-knitters. He preferred to preach to this

---

[18] Gregory, *Works*, 1:97.
[19] Gregory, *Works*, 1:103.

Breakdown and New Beginnings

kind of congregation rather than to the refined audience of Cambridge. His Leicester congregation were different, "simple-hearted, affectionate, praying people."[20]

Marriage

Shortly after he became pastor in Leicester, he married Eliza Smith, whom he had first met at the house of Thomas Edmonds, pastor of the church in Clipstone. Many were horrified at his choice of bride and by the suddenness with which his marriage took place. Clearly they did not understand Robert Hall.

He had known his bride-to-be for less than a year. Yet he was not seeking a woman of rank, property, or intellectual talents, rather a lady whose Christian graces would adorn family life. If someone commended a learned or ingenuous lady to him Morris said he would reply impatiently, "I do not want a wife to read Greek, sir. I can read Greek myself."[21] Eliza was an uneducated servant girl. She stayed for a while with the Edmonds and then spent six months with Joseph Timms and his wife in Kettering. They were friends of the Hall family. (Joseph Timms had been present at the first meeting of The Particular Baptist Society for the Propagation of the Gospel among the Heathen, held in Kettering in 1792.) The Edmonds and the Timms invested their time and energy into preparing Eliza for her life as the wife of Robert Hall.

Hall was now forty-three years of age. He declared March 25, 1808 to be the happiest day of his life. Casting his mind back to the disappointments of his days in Bristol, he saw his marriage to Eliza as an end "to eighteen years of anxiety and regret already

---

[20] Gregory, *Works*, 1:301.
[21] J.W. Morris, *Biographical Reflections of the Rev. Robert Hall, A M.* (India, New Delhi: Isha Books, 2013), 216.

endured."[22] Ten months after their wedding he wrote to John Ryland and spoke of his pleasure at having moved to Leicester, adding a "p.s.: In gratitude to God, and to my dear companion, I must add, that marriage has added (a little to my cares), *much* to my comfort, and that I am indulged with the best of wives."[23] They were to have three daughters, and two sons, one of whom died in infancy. Despite the grief of that loss, Robert Hall found in Eliza a true life-companion who became "the solace of his remaining days."[24]

Conversion and dedication to God

Hall had professed faith in Christ and was baptised at the age of fourteen. As Hall reflected on his experiences of 1804 and 1805 it appears that he called into question the genuineness of his professed conversion. Letters written to William Hollick and James Phillips during his period of recovery in Leicestershire record the deep impression his afflictions made on him, but these letters contain no specific evidence that he thought of himself as being unconverted before 1805. Writing to Phillips he records, "I am a monument of the goodness and severity of God."[25] Likewise he records "with the sincerest gratitude I would acknowledge the goodness of God in restoring me," adding a few sentences later, "During my affliction I have not been entirely forsaken of God, nor left destitute of that calm trust in his providence which was requisite to support me; yet I have not been favoured with that intimate communion and that delightful sense of his love which I

---

[22] Morris, *Biographical Recollections*, 218.

[23] Gregory, *Works*, 1:301. A letter to Rev James Phillip, dated 1 September 1809 expresses similar happiness. Hall spoke of "being blessed with an affectionate, amiable woman, and a lovely little girl, about five months old." Gregory, *Works*, 1:306.

[24] Morris, *Biographical Recollections*, 217. A further letter to Rev James Phillip, dated 1 September 1809 expresses a similar spirit.

[25] Gregory, *Works*, 1:94.

Breakdown and New Beginnings

have enjoyed on former occasions."[26]

Those letters are not conclusive however, for they only provide some of Hall's own testimony. On the basis of personal conversations with Hall, Gregory records the impact of the illness on his friend:

> The permanent impression on his character was exclusively religious. His own decided persuasion was that, however vivid his convictions of religious truth, and of the necessity of a consistent course of evangelical obedience had formerly been, and however correct his doctrinal sentiments during the past four or five years, yet he did not undergo a thorough transformation of character, a complete renewal of heart and affections until the first of these seizures.[27]

Gregory continued by noting that some of his Cambridge friends who had heard his penitent confession when Psalm 51 was being read to him were "rather inclined to concur with him as to the correctness of his opinion."[28] David Bennett, a contemporary of Hall and, who, with David Bogue, wrote a history of Dissent, observed that Hall's "religious character was so much improved by his afflictions, that he deemed them the means of his *first* acquaintance with the genuine religion of the heart."[29]

Robert Oliver is also persuaded by Hall's own testimony that he was not converted until 1804.[30] Hall's close friend and biographer remained undecided. Gregory said "the wonderful revelations of "the great day" can alone remove the doubt."[31] However,

---

[26] Gregory, *Works*, 1:290.
[27] Gregory, *Works*, 1:93.
[28] Gregory, *Works*, 1:93.
[29] James Bennett, *The History of Dissenters During the Last Thirty Years, 1808-1838* (London: Hamilton, Adams and Co., 1839), 488.
[30] Robert W. Oliver, *History of the English Calvinistic Baptists, 1771-1892: From John Gill to C. H. Spurgeon* (Edinburgh: The Banner of Truth Trust, 2006), 236.
[31] Gregory, *Works*, 1:93.

what is clear is that Hall was a changed man as a result of his experience—more dependent on God, more devotional in his habits, and more fervent and elevated in his spiritual exercises.[32]

William Steadman also knew Hall well and made some significant observations about his first preaching in Bristol. It "had not then an evangelical cast. Seldom did he insist on the peculiarities of the Gospel; when, however, he did, he did it well."[33] Hearing him in Plymouth in 1801, he recorded that Hall "preaches with a brilliant eloquence as well as great seriousness but introduces only a small degree of evangelical truth into his discourses, much as he did at Bristol."[34] That same year he heard Hall again and felt the same deficiency: "his sermon was ... rather barren of evangelical truth."[35] He recorded that,

> From several persons, and amongst them Mr. Nicholls of Collingham, I have heard that he [Hall] had said, that when at Bristol, he was not converted, and that if he had died then, he should have perished. He then dated his conversion from his affliction, in 1804.[36]

He admitted though that he did not know what to say about Hall becoming a Christian in that crisis. However, he had observed a marked change in Hall:

> Since his recovery and settlement in Leicester, and also his removal to Bristol, he appeared to have been greatly and constantly under the influence of vital godliness, and to have manifested much of the spirit of genuine devotion. His

---

[32] Gregory, *Works*, 1:93.
[33] Thomas Steadman, *Memoir of the Rev. William Steadman, D.D.* (London: Thomas Ward and Co., 1838), 422-423.
[34] Steadman, *Memoir of the Rev. William Steadman*, 202.
[35] Steadman, *Memoir of the Rev. William Steadman*, 202.
[36] Steadman, *Memoir of the Rev. William Steadman*, 422-423.

Breakdown and New Beginnings

preaching was in general evangelical, as plain as he could make it and manifestly conducted with a view to save souls. Though conscious of his great abilities, he was humble, affable, and attentive to everyone, however inferior. He certainly gave great weight to the denomination and the cause of Christianity.[37]

Yet Hall was not without inward turmoil after his conversion. Despite the profound impact of what happened in 1804 he was on occasions still a troubled man. In the very same letter he wrote to John Ryland telling him of his domestic happiness, and the pleasure he derived from his new congregation in Leicester, he entreated Ryland's prayers. He wrote, "For myself, my mind and body are both much out of order; awful doubt and darkness hanging on the former, and much affliction and pain in the latter."[38] Hall gave no details. No doubt the bodily pains were caused by his kidney stones. He told Morris that for weeks he could seldom sit up for one hour.[39]

The causes of his doubts and darkness are not easy to identify but he did give some indication. He explained to Morris that his mind was "filled with awful and disquieting apprehensions respecting a hereafter."[40] Trestrail records an incident related to him by an inn-keeper, a fine Christian man, known as Master York. Hall was returning home from Clipstone. He decided to stop at the inn because it was a stormy winter's night. Master York seized the initiative and went around the village of Sibbertoft, inviting the villagers to come and hear their unexpected visitor preach. Hall preached an impromptu sermon on heaven, from Revelation 21:12: "I saw no temple therein." Master York

---

[37] Steadman, *Memoir of the Rev. William Steadman*, 423.
[38] Gregory, *Works*, 1:301.
[39] Morris, *Biographical Recollections*, 225.
[40] Morris, *Biographical Recollections*, 225.

was enraptured and told Trestrail, "he talked in so wonderful a manner about the glory of heaven, and the worship which the saints would offer to God, that I forgot where I was, and thought I was up there."[41]

Once everyone had gone Hall fell silent and sighed deeply several times. Asked if anything was the matter, he replied, "Yes, Master York, very much. I am in great doubts as to my state. I sometimes fear I have never been converted, and it distresses me exceedingly."[42] The hour was past midnight but the exchanges between the preacher and the inn-keeper drew out another sermon from Hall. By the end of that sermon his fears and doubts were turned into peace and joy. Hall had preached to one man about sin and the ruin it had caused, about God's pity and love for poor sinners, sending his Son to die for sinners, and finally about pardon and everlasting life. When he finally came to leave he expressed his warm thanks to his host telling him that he had "lifted a load off my mind ... I shall sleep in peace. Good-night." Overcome by the fact that he had been a help to such a man as Hall, Master York said, "I stood there and cried like a babby [sic]."[43] This event probably took place in 1806 or 1807, before he became the pastor at Harvey Lane. What was the cause of Hall's distress? Was he lacking assurance of salvation? Was he being assailed by Satan? How well at this point in his life did he understand union with Christ, justification by faith in Christ? Did he believe that Christ's righteousness had been imputed to him and that this righteousness was the ground of his acceptance with God? We can only ask those questions but cannot provide definite answers from Hall. Some have suggested that his mental turmoil was the result of his Calvinistic background but that is a misleading and

---

[41] Frederick Trestrail, *Reminiscences of College Life in Bristol During the Ministry of Rev. Robert Hall, A.M.* (London: E Marlborough and Co., 1879), 146.

[42] Trestrail, *Reminiscences of College Life*, 146.

[43] Trestrail, *Reminiscences of College Life*, 147.

Breakdown and New Beginnings

prejudiced conclusion.

By May 2, 1809 his fears and doubts seem to have been resolved. Hall solemnly dedicated himself to God on his forty-fifth birthday, something he renewed each year on the same day. By this time he was a pastor in Leicester. In this document he made a confession of his sins before God, conscious that none of them were hidden from his eyes. Quoting Psalm 51:5, the psalm that had made such a deep impression on him a few years before, he confessed:

> I am an apostate, guilty branch of an apostate guilty root, and my life has been a series of rebellions and transgressions, in which I have walked "according to the course of this world, according to the Prince of the power of the air, the spirit that now worketh in the children of disobedience." How shall I confess my transgressions before thee, what numbers can reach; what words can adequately express them! "My iniquities have increased over my head, and my transgressions have grown up into Heaven." O Lord, I esteem it a wonderful mercy that I have not long since been cut off in the midst of my sins, and been sent to hell before I had an opportunity or a heart to repent. Being assured from the word of God of thy merciful and gracious nature, and of thy willingness to accept penitent believing sinners on the ground of the blood and righteousness of thine own adorable Son, "who died, the just for the unjust, to bring them to God," and that "him that cometh to him he will in no wise cast out," I do most humbly prostrate myself at the footstool of his cross, and through him enter into thy covenant. I disclaim all right to myself from henceforth, to my soul, my body, my time, my health, my reputation, my talents, or anything that belongs to me. I confess myself to be the property of the glorious Redeemer, as one who I humbly hope he has redeemed by his blood to be part of "the first fruits of his creatures."[44]

---

[44] Gregory, *Works*, 1:94–95.

The Theology of Robert Hall Jr.

As part of his solemn dedication of himself to God he renounced the Devil and all his works, the flesh, and the world, regretting that he had been enslaved by them for so long. He spoke of Christ as his Priest, Prophet, and King, saying, "I dedicate myself to him, to serve, love, and trust in him as my life and my salvation and my life's end."[45] He owned the Holy Spirit as his sanctifier and comforter, praying that the Holy Spirit would take perpetual possession of his heart, and dwell there. Hall's words reflect a full Trinitarianism:

> I do most solemnly devote and give up myself to the Father, the Son, and the Holy Ghost, agreeably to the terms of the Gospel covenant, and in humble expectation of the blessings it ascertains to sincere believers. I call thee to witness, O God! The truth and reality of the surrender of all I have, and all I am, to thee: and, conscious of the unspeakable deceitfulness of my heart, I humbly and earnestly implore the influence of thy Spirit to enable me to stand steadfast in thy covenant, as well as an interest in the blood of thy Son, that I may be forgiven in those instances (alas! that such an idea should be possible,) in which I may, in any degree, swerve from it.[46]

His solemn dedication shows him to be a man of great sincerity and intense earnestness, devoted only to serving God. Furthermore, the scriptural language he uses, the conviction and confession of sin, his evident repentance, grasping hold of the mercy of God and his willingness to forgive believing sinners, his faith in the Lord Jesus Christ and the shedding of his blood on the cross, his reliance on the Holy Spirit to sanctify him, his determination to remain steadfast in dependence on the same Spirit, and his desire to serve God faithfully with his whole being, speak eloquently

---

[45] Gregory, *Works*, 1:95.
[46] Gregory, *Works*, 1:95–96.

Breakdown and New Beginnings

of a genuine conversion to Christ, whatever doubts and fears he had expressed after his breakdown. Nothing as personal, or as full as this solemn dedication, exists in Hall's writings prior to 1809.

However, an intriguing and crucial question remains. Some of Hall's theological convictions were in place long before he began his ministry in Leicester. There is a little evidence, which will be considered in later chapters, to suggest that he modified some of his sentiments once he left Cambridge. However, we have to ask whether he formulated his doctrinal convictions, such as universal atonement, as a converted or an unconverted man. Other doctrinal convictions, for example, the imputation of Christ's righteousness Hall may have adopted relatively late in his life. Consequently, some doctrinal matters were omitted by him in his public ministry. Anyone listening to him over a longer period of time would not have been exposed to Calvinistic doctrines, distinctively and vigorously presented.

Gregory found it hard to accept that Hall became a converted man during his recovery from his mental breakdown. Hall, though, appeared decided. The question arises, how could Hall have exercised such an influential ministry in Cambridge prior to 1804? What are we to make of his profession of faith at the age of fourteen and his being set apart in August 1780 by his father's church in Arnesby to preach the word of God, when he was only sixteen years of age?

Robert Hall was not the first or the last person to engage in preaching while not converted to Christ. John Wesley (1703-1791) and Hall's peer, Thomas Chalmers (1780-1847) are famous examples of such men. Wesley had founded the "Methodist" or "Holy Club" in Oxford in 1729, and went to Georgia with his brother intent on securing the conversion of the native Americans, but he was not converted until 1738. Chalmers, who on occasions deliberately travelled via Leicester from Scotland to London to hear Hall preach, was first appointed a minister in 1802 but

The Theology of Robert Hall Jr.

was not converted until five or six years later. Hall was gifted with remarkable eloquence both in preaching and in writing and became widely accepted as the voice of Dissent while in Cambridge. But gifts, even of great eloquence, are no substitute for the grace of God converting a man to Christ.

Sealed by his solemn dedication to God Hall began afresh in Leicester. On his recovery he made it plain that he had undergone a profound spiritual experience that permanently changed him. Though some of his friends disagreed with his conclusion, he was of the opinion that when he first received the invitation to go to Cambridge he possessed, "just a sufficient quantum of orthodoxy to pass muster with the pious part of the members, and not too much to be refused by the refined and speculative part of the congregation."[47] Greene was one of those friends and declared it was a mistake to suppose that Hall's religious sentiments were not evangelical before 1804.[48] However, even holding formal evangelical sentiments is no guarantee of the grace of God in the heart.

Whatever his friends thought, Hall was fully persuaded that he had undergone a transformation of his character, and a complete renewal of his heart and his affections. As far as we know he never made any further reference to his previous profession of faith and his baptism at the age of fourteen. No one at the time seemed to question the genuineness of his profession of faith, nor to question his suitability as a preacher when he was ordained to the ministry. The church in Arnesby was satisfied by what they saw in this young man. He was gifted and stood out as a consequence. They had heard

> his speaking in his turn at conference meetings from various portions of Scripture; in which, and in prayer, he had borne a part for upwards of four years before; and having when at

---

[47] Gregory and Belcher, *Works*, 4:12.
[48] Gregory and Belcher, *Works*, 4:12.

Breakdown and New Beginnings

home, at their request, frequently preached on Lord's day mornings, to their great satisfaction. They therefore earnestly and unanimously requested his being in a solemn manner set apart to public employ.[49]

The same was true in the Academy at Bristol where Caleb Evans prepared him for his studies in King's College, Aberdeen. Questions about his suitability arose only after he had been appointed as a co-pastor and a tutor in Bristol.

In an address given a few years later in 1811 or 1812, on behalf of the new London Academy in Stepney, Hall identified "An unconverted ministry ... as the greatest calamity that can befall the church: nor would we be supposed to insinuate, by the preceding observations, that education can ever be a proper substitute for native talent, much less for real piety."[50] It would not have been appropriate on this occasion for Hall to have commented on his own personal situation, but perhaps these comments help to explain why he destroyed the Sunday morning sermons he had preached while in Cambridge between 1791 and 1804. He described them as "good for nothing" and as having "very little gospel in them."[51]

---

[49] Morris, *Biographical Reflections*, 45.
[50] Gregory, *Works*, 4:363–365.
[51] Gregory and Belcher, *Works*, 4:12. Greene also records that when the Rev. John Mack, a friend of Hall, visited him in Leicester he rescued a number of the sermon manuscripts while Hall was out of the room. Hall had put them by the fireside, having consigned them to be used as paper-lights for their pipes.

8
The Erosion of Calvinistic Distinctives

The ministers of the Northamptonshire Association, and Andrew Fuller in particular, together with men like Caleb Evans, wholeheartedly professed adherence to evangelical Calvinism. Robert Hall was of a different persuasion. By regarding the differences between Calvinism and Arminianism as non-essential, he contributed to the erosion of Calvinistic distinctives in his and succeeding generations. On a wider front there was a decline in doctrinal awareness among evangelicals in the early decades of the nineteenth century. Sadly, Hall was part of this drift.

In 1790, he had declared his rejection of specific Calvinistic doctrines. Before Hall's letter of explanation was read out to the Broadmead church he had told Caleb Evans a few days earlier that he was not a Calvinist like his older colleague. In his letter dated December 9, 1790, he made this known in more detail. He had told the church frankly that he was, "not a Calvinist, in the strict and proper sense of that term."[1] It is at this point that we see clearly the "erosion of distinctives" referred to earlier and the way in which Hall was rejecting the Calvinism that had characterised Particular Baptists for over one hundred and fifty years. Hall affirmed to the Bristol church:

> I do not maintain the federal headship of Adam, as it is called, or the imputation of sin to his posterity; and this doctrine I have always considered, and do still consider, as the foundation of that system. I believe we have received from our first parents, together with various outward ills, a corrupt and irregular bias of mind; but at the same time, it is

---

[1] Gregory, *Works*, 1:32.

my firm opinion that we are liable to condemnation only for our own actions, and that guilt is a personal and individual thing. I believe in the doctrine of the Divine Decrees, and of course in the predestination of all events, of which the number of the finally saved is one. But this appears to me a different thing from the doctrine of absolute election and reprobation, as it has been ever explained by Calvinists, which does not meet my approbation. Without going into a large field of metaphysical discussion, this is all I think it is requisite to say respecting my orthodoxy.[2]

This statement is quite brief but important. It is one of the few statements he made about his sentiments. Placed alongside his rejection of particular atonement and his recasting of the doctrine of election, considered in an earlier chapter, it becomes evident that Hall in fact was far from being a persuaded and distinctive Calvinist in 1790. Hall stated that he believed in the doctrine of the divine decrees and in the overarching sovereignty of God in the predestination of all events. But such a general statement about the sovereignty of God does not mean that Hall was a Calvinist in the same way as his father's generation, or as the Particular Baptist forefathers of the seventeenth century.

Fuller and "the five points"

The "five points of Calvinism" were enunciated at the Synod of Dort in 1618–1619. It was an international gathering of theologians which answered points of controversy that had emerged as a result of the rise of what became known as Arminianism. Those "five points"—total depravity, unconditional election, particular redemption, irresistible grace, and the perseverance of the saints— are not a full expression of Calvinism but they form a convenient summary of the main points. As has been stated, these five points

---

[2] Gregory, *Works*, 1:32.

The Erosion of Calvinistic Distinctives

were adopted by the Northamptonshire Association of Particular Baptist Churches and by individual congregations, including Carey's Leicester congregation, as a statement of their commitment to a full-orbed evangelical Calvinism.

Having rejected his hyper-Calvinistic background Fuller remained committed throughout the remainder of his life to each of the five points. In *The Memoir of Mr. Fuller*, a journey to Scotland in 1802 is recorded, with a conversation he had regarding the different shades of Calvinism—high, moderate, and strict. The first group Fuller reckoned bordered on Antinomianism, the second he regarded as half-Arminian or as holding Baxterian views. He declared himself among the third group, that of a strict Calvinist, "one who really holds the system of Calvin. I do not believe everything Calvin taught, nor anything because he taught it; but I reckon strict Calvinism to be my own system."[3] Brewster has an extended account of what Fuller believed and the impact he made on his and subsequent generations of Particular Baptists.[4] He pointed out "that Fuller never disowned Calvinism and never felt the slightest need to modify the seventeenth-century Calvinistic Baptist confessions of faith."[5] John Ryland was of the same opinion. Hall recognised this fact in his funeral oration for Ryland in 1825, when he identified him as "a Calvinist, in the strictest sense of the word, and attached to its peculiarities in a higher degree than most of the advocates of that system."[6]

Fuller's convictions and his insistence on the duty of all men to believe the gospel earned him the opposition of some nineteenth-century English Baptists. Yet Fuller was not responsible for the erosion of Calvinistic distinctives either among his

---

[3] Andrew Fuller, *The Complete Works of the Rev. Andrew Fuller*, 3 vols. (Harrisonburg, VA: Sprinkle Publications, 1988), 1:77.

[4] Paul Brewster, *Andrew Fuller: Model Pastor-Theologian* (Nashville, TN: B&H Publishing Group, 2010), 76–97.

[5] Brewster, *Andrew Fuller*, 107.

[6] Gregory, *Works*, 5:59–60.

Particular Baptist peers or in the following decades of the nineteenth century. An explanation for that erosion must be found elsewhere. The tide of opinion was turning against Calvinism and slowly accelerating during the "long eighteenth century," gaining speed in the nineteenth.

To suggest, therefore, that Robert Hall shared the same Calvinistic sentiments as Fuller and Ryland misrepresents both parties. Hall adopted some Arminian teachings and developed his own system of doctrine. The original five points are scarcely recognisable in Hall's presentation of the gospel. It was men like Robert Hall who, by following other sentiments, were abandoning some of the doctrines of their forefathers. The effect was serious and far more dangerous than they realised. By doing so they opened the door to Arminianism, and thus undermined the evangelical Calvinism that had reached its fullest expression in *The Second London Confession of Faith*.

Hall rejected Calvinism as a system. It would have a marked effect on his preaching. He did not enter into controversy in the pulpit or attack Calvinism publicly, for he hated controversy. On the contrary, because he did not believe these doctrines he tended therefore to omit them, preaching positively on what he regarded to be the essentials of the evangelical faith and emphasising the importance of Christian character together with sincere and genuine holiness, or piety. The long term effects of that are incalculable. It meant, for example, that during his seventeen years ministry at Leicester from 1807–1824, his congregation would have listened to a man, who, was regarded by many as the leading evangelical voice in England, but he was not distinctly and robustly Calvinistic, even though in a few sermons he displayed a greater sympathy for Calvinism than he did in 1790.

It would have taken a very discerning hearer to realise what was happening, especially as Hall did not make it his habit to declaim against those with whom he disagreed. One of Hall's

The Erosion of Calvinistic Distinctives

concerns was to avoid extremes and another was to avoid promoting a party spirit, but by preaching in this manner he was doing so at the expense of promoting and defending the faith of his fathers. Even allowing for some changes in his views more in sympathy with Calvinism, they did not constitute any major changes in his preaching style and content. Indications of changes in Hall's theology remained isolated and were very few in number.

Hall, original sin, and human depravity

Hall knew he was striking at the heart of Calvinistic teaching. He possessed an acute awareness of the importance of key doctrines. In his 1790 letter he rightly identified the federal headship of Adam and the imputation of sin to his posterity as a pillar of the whole system. By his mid-twenties Hall had rejected original sin. His position contradicted chapter 6 and paragraph 3 of *The Second London Baptist Confession of Faith*.

> They [our first parents] being the root, and by God's appointment, standing in the room and stead of all mankind, the guilt of the sin was imputed, and corrupted nature conveyed, to all their posterity descending from them by ordinary generation, being now conceived in sin, and by nature children of wrath, the servants of sin, the subjects of death, and all other miseries, spiritual, temporal, and eternal, unless the Lord Jesus set them free.

Sin and guilt were an individual and personal matter as far as Hall was concerned, although he admitted that there were various consequences for the human race as a result of Adam and Eve's disobedience. He did believe in the depravity and sinfulness of the human race and in the wrath of God against sin, the necessity of the atonement, and the need of divine power to change the heart of a sinner. In two sermons *On spiritual leprosy*, preached in Leicester in 1810 he spoke of "the inherent defilement attached to sin," as well as "the necessity of being purified from it by a method of God's devising."⁷ He told his congregation:

> The leprosy of sin is not like some other disorders which affect some individuals alone, while others escape; it is a universal malady,—no child of Adam escapes it; it attaches to the whole human race; and the only persons who are not now involved in that calamity are such as are *cured*, *saved*, redeemed from among men ... the bitter fruits of human apostasy extend to each individual of the human race, as may be sufficiently inferred from the very appellation of Christ, the Saviour of the world ... as well as from the most express declarations of scripture respecting the universal prevalence of guilt and corruption, in all instances where it has not been counteracted and controlled by divine grace.⁸

He pressed the truth home to the consciences of his hearers: "the cure of sin must be preceded by a sense of the malady, by a humiliating conviction of defilement urging us to cry with the leper, 'unclean, unclean.' He asked 'did ever any witness in you this appearance of concern for sin, this apprehension of your misery as a guilty creature before God?'"⁹

Insofar as he believed and preached these doctrines he appeared orthodox. However, it is very difficult to discover anywhere in his published sermons that at this time in his life he believed in the federal headship of Adam and in the doctrine of original sin as, for example, it is set out in Romans 5:12–21.

Hall could be a fierce opponent in private discussion as his father had discovered. Morris recorded an occasion when Fuller was completely caught off-guard and was out-manoeuvred by Hall. The subject matter was the doctrine of the universal and

---

⁷ Gregory, *Works*, 5:229.

⁸ Gregory, *Works*, 5:233. Hall quoted Acts 13:47 and Ephesians 2:3 to substantiate his statements.

⁹ Gregory, *Works*, 5:234.

total depravity of the human race. There were known differences of opinion between the two men, in particular over original sin. Fuller was not prepared for the discussion but having set out what he believed to be the scriptural teaching he found himself under a barrage of argument that left him flummoxed. Hall at one point sarcastically remarked that the doctrine he opposed "was a libel on human nature."[10] Fuller, for his part, was left complaining

> of being reluctantly brought into competition with one whom he so much admired, but who instantly anticipated all he had to say, eat up all his words, and gave no quarter, but cleared the field of every argument, and slew indiscriminately all the host, by logic, by sophistry, or by sarcasm.[11]

Hall was a formidable figure, especially in private debate and discussion. On this occasion Fuller was no match for Hall's powerful and acute intellect, that "pounces upon a statement with the quickness of lightning, and shatters it at once into a thousand pieces."[12] He would much rather have been engaged in the calmer atmosphere of a written debate. Fuller believed that original sin was biblical, Hall did not.

There is evidence of a change of convictions after fourteen years of ministry in Leicester. Having rejected the doctrines of the federal headship of Adam and also of original sin over thirty years earlier in 1790, he now affirmed that sin had been transmitted from Adam to his children and that he was not acting for himself alone. The fuller significance of this will be examined in the next chapter in connection with Hall's understanding of justification by faith.

---

[10] J.W. Morris, *Biographical Reflections of the Rev. Robert Hall, A.M.* (India, New Delhi: Isha Books, 2013), 154.
[11] Morris, *Biographical Recollections*, 154.
[12] Morris, *Biographical Recollections*, 154.

Hall and election

Hall did not believe in unconditional election, the second of "the five points." He told the church in Bristol that he believed in the divine decrees but then immediately qualified his statement by adding, "but this appears to me a different thing from the doctrine of absolute election and reprobation, as it has been ever explained by Calvinists, which does not meet my approbation."[13] The Calvinistic understanding of Christ's death states that God the Father had ordained his Son to die on the cross as a result of a certain and definite decree to save the elect.

Between 1819 and 1823, Robert Balmer had asked Hall about the extent of the atonement and whether election and particular redemption were inseparably connected. He pointed out that if someone believed in election that implied a limitation on the extent of the atonement. Hall's reply is a telling one, revealing again his re-shaping not only of particular redemption but also of election. Quoting Hall, Balmer recorded:

> I believe firmly in election but I do not think it involves particular redemption; I consider the sacrifice of Christ as a remedy, not only adapted, but intended, for all, and as placing all in a salvable state; as removing all barriers to their salvation, except such as arise from their own perversity and depravity. But God knew that none would accept the remedy, merely of themselves, and therefore, by what may be regarded as a separate arrangement, he resolved to glorify his mercy, be effectually applying salvation to a certain number of our race, through the agency of the Holy Spirit. I apprehend, then, that the limiting clause implied in election refers not to the purchase, but to the application of redemption.[14]

---

[13] Gregory, *Works*, 1:32.
[14] Gregory, *Works*, 1:160.

The Erosion of Calvinistic Distinctives

At this point Hall was driving a wedge between the purpose and the extent of the atonement and election. In his view election was "a separate arrangement" brought in by God the Father after atonement had been made for all men by the incarnate Son of God. Therefore, the death of Christ only made redemption a possibility. It placed everyone in a "salvable state" but did not actually secure the salvation of any particular individual. It was only by the work of the Holy Spirit, effectually applying the redemptive work of Christ, that anyone would be saved. The purpose of atonement was universal, the application was particular. According to Hall, election secured this salvation, guaranteeing that sinners would accept the remedy God had provided in Christ.[15]

In contrast the Synod of Dort had positively stated that when some receive the gift of faith from God and others do not, that difference "proceeds from God's eternal decree."[16] The synod affirmed on the basis of Ephesians 1:4–6 and Romans 8:30 that:

> Election is the unchangeable purpose of God, whereby before the foundation of the world, He has out of mere grace, according to the sovereign good pleasure of his own will, chosen from the whole human race, which had fallen through their own fault from their primitive state of rectitude into sin and destruction, a certain number of persons to redemption in Christ, who He from eternity appointed the Mediator and Head of the elect and the foundation of salvation. This elect number, though by nature neither better nor more deserving than others, but with them involved in our common misery, God has decreed to give to Christ to

---

[15] For a contemporary treatment of this subject see Matthew S. Harmon, "For the Glory of the Father and the Salvation of his People," in Gibson and Gibson, eds., *From Heaven He Came and Sought Her: Definite Atonement in Historical, Biblical, Theological and Pastoral Perspective* (Wheaton, IL: Crossway, 2013), 269-272.

[16] The Canons of Dort, First Head of Doctrine, Divine Election and Reprobation, Article 6, in Peter Y. De Yong, ed., *Crisis in the Reformed Churches* (Grand Rapids: Reformed Fellowship Inc., 1968), 231.

be saved by Him, and effectually to call and draw them to His communion by His Word and Spirit; to bestow upon them true faith, justification and sanctification; and having powerfully preserved them in the fellowship of His Son, finally to glorify them for the demonstration of His mercy, and for the praise of the riches of His glorious grace.[17]

The same truth about election was set out by the Particular Baptists in *The Second London Confession of Faith*:

As God hath appointed the elect unto glory, so he hath, by the eternal and most free purpose of his will, foreordained all the means thereunto; wherefore they who are elected, being fallen in Adam, are redeemed by Christ, and effectually called unto faith in Christ, by his Spirit working in due season, are justified, adopted, sanctified and kept by his power through faith unto salvation; neither are any other redeemed by Christ, or effectually called, justified, adopted, sanctified and saved, but the elect only.[18]

Hall rejected this understanding of the decrees of God. He was effectively conflating election with irresistible grace (the fourth of "the five points") and effectual calling, separating them from the Father's eternal purpose concerning the intended extent of the death of his Son. Hall may have used the term "election" in his preaching and conversation, but it is quite clear that he had invested it with a different meaning.

Did Hall reverse his convictions on election? In an undated sermon, *On conversion as illustrated by that of St. Paul*, based on Galatians 1:15-16, Hall uses language more in keeping with the five points. While he did not use the term "election" he stated:

---

[17] The Canons of Dort, Article 7, 231-232.
[18] *The Baptist Confession of Faith of 1689* 3.6. This statement was grounded in the following scriptural passages: 1 Peter 1:2, 5; 1 Thessalonians 5:9, 10; 2 Thessalonians 2:13; Romans 8:30; John 6:64; 10:26; and 17:9.

The Erosion of Calvinistic Distinctives

We cannot suppose the purposes of God to be of recent date, or to have taken rise from any limited point of time. What he designs, he designs from eternity. Whatever he accomplishes is agreeable to his eternal purposes and word: "Who hath saved us, and called us with an holy calling, not according to our works, but according to his own purposes and grace, which was given us in Christ Jesus, before the world began."[19]

A few sentences further on he speaks of an effectual call, the consequence of predestination, quoting Romans 8:30, "Whom he predestinated, them he also called." He explained:

There is a general call in the gospel, addressed to all men indiscriminately. Gracious invitations are given, without exception, far as the sound of the gospel extends; but this, of itself, is not effectual. There is, in every instance of real conversion, another and inward call, by which the Spirit applies the general truth of the gospel to the heart.[20]

The precise significance of these statements as used by Hall is difficult to gauge. As with his statements with regard to Adam's headship and original sin they are made without any further comment or explanation. Nowhere does Hall say he had changed his mind. Nowhere does he acknowledge that he had been mistaken in the past. And nowhere does he provide any reasons for any of these changes if that is what they are.

Hall and the extent of the atonement

Hall's rejection of particular redemption has already been considered in an earlier chapter. The language of the Canons of Dort and the 1689 *Confession of Faith* set out the biblical understanding of

---

[19] Gregory, *Works*, 5:200.
[20] Gregory, *Works*, 5:201.

the death of Christ. God the Father's intention was that "the quickening and saving efficacy of the most precious death of His Son should extend to all the elect, for bestowing upon them alone the gift of justifying faith, thereby to bring them infallibly to salvation."[21] Likewise, the same *Confession of Faith* speaks of Christ's having "procured reconciliation, and purchased an everlasting inheritance in the kingdom of heaven for all those whom the Father hath given unto him."[22]

Hall believed that to place limitations on the death of Christ was to place limitations on the gospel invitation and the commands and invitations to come to Christ for salvation. Hall preached powerful sermons on the death of Christ. One of the most famous was from Isaiah 53:8: "The innocent for the guilty." It was preached in Leicester in 1822. He believed that "the sufferings of the Redeemer were vicarious and piacular, that he appeared in the character of a substitute for sinners, in distinction from a mere example, teacher, or martyr."[23] Hall asserted that the doctrine of the voluntary, penal, substitutionary atonement of Jesus Christ, the incarnate Son of God, was a fundamental of the Christian faith. It was a clear teaching of the scriptures and if it was not believed this was due to a failure to submit to the authority of divine revelation. The blood of Jesus Christ provided the only basis for the forgiveness of sins and "forms the grand peculiarity of the gospel and was the principal theme of the apostolic ministry and is still pre-eminently the power of God to salvation."[24] Hall concluded his sermon by saying that Christ's substitution was "the only foundation of human hope" and that:

---

[21] Canons of Dort, Second Head of Doctrine, The death of Christ, and the redemption of men thereby, Article 8, 241.
[22] *The Baptist Confession of Faith of 1689*, 8.5.
[23] Gregory, *Works*, 5:78.
[24] Gregory, *Works*, 5:101.
[25] Gregory, *Works*, 5:103.

The Erosion of Calvinistic Distinctives

the merit of the Saviour, arising from his matchless condescension and love, in becoming obedient unto death, even the death of the cross, is of so elevated and transcendent a kind, as to disclaim all association with the imperfections of human virtue as the basis of justification. The price of redemption (to use a scriptural metaphor) has been paid; the justice of God is satisfied; a full and complete atonement has been made.[25]

At this point Hall was being inconsistent. He was preaching a full and complete atonement, suggesting that Christ's death has secured redemption, language that could be used by any Calvinistic preacher. Yet, in fact, because he believed that Christ died for all men he was, in effect, only preaching a potential salvation, and that sinners were now redeemable. He was obliged to say that Christ's death secures salvation "of an innumerable multitude of mankind, *and if duly improved*, [emphasis mine] a sufficient source for the salvation of all."[26] This seems to suggest that salvation is conditional on faith. On the other hand, the Calvinistic preacher using the same language proclaimed a salvation that secures the ends for which God intended, that is the actual redemption and salvation of all the elect and received by faith. It is doubtful whether anyone listening to the preaching of Hall at this point would suspect him of not being a consistent Calvinist.

In his sermon on Isaiah 53, Hall appears to have assumed that the passage proclaimed an atonement that is general or universal. Yet the whole tone of Isaiah 53 is that the death of Christ effectively secured the salvation of a particular number, delineated in the passage as "the many," and "my people." Alec Motyer in his contemporary treatment of this chapter insists that verses like

---

[26] Gregory, *Works*, 5:80.

verses 4–6, "commits the unprejudiced interpreter to an effective, particularistic understanding of the atonement."[27]

Few hearers of Hall's sermons or readers of his published sermons recorded by Gregory in *Works*, would have reason to question whether he was a consistent Calvinist. The same is true of over two hundred unpublished sermons preached by Hall at Leicester between 1812 and 1823.[28] These were originally taken down in shorthand by G.W. Riley and then transcribed by him. They are certainly evangelical in tone and substance but there is nothing consistently, distinctly, and robustly Calvinistic about the language and content of these or any other of his later sermons.

Hall and the perseverance of the saints

The last of "the five points" concerns the perseverance of the saints. At first sight it would appear that Hall believed this doctrine. However, once again, he qualified what he believed in a similar way to the way he qualified election. The 1689 *Confession of Faith* follows the line of teaching set out by the Synod of Dort under the fifth head of doctrine. Chapter 17 of the Confession, article 2 states:

> The perseverance of the saints depends not upon their own free will, but upon the immutability of the decree of election, flowing from the free and unchangeable love of God the Father, upon the efficacy and merit of the intercession of Jesus Christ, and union with him, the oath of God, the

---

[27] J. Alec Motyer, "Stricken for the Transgression of My People" in David Gibson & Jonathan Gibson eds., *From Heaven He Came and Sought her: Definite Atonement In Historical, Biblical, Theological and Pastoral Perspective* (Wheaton IL: Crossway, 2013), 261.

[28] Robert Hall: Two hundred and nineteen unpublished sermons preached at Leicester 1812–1823, 8 vols. Taken down in shorthand and transcribed by G. W. Riley. Donated by Dr. E. B. Underhill to the Angus Library, Oxford in 1886 (Angus Library Catalogue Nos. 35.g.16–23). The list of sermons was edited by Austin Walker, 2010.

The Erosion of Calvinistic Distinctives

abiding of his Spirit, and the seed of God within them, and the nature of the covenant of grace, from all which ariseth also the certainty and infallibility thereof.

Morris identified Hall's disagreement with the perseverance of all the regenerate back in the 1780s, stating that his sentiments were rather like those espoused by Richard Baxter, who admitted the perseverance of all the elect.[29] That is not the same teaching as expressed by Dort and *The Second London Confession of Faith*. Hall had made perseverance contingent on election, but not the eternal decree of election, but rather the "election" that follows the atonement resulting in the effectual application of the redemption secured by Christ. Hall has effectively broken up the unity of the triune God's saving purpose that begins with election before the foundation of the world, that accomplishes the redemption of all the elect, undergirds their perseverance and guarantees their glorification. Hall made election, as he understood it, a separate arrangement. His understanding of perseverance follows the same pattern.

It would appear that by 1807, when he began his ministry in Leicester, he was fairly settled in his convictions. Hall did modify some of them as he grew older. Morris commented that Hall felt "a growing conviction of the truth and importance of the Calvinistic system, and found in it a rich source of consolation."[30] On October 4, 1818, Hall had preached two sermons from John 17:24, the morning sermon being on election. That evening in conversation with his family he commented: "On the Arminian hypothesis, God did not actually choose any to eternal life; but all who are saved make choice of him, and are saved in consequence of such a choice; so that the destiny of eternal life originates in themselves

---

[29] Morris, *Biographical Recollections*, 57–58.
[30] Morris, *Biographical Recollections*, 389.

and not in God."[31] By such a comment Morris was implying that Hall was increasingly distancing himself from Arminianism. As far as I am aware, however, none of Hall's first biographers have drawn any attention to changes relating to the headship of Adam and original sin.

Did Hall then believe that doctrine was not important? That would be a wrong conclusion. He was vigorously opposed not only to hyper-Calvinism but also to Socinianism and Antinomianism. In these matters he and Fuller were of the same mind. In 1823, Hall delivered *Twelve lectures on the Socinian controversy*, basing them on the text from Jude 3, "It was needful for me to write unto you, and exhort you, that ye should earnestly contend for the faith which was once delivered to the saints."[32] He was ruthless in exposing Antinomianism. He defended the need for controversy in religion on the grounds that despite the way controversies have been handled they assist each generation to discover and state the truth. He opposed hyper-Calvinism, Socinianism, and Antinomianism because they attacked the fundamentals of the Christian religion, but he did not believe the differences between Calvinists and Arminians should be dealt with in the same manner. The hope of salvation remained secure on either system.[33] However, the conclusions of the anonymous contributor to the *The Pulpit* are confirmed. Hall did not present the truth in any decisive character, either Calvinistic or Arminian.

The aftermath

Sadly, such an approach tended to further diminish confessional

---

[31] Morris, *Biographical Recollections*, 389.

[32] Gregory *Works*, 5:118–125.

[33] I am not suggesting either that the differences between Calvinism and Arminianism are of the same order as, for example, the differences between Socinianism and the orthodox doctrine relating to the person and work of Christ. Earlier we noted that John Ryland doubted whether a Socinian could really be a Christian. The same doubt cannot be applied to those who differ on Calvinism and Arminianism.

The Erosion of Calvinistic Distinctives

awareness and doctrinal distinctiveness among Particular Baptists. Hall had effectively ignored the articles of faith of Carey's former congregation when he became the pastor in Leicester in 1807. They would inevitably be forgotten if no one drew attention to them, regularly preached them, demonstrating their scriptural basis. Within a few years, certainly within a generation, no one would believe they were of any real significance any longer. Hall had moved a considerable distance from the convictions of his father, of his early instructors, those of Benjamin Beddome, Caleb Evans, and the doctrinal foundations of Bristol Academy established by Bernard Foskett, and of Andrew Fuller and John Ryland. That was true from 1790 until perhaps the middle years of his Leicester ministry, a period of twenty-five to thirty years.

Some might argue that this was progress and that the declining influence of Calvinism not only among Particular Baptists but also among other Dissenters and the Church of England simply needs to be recognised as a natural progression. Others might conclude that the assessment of Hall presented in this book is the result of an overly scrupulous, suspicious, and cynical approach to him and his views. However, error sometimes creeps in from people who have come to be regarded as trusted guides. Hall was considered to be the mouthpiece of English evangelical dissent in the first part of the nineteenth century. He was a very gifted orator and it was all too easy to be captivated by the eloquence of the preacher. Evidence suggests that Hall's eloquence tended to obscure what Hall was really saying.

Christians need to understand not only the great theologians but also the significant controversies of church history and be able to discern both the causes and the consequences of those controversies. The seeds of the Downgrade Controversy that so profoundly affected Spurgeon and the Baptist Union in the late 1880s, were sown in the early decades of the nineteenth century and Robert Hall had a marked influence among the Particular

Baptists of his generation and succeeding generations of Baptists. The erosion of Calvinistic distinctives in the early nineteenth century was characteristic of Nonconformity, including Particular Baptists.

Men rarely perceive the consequences of their opinions, and Hall would have been no exception. With the benefit of hindsight, Tom Nettles attributes the long-term effects of Robert Hall's influence in helping to form "the climate for the energetic modernism of John Clifford."[34] That is not to say Hall was directly responsible for the down-grade identified by Spurgeon. The downgrade was not so much about the loss of Calvinism but the departure from some of the fundamentals of the biblical gospel. Nevertheless, Hall's approach inflicted severe blows on evangelical Calvinism.

It was Clifford who stood opposed to Spurgeon in the Downgrade Controversy. Nettles concludes, "The ideas that Hall set in motion, both of open communion and diminished confessional consciousness, led to Clifford's powerful influence over the Baptist Union."[35] This "diminished confessional consciousness" was not unique to Robert Hall. It was a reflection of the changing mood of evangelical religion in England in which he played a key part, and in particular the dumbing-down of evangelical Calvinism and thus its inevitable decline.

Twenty-five years or so before the Downgrade Controversy erupted, the church of which Charles Spurgeon was pastor completed the building of the Metropolitan Tabernacle. Spurgeon was an unashamed Calvinist. "I have my own private opinion that there is no such thing as preaching Christ and Him crucified

---

[34] Thomas J. Nettles, *The Baptists: Key People Involved In Forming the Baptist Identity*, 3 vols. (Fearn, Ross-shire: Mentor Imprint for Christian Focus Publications, 2007), 58.

[35] Nettles, *The Baptists*, 58.

The Erosion of Calvinistic Distinctives

unless we preach what nowadays is called Calvinism; it is a nickname to call it Calvinism; Calvinism is the gospel and nothing else."[36] In 1861 soon after he had preached the first sermon at the Tabernacle, he organised a conference where the doctrines of grace were expounded. Five different men preached on the "five points of Calvinism." Spurgeon was persuaded that the need to explain the nature of Calvinism was one of the needs of the hour. It would not have been possible for Robert Hall to speak at such a conference because he was not a distinctive Calvinist like Spurgeon.

In 1855, six years before that conference, Spurgeon republished *The Second London Baptist Confession of Faith*. It was only the second year of his ministry at the New Park Street Chapel, Southwark. He wanted to testify plainly to the leading doctrines of the gospel. It was another piece of evidence that Calvinism had been in decline. Spurgeon was determined to do what he could to stem that tide. Barely thirty years had passed since the death of Robert Hall.

---

[36] *Spurgeon's Autobiography*, 4 vols. (London: Passmore and Alabaster, 1899), 1:167.

9
Justification by Faith

Mention has already been made of Robert Balmer's conversations with Hall between 1819 and 1823 about the extent of the atonement. Hall had recommended Joseph Bellamy's, *True Religion Delineated*.[1] Bellamy (1719-1790) was an exponent of the New Divinity theology. Their understanding of justification by faith bears some resemblance to Hall's own view but there is no direct evidence, apart from this one reference to Bellamy, that Hall drew his theology of justification from New England sources. Bellamy suspected that any understanding of the righteousness that saves derived from the imputation of the merits of Christ to the repentant believer led to moral laxity, and that the work of salvation then required nothing from a sinner. This was a real fear for promoters of New Divinity theology.

This suspicion and fear brought the New Divinity "into conflict with what had been a central belief of Calvinist orthodoxy since the sixteenth century, and for that matter, the Protestant reformation itself."[2] The next generation of New Divinity theologians, like Nathan Strong (1748-1816), were prepared to jettison the notion of imputation. Hall had stated his objections to the imputation of Adam's sin in his letter to the Bristol congregation in 1790. There is no evidence that he preached justification by faith through the imputed righteousness of Christ during the earlier part of his ministry. If that was so then Hall was aligning himself, consciously or otherwise, with those who were departing from

---

[1] Gregory, *Works*, 1:160-161.
[2] Douglas A. Sweeney and Allen C. Guezlo, eds., *The New England Theology: From Jonathan Edwards to Edwards Amasa Park* (Grand Rapids MI: Baker Academic, 2006), 109.

some of the fundamentals of Calvinism held not only by Particular Baptists but Protestantism itself. In his solemn dedication of himself to God in May 1809 Hall expressed his persuasion of God's willingness "to pardon and accept penitent believing sinners on the ground of the blood and righteousness of thine own adorable Son, 'who died the just for the unjust.'"[3] At that point Hall did not explain precisely what he understood by Christ's blood and righteousness being the ground of his acceptance before God.

Preaching in Broadmead in 1829, two years before his death, preparatory to the Lord's Supper, stressing the value of the gospel from 1 Timothy 2:10, Hall exhorted his congregation:

> never indulge the vain conceit that, if our conduct is consistent, it matters little what is our faith. Good works are doubtless necessary; but, to be good works, they must proceed from right principles. The great design of Jesus Christ is to justify and sanctify his people: all depends upon that turning-point, the justification of a sinner before God; and this can be only by faith in the Lord Jesus Christ. He came, at the same time, to purify for Himself a peculiar people, zealous of good works; to make us partakers of his holiness and His Spirit. Unless this great design of the gospel be accomplished in us, it has left us where it found us, "dead in trespasses and sins!" Hold fast these vital points, in which all true Christians unite.[4]

There is no specific mention of imputed righteousness in this sermon. Hall's concern was to establish the necessity of justification and sanctification. The evidence we have suggests that throughout his life Robert Hall believed in justification by faith, grounded in the blood and righteousness of Jesus Christ. He

---

[3] Gregory, *Works*, 1:95.
[4] Gregory and Belcher, *Works*, 4:185. This sermon was published from the notes of Rev. T. Grinfield and not from a manuscript of Hall.

denied any role for good works in justification and taught that forgiveness of sins and peace with God were secured only by faith in Jesus Christ. But what exactly did he mean by justification?

Hall's earlier views of justification

There are some grounds for believing that in the years prior to Hall's ministry in Leicester, he believed that justification was only God's forgiveness for sins committed, with no element of imputed righteousness. Hall had a very real fear of Antinomianism as had Richard Baxter and Joseph Bellamy. That may have led Hall to downplay the imputation of Christ's righteousness.

This is an important issue because if the denial of imputed righteousness was and remained Hall's doctrine then we are facing a serious omission from the recognized Protestant doctrine of justification by faith. It is very difficult to trace the changes in Hall's thinking. At no point does Hall say he has changed his views. Any changes have to be painstakingly gleaned from his published and unpublished sermons. There are at least four reasons for investigating this matter and asking what Hall believed and what he preached.

Firstly, as we have already seen, Hall openly denied the doctrines of original sin, the federal headship of Adam and the imputation of Adam's sin to his posterity in his 1790 letter to the Broadmead church. It would be jumping to the wrong conclusion to assert solely on the basis of his denial of these doctrines that Hall did not, therefore, believe in the headship of Christ and the imputation of our sins to Christ and the imputation of Christ's righteousness to believers. Nevertheless, it raises the question of whether the imputation of our sin to Christ and of the righteousness of Christ to us did become part of Hall's understanding of justification.

Secondly, from reading through his sermons, his letters and other published material, and the comments of his friends recording his conversations, there appear to be few, if any, references anywhere to imputation, either of sin or of righteousness. In his published works there is a marked absence of sermons from the key chapters in the New Testament, Romans 3–5, and Galatians 3. There are however, a large number of unpublished transcribed sermons which do contain a few sermons both from Romans chapter 3 and chapter 5.[5]

Hall had been honest with John Greene during his days in Cambridge. Greene observed that it was Hall's habit of expounding books of the Scriptures at the morning service and single texts in the afternoon. Hall preached through John's Gospel, Acts, Philippians, 1 and 2 Peter, and the three letters of John. Greene asked Hall why he had omitted Romans. Hall's candid reply was, "I do not understand it, sir, The Apostle Peter says, there are *many things hard to be understood:* I shall reserve the exposition of that Epistle for the last work of my life."[6]

The comment by Hall about Romans may be significant, providing a window into his understanding of the gospel during his ministry in Cambridge. It would be unfair to place too much weight on one statement but it may indicate that he had not grasped the overall message of Romans and the ways in which God's plan of salvation was the outworking of one harmonious plan beginning with eternal election. Hall never undertook the exposition of Romans, but he did preach some significant sermons from Romans and Galatians which indicate a change in his understanding and convictions.

Romans has invariably been regarded as the high point of Scripture. Luther and Calvin had treated it that way in their commentaries. Luther, for example had said, "this epistle is really the

---

[5] Hall, "Sermons preached at Leicester 1812–1821, 1821–1823" taken down in shorthand and transcribed by G.W. Riley.

[6] Greene, *Reminiscences of the Rev. Robert Hall* in Gregory and Belcher, *Works*, 4:17.

Justification by Faith

chief part of the New Testament and purest Gospel."[7] More recently Martyn Lloyd-Jones noted that in Romans "we are face-to-face with all the foundation truths of the Scripture," and that it has been, "the universal opinion in the Christian church throughout the centuries that Romans is the Epistle above all which deals with fundamentals."[8] J.I. Packer made similar comments about the importance of Romans, "it gives you all the main themes [of doctrine] integrated together."[9]

Perhaps it was significant that Hall's comment about Romans being hard to understand was made before his conversion. The question must be asked therefore as to whether Hall, in his late thirties and early forties, had really grasped the biblical gospel and the way in which it was all one piece. He had previously denied some of its key elements and therefore it would not be surprising if he could not make much sense of Romans, including the key doctrine of justification by faith.

Greene was also responsible for transcribing Hall's sermons on Philippians. They were preached in Cambridge in 1801 and 1802 and are found only in the American edition of his works. The sermons on Philippians 3 display a marked absence of any reference to the imputed righteousness of Christ.[10] It has already been stated, that Hall would omit in his public preaching any reference to subjects that he regarded as controversial. Furthermore, it would seem that whatever happened to Hall as a result of his mental breakdown of 1804–1805 there was no significant or immediate change in his understanding and preaching of justification by faith.

---

[7] Quoted by Ewald M. Plass, *What Luther Says: A Practical In-Home Anthology for the Active Christian* (St. Louis: Concordia Publishing House, n.d.), 989.

[8] D. Martyn Lloyd-Jones, *Romans: An Exposition of Chapter 1, The Gospel of God* (Edinburgh: The Banner of Truth Trust 1985), 3.

[9] J.I. Packer, *Knowing God* (London: Hodder and Stoughton, 1973), 230.

[10] Gregory and Belcher, *Works*, 4:605–606. These sermons were taken down in shorthand by John Greene.

The Theology of Robert Hall Jr.

Thirdly, attention has already been drawn to Hall's fierce opposition to Antinomianism. This was not peculiar to Hall. It also characterised many other Particular Baptists. For example, in 1787 Ryland had addressed the matter in *The Law Not Against the Promises of God*. He argued that genuine love to God was expressed by obedience to the law. Antinomianism was a "false gospel."[11] Later Andrew Fuller also uncovered Antinomianism's real character and identified it as a "false religion," masquerading under "the names and forms of orthodoxy."[12] He defined Antinomianism as "whatever goes to disown or weaken the authority of [God's] law, goes to overturn the gospel and all true religion."[13]

In similar fashion Hall regarded Antinomianism as a heresy that would lead to the subversion of religion. He was reacting, on justifiable grounds, to some of the beliefs and practices he had observed in both Calvinistic and hyper-Calvinistic circles. Perhaps he was thinking of churches where sin was excused under such pretexts as, "Unless the Lord keeps me, there is nothing I can do about it." He wrote, "In the New Testament, the absolute subserviency of doctrinal statements to the formation of the principles and habits of personal piety, is never lost sight of; we are continually reminded that obedience is the end of all knowledge, and of all religious impressions."[14] He contended that too many Calvinistic preachers had emphasised the privileges, to the exclusion of the precepts and sanctions in the Scriptures, and that by presenting the promises of the gospel as being unconditional they had paved the way for Antinomianism.

---

[11] Michael A.G. Haykin, "'The Sum of All Good': John Ryland, Jr. and the Doctrine of the Holy Spirit," *Churchman* 103/104 (1989): 338.

[12] Andrew Fuller, "Antinomianism contrasted with the Religion Taught and Exemplified in the Holy Scriptures" in *The Complete Works of Andrew Fuller*, 3 vols. (Harrisonburg, VA: Sprinkle Publications, 1988), 2:737.

[13] Fuller, *Complete Works*, 2:744.

[14] Robert Hall, "Preface to Rev. Samuel Chase's 'Antinomianism Unmasked,'" in Gregory, *Works*, 6:387.

Justification by Faith

Fuller, however, in his opposition to Antinomianism, did not call into question the imputed righteousness of Christ to the sinner as Hall appeared to do. In the 1640s Richard Baxter had been troubled by the excesses of Antinomianism and had subsequently come to reject the biblical doctrine of the imputation of Christ's righteousness. Was Hall travelling along the same path? While Hall rejected meritorious conditions he pointed out that gospel promises are made indefinitely to persons of a specific character, such as the penitent, the believing, and the obedient. However, there is no mention of our sins being imputed to Christ or to Christ's righteousness being imputed to the sinner.

Fourthly, some statements Hall made in an extensive review of James Bean's *Zeal without Innovation*, published in 1808, lead us to think that at that time he had a restricted view of justification by faith. He told a friend to whom he wrote that he had read the book with a feeling of "extreme disgust."[15] Bean was a high churchman who thought that developments in England since the sixteenth-century Reformation were a mistake. He was hostile to the evangelical wing of the Anglican Church as well as to evangelical Dissenters, and thought the Toleration Act of 1689 had been perverted. In Hall's eyes Bean betrayed a party spirit because, as a churchman, he laid exclusive claim to purity and orthodoxy. Bean's book was more than Hall could stomach and he rose to the defence not only of Dissenters but also of the evangelical clergy within the Church of England.

Hall commended the evangelical party for their moderation, "those intricate points which unhappily divide the Christian church," for freely tolerating and indulging a diversity of opinion without adopting the extremes of Pelagianism and Antinomianism. According to Hall, provided the Calvinism was practical and

---

[15] Gregory, *Works*, 1:302. Hall's review is to be found in Gregory, *Works*, 2:269-320.

moderate and the Arminianism evangelical and devout, it was to be tolerated. He also believed that most evangelical clergy accepted general redemption, being "much less anxious to establish a polemical accuracy than to 'win souls to Christ.'"[16] Given the other strands of evidence, it is at least reasonable to suppose that Hall was commending in others the convictions which he himself held.

Maintaining that faith without works is dead, and that the duties of a holy life are essential, Hall said these evangelical clergymen ascribe the transition from a state of death to a state of justification solely to faith in Christ previous to good works actually performed. At the same time they equally insist on a performance of those works as evidence of justifying faith, and the indispensable condition of final happiness. For them the law is the perpetual standard of rectitude in Christ's kingdom. Then he makes the following intriguing statement:

> The matter of duty they look upon as unalterable, and the only difference is this; that, whereas, under the covenant of works, the condition of life was sinless obedience, under the new covenant, an obedience sincere and affectionate, though imperfect, is accepted for the sake of the Redeemer. At the same time, they do not cease to maintain that the faith which they hold to be justifying comprehends in it the seminal principle of every virtue; that is genuine, it will not fail to be fruitful; and that a Christian has it in his power to show his faith "by his works," and by no other means.[17]

This emphasis on "an obedience sincere and affectionate, though imperfect," reflects a Neo-nomian or Baxterian sentiment. It makes evangelical obedience the basis of acceptance with

---

[16] Gregory, *Works*, 2:303-304.
[17] Gregory, *Works*, 2:301.

Justification by Faith

God. Such an understanding effectively denies not only the actual imputation of Christ's righteousness to the believer but also the need for the active obedience of Jesus Christ.[18]

If that quotation accurately expresses Hall's own view in 1808 then we are faced with the fact that Hall espoused an unbiblical doctrine of justification. On a number of occasions in conversation with friends Hall acknowledged that he had sympathy for the theological views of Baxter. For example, recall the statement Greene included in his biography of Hall, "If there are any sentiments to which I would subscribe, they are Baxter's."[19]

If these were and remained the sentiments of Hall then we would have to conclude that in his early years he had abandoned a key element in one of the central beliefs of Protestant orthodoxy. It would appear that for a number of years he did not believe in justification by faith through the imputed righteousness of Christ. However, he may have changed his convictions, though it is not clear precisely when he did this. Frustratingly, nowhere does Hall explain how or why he had changed.

Hall's embracing of the imputed righteousness of Christ

There are some indications of a change in 1821. In a sermon based on Romans 7:26, Hall affirmed:

> We have all sinned and the wages of sin is death—To be united to the first Adam is to share in his apostacy—How necessary is it that we should look to Jesus Christ by a lively faith—believe in his blood—be partakers of his spirit—If any man believe on Jesus Christ there is no condemnation to him.[20]

---

[18] For a fuller description of Baxterianism and how the seventeenth-century Particular Baptist, Benjamin Keach, opposed it see Austin Walker, *The Excellent Benjamin Keach* (Kitchener, ON: Joshua Press, 2015), 343-373.

[19] Gregory and Belcher, *Works*, 4:75.

[20] Hall, "Sermons preached at Leicester 1812-1821, 1821-1823" taken down in shorthand and transcribed by G.W. Riley, Set A, 3:6.

In this same sermon it appears that Hall had altered his views of original sin and the federal headship of Adam. Having denied it in the 1790 letter he now affirmed that sin had been transmitted from Adam to his children and that he was not acting for himself alone. Hall appears to have come to believe that Adam and Christ were key figures in deciding the destiny of the human race. Adam's sinful disobedience had a devastating effect on his posterity. "Death, natural Death, has been levelled on the whole human race and hence it is evident that all have sinned."[21] He continued:

> It is plain that the corruption of nature has been transmitted from Adam. He lost the image of God—he became spiritually dead—he became alienated from God—he lost his integrity and therefore all confidence in God; and it is plain that this has been transmitted to his children. Hence, he acted not for himself since actual guilt is the necessary consequence of that state of mind which he brought into the world by his apostacy. But in this instance he was a figure of him that was to come; as he brought death upon all men by this disobedience, so eternal life is permitted to all that believe by virtue of Christ's obedience—As death passed upon all men, so thro' Jesus Christ, Justification passes upon all who are united to him by faith in his name and are virtually his posterity.[22]

The same tendency can be identified in an earlier sermon that was probably preached in late 1811. Basing his observations on Romans 5:1, Hall pointed out that the way in which Abraham was justified was the method by which sinners receive justification through the gospel—it was by faith. "The proper and meritorious ground of the acceptance of sinners is laid in the interposition of

---

[21] Hall, "Sermons preached at Leicester," Set A, 3:2.
[22] Hall, "Sermons preached at Leicester," Set A, 3:3.

Justification by Faith

the merits or in the grace of our Lord Jesus Christ, who that he might offer himself a sacrifice became obedient unto death, even the death of the cross."[23]

Imputed righteousness is implied by Hall in both of these sermons from 1811 and 1821. They reflect the fact that Hall had reached a better understanding of the teaching of Romans, considering what he had told John Greene during his days in Cambridge. What was implicit in these two sermons is made explicit in two further sermons that Hall preached, one in September 1827 in Melbourne, near Royston, Hertfordshire, and the other in July 1830 in Broadmead, Bristol, seven months before his death.

The first sermon was from Galatians 4:4-5: *Christ's mission for the adoption of sons in the fullness of time.* He was concerned to convey three things—the mission of Jesus Christ, and the manner in which he manifested himself; the design of his mission; and the fitness of the season which God had appointed for this purpose. Concluding his first point he dealt with the perfect obedience of Jesus Christ, the mediator. He affirmed:

> Standing in the stead of sinners, representing their persons, and being exposed to the penalties of a broken law, he endured the wrath of God which was kindled against us, submitted to that death which was denounced against our transgressions, and "by death destroyed death." He came into the world under the necessity of suffering; he came into it principally for the purpose of dying; death was the end of his life, the very design of his being. He came not to reign, but to obey; not to rejoice, but to sorrow; not to live a life of ease and comfort, of dignity, and splendour, but of poverty, self-denial and reproach; and then to expire in agony upon the cross.[24]

---

[23] Hall, "Sermons preached at Leicester," Set A, 1:91-92.
[24] Gregory, *Works*, 6:309-310.

Then with that understanding of the death of Christ established he undertook to explain the purpose of redemption and how it was accomplished:

> Jesus Christ was made under the law, who was not originally under it, for the purpose of producing that righteousness, and creating that fund of merit in the eyes of an infinitely wise and holy Being, which should be imputed for the benefit of penitent believers, by dying on the cross a death which he never merited; and thus working out a justification, from which the spiritual wants of all mankind should be supplied, if they received his testimony and believed on his name.[25]

He continued in the same vein:

> The immediate effect of Christ's death is the imputation of his righteousness to the believer, and this righteousness produces an instant acquittal from punishment; but such was the exuberance of his merits, such the dignity of his person, and the high complacency of the Father in his work, that is was worthy of him to bestow on them that were members of his Son, greater blessings than those which their first parents had forfeited. It was not merely to relieve from misery that Christ died; it was not only justification that was the fruit of his sufferings; but adoption into the family of heaven, the privileges of sons and daughters for all his believing people.[26]

The second sermon was preached from Matthew 11:28–30, *Invitation of Christ to sinners*. Hall chose to deal with the different kind of people who were labouring and heavy laden. One such group were those oppressed and burdened with a sense of their

---

[25] Gregory, *Works*, 6:311.
[26] Gregory, *Works*, 6:315.

Justification by Faith

guilt, sensing themselves to be under the wrath of God. He directed such people to Christ for:

> There we find hope arising even in the valley, there we find an avenue by which we may enter the presence of God with acceptance. He is the way to the Father, having removed all the obstructions that lay in the way of justice. He has brought in everlasting righteousness, in his endurance of the penalty, in his performance of the obedience due to the law. In his sacrifice we see an adequate provision made, whereby God can be just and yet the justifier of everyone that believeth on Jesus. Here is the true foundation of peace which God himself has laid. It is not presumption, therefore, to rest upon it: for in resting our weary souls on the promises of Christ, we follow the dictates of his holy teaching, we obey the great command of his gospel, which is, that we should "believe on Him whom God hath sent, for Him hath God the Father sealed."[27]

Some observations

There is little doubt then that Hall eventually came to believe that the righteousness of Christ was imputed to the sinner who believed in Christ. This was something he had not preached for many years. How often he mentioned imputed righteousness in his sermons during the latter days of his ministry remains unknown. We do not possess all the sermons Hall preached. In the sermons we do possess Hall used the actual language of "imputation'" only twice and that in the same sermon from Galatians 4:5-6. Imputation, however, is implied in some other sermons.

Any reader of Hall's sermons may well feel frustrated. For Hall, the Scriptures were always the final authority, but he did not always enunciate scriptural doctrine fully and clearly. There were exceptions where, for example, he was dealing with fundamentals

---

[27] Gregory and Belcher, *Works*, 6:430.

such as the deity of Christ, over against Socinianism, or in exposing Antinomianism. Many of his sermons concentrated on piety and the Christian life and did not have a distinctive flavour. They were broadly evangelical and would have fitted comfortably in with the moods and tastes of the evangelical world at large.

Robert Hall was the greatest preacher in England of his day. Yet he was a preacher who tended to minimise theology in his sermons. He avoided presenting the truth in any decisive character. Furthermore, even in the sermons that mention the imputation of Christ's righteousness he made no attempt to substantiate and to explain the significance of such doctrine and no attempt to vigorously defend that biblical view over against contrary teaching, as expressed for example in Baxterianism. Neither did he appear to take the opportunity to tell his congregation that he had once held different views but that now he had reached more scriptural, settled and mature convictions. If these were matters he had not preached to his congregations before it would have provided an opportunity for him to ensure that his present congregation understood the full meaning of justification by faith. The fact remains that for much of his life Hall was not preaching that full meaning.

By way of contrast to Hall, the Particular Baptist leader, Benjamin Keach, preaching in London until his death in 1704 had repeatedly exposed the errors that Baxter promulgated on justification. John Bunyan affirmed the Protestant doctrine of justification; likewise, the Presbyterian preacher Robert Traill (1642-1716) and the majority of the Puritans. The Particular Baptist confession of faith affirms that God freely justifies sinners

> by pardoning their sins, and by accounting and accepting them as righteous; not for anything wrought in them, or done by them, but for Christ's sake alone; not by imputing faith itself, the act of believing, or any other evangelical

Justification by Faith

obedience to them, as their righteousness; but by imputing Christ's active obedience unto the whole law, and passive obedience in his death for their whole and sole righteousness, they receiving and resting on him and his righteousness by faith, which faith they have not of themselves; it is the gift of God.[28]

Spurgeon likewise, was unashamedly committed to evangelical Calvinism and Protestant orthodoxy. Hundreds of Spurgeon's sermons have been printed, listed in *A Complete Index to C.H. Spurgeon's Sermons (1855-1917)*.[29] Just to survey the titles in that index demonstrates how Spurgeon was richly doctrinal in his preaching. Evangelistic messages and sermons of pastoral encouragement may have been dominant, but Spurgeon never avoided opening, illustrating, and applying the grand doctrinal themes of Holy Scripture. He was a convinced Calvinist who held Andrew Fuller in the highest esteem. They shared the same commitment to evangelical Calvinistic orthodoxy. In the early 1880s when Fuller's son, Andrew Gunton Fuller, sent him a complimentary copy of the biography of his father, part of a series entitled *Men Worth Remembering*, he received a brief letter of appreciation from Spurgeon. He wrote, "I have long considered your father to be the greatest theologian of the century."[30] Spurgeon was never embarrassed about his own Calvinistic convictions and almost from the very beginning of his ministry in London he preached specific messages on every one of the five points of Calvinism. He also preached a full biblical doctrine of justification by faith.

These were not pervasive themes in Robert Hall's sermons and this may be one of the reasons why Hall's sermons are rarely

---

[28] The Second London Baptist Confession of Faith, chapter 11.

[29] *A Complete Index to the Sermons of C.H. Spurgeon, 1855-1917* (Pasadena, TX: Pilgrim Publications, 1980).

[30] Michael A.G. Haykin, https://pastorhistorian.com/2014/05/12/letter-from-c-h-spurgeon-to-a-g-fuller-commending-andrew-fuller/. Also cited in Laws, *Andrew Fuller*, 127.

read today, whereas Spurgeon's sermons abound in print and on the internet. Hall's failure to steadfastly propagate and staunchly defend Calvinism and the full doctrine of justification by faith was one reason why Particular Baptists lost their distinctiveness.

10
Piety: The Basis for Friendship

Almost everyone who has written about Robert Hall has drawn attention to his piety. John Greene was typical of many when in the concluding paragraph of his *Reminiscences of Rev. Robert Hall* he wrote:

> We may, however, be permitted to observe, that, while, Mr. Hall obtained an almost unexampled popularity by the productions of his mighty mind, it was ardent and unaffected piety that endeared him to those who enjoyed his society and friendship. Devotedness to God was his peculiar characteristic. If in the great congregation he was revered as the *head* among the thousands of Israel; when leading their devotions, and pleading their cause at the footstool of mercy, he was, emphatically, *as a little child*. Amid the socialities of the family circle, Mr Hall was lively and interesting; adding to its pleasures by the amiability of his disposition and the inexhaustible variety of his conversation.[1]

The primacy of piety

Piety, or that Christian character and conduct expressive of love for and obedience to God, was of great importance to Hall. It was a prominent theme in his sermons. He made personal piety the criterion for his many friendships. This was true throughout his life. When Hall was asked during his Cambridge ministry whether he was an Arminian or a Calvinist, he had replied:

> Neither, Sir: but I believe I recede farther from Arminianism than from Calvinism. If a man profess himself a decided

---

[1] Gregory and Belcher, *Works*, 4:99-100.

Arminian, I infer from it that he is not a good logician; but, Sir, it does not interfere with his personal piety; look at good Mr. Benson, for example. I regard the question more as metaphysical than religious.[2]

Those comments provide us with insights into Hall's priorities. He was averring that while he was less inclined to Arminianism than he was to Calvinism he regarded the question as being speculative. He wanted to emphasize that such doctrinal issues have very little bearing on a man's heart and life, on his personal piety. For Hall it did not matter so much what a person believed, so long as he was marked by Christian character and conduct that was the result of the grace of God in the heart.

So, for example, paying tribute to his friend Joseph Freeston in 1821, he could attest:

> Though he exercised his ministry through the whole of his life among the General Baptists, his sentiment approached nearer to those of Mr. Baxter than the system of Arminius, nor could his statement of christian doctrine have given the slightest offence to a congregation of moderate calvinists. But to polemical theology he was not attached; his religion was entirely of a practical and experimental character; nor did he attach the smallest importance to correct views of christian doctrine, any further than they tended to influence the heart.[3]

Hall was perhaps reflecting and drawing on his experiences in Aberdeen. He had not been impressed by the Calvinism he saw there—"frosty spirited" was the term he used. One of his criticisms of Gill had been that while he presented a system of theology, he failed to emphasise practical Christian living. His

---

[2] Gregory, *Works*, 1:60.
[3] Gregory, *Works*, 4:324.

Piety

insistence on the necessity of holiness of life was also one of the reasons for his fierce opposition to Antinomianism. It may be that at this point Baxter's outlook influenced Hall. Carl Trueman draws attention to the fact that in the 1640s Baxter became very concerned about the proliferating sectarianism of the 1640s and the related spread of antinomianism. He observed that,

> these twin fears made him ecumenical in ambition, in that he was always trying to find a bridge or middle position between two extremes, and earnest in his commitment to formulating his understanding of salvation in a way that accented the moral imperatives of the Christian life.[4]

The same two concerns seem to be mirrored in Hall.

The question though arises whether Hall was right in asserting the primacy of piety over against correct views of Christian doctrine. He seemed to imply that it was an "either/or issue" rather than a "both/and issue." For Hall, Calvinism was not of primary significance in the cultivating of Christian relationships and friendships. He was critical of Andrew Fuller because he thought that Fuller tended to make doctrine paramount in his relationships with other Christians who held different convictions. Fuller made an acute observation about the gap that sometimes exists between a person's doctrinal views and their piety. In a letter, written in February 1815, shortly before his death, he observed

> I perceive that men's characters are not always formed by their avowed principles; that we may hold a sound faith without it's having that hold of us as to form our spirit and conduct; that we profess an erroneous creed, and yet our

---

[4] Carl R. Trueman, "Atonement and the Covenant of Redemption" in David Gibson and Jonathan Gibson eds., *From Heaven He Came and Sought Her: Definite Atonement In Historical, Biblical, Theological and Pastoral Perspective* (Wheaton, IL: Crossway, 2013), 209.

spirit and conduct may be formed nearly irrespective of it; in short, that there is a difference between principles and opinions; the one are the actual moving causes which lie at the root of the action, the other often float in the mind, without being reduced to practice.[5]

There is no evidence to suggest that Fuller was thinking of Hall when he made this observation. Nevertheless, it helps to explain what Hall had said, for example, about his friend Joseph Freeston. A man may be a better Christian than he is a theologian. Our problem with Hall, however, is that he was implying that what a man believed did not matter as much as his piety.

Spurgeon, on the other hand, told his students, "to be effective preachers you must be sound theologians." He warned them that, "those who do away with Christian doctrine are, whether they are aware of it or not, the worst enemies of Christian living ... [because] the coals of orthodoxy are necessary to the fire of piety."[6] Hall did not want to do away with Christian doctrine but he did change some key things toning down doctrinal distinctives in the process. Spurgeon was not an "either/or" man. Doctrinal truth was the foundation and superstructure of all his life, labours, and piety. "For Spurgeon spiritual health depended on right doctrine, for it is doctrine rightly understood, and that in Calvinistic terms, which had enabled him to interpret his own experience."[7]

Spurgeon would have been of one mind with John Ryland on

---

[5] John Ryland, *The Work of Faith, the Labour of Love, and the Patience of Hope Illustrated: In the Life and Death of the Reverend Andrew Fuller, late Pastor of the Baptist Church at Kettering, and Secretary to the Baptist Missionary Society, from Its commencement In 1792* (London: Button and Son, 1816), 57.

[6] "The 110th anniversary of the death of Spurgeon," Banner of Truth, February 4, 2002 (https://banneroftruth.org/uk/resources/articles/2002/the-110th-anniversary-of-the-death-of-spurgeon/).

[7] James M. Gordon, *Evangelical Spirituality: from the Wesleys to John Stott* (London: SPCK, 1991), 170.

Piety

this matter. Writing to John Sutcliff in 1774, Ryland stated, "'Tis the wisdom as well as the duty of the Dissenters to be friendly with the *orthodox* Methodists." Haykin, quoting Ryland, says by "orthodox" Ryland meant Calvinistic, because he added with regard to the Wesleys, "Both their doctrine and Policy are inimical to Dissenters and I think contrary to the Word of God."[8]

Hall's portrait of John Ryland's piety

On June 8, 1825, he preached a funeral sermon for John Ryland, the esteemed father-figure among Particular Baptists who had succeeded Caleb Evans in Bristol in 1793, shortly after Hall's departure to Cambridge. A great deal had changed in those thirty-four years, so much so that not only did Hall return to Bristol to preach at Ryland's funeral but he also succeeded him in the ministry of the Broadmead church.

The most succinct statements Hall made on piety may be found in Ryland's funeral sermon. His text was John 20:7: "the disciple whom Jesus loved." In his tribute to Ryland he readily confessed that, "his piety was of the same mould and complexion with that which distinguished the beloved disciple," and that he was, "so eminent a pattern of Christian excellence."[9] Hall owed a great deal to Ryland, who was eleven years his senior. It was Ryland who had taken the trouble to write to Hall, believing he was in grave danger of adopting the Socinianism of Joseph Priestley.

During his life Ryland had been a prodigious preacher. According to Hall he had preached at least eight thousand six hundred and ninety-one sermons in two hundred and eighty-six distinct places.[10] Hall claimed that while Ryland was not the most

---

[8] Cited in Michael A.G. Haykin, "'The Sum of All Good': John Ryland, Jr., and the Doctrine of the Holy Spirit" *Churchman* 103/104 (1989), 333.

[9] Gregory, *Works*, 5:53.

[10] Gregory, *Works*, 5:55.

popular preacher of his day, it was his sincerity that impressed his hearers. It was his particular Christian character and his piety that marked him out, placing him head and shoulders above other men. Hall described this in the following ways.

> Devotion appeared to be the principal element in his being: it was next to impossible to converse with him without perceiving how it entirely pervaded his mind, and imparted to his whole deportment an air of purity, innocence and sanctity, difficult for words to express. His piety did not display itself in a profusion of religious discourse, not infrequently alluding to the interior exercises of his mind on spiritual subjects. He was seldom known to speak of his religious joys or sorrows: his devotional feelings were too deep and sacred to suffer themselves to evaporate in ordinary conversation. His religion appeared in its fruits; in gentleness, humility, and benevolence; in a steady, conscientious, performance of every duty; and a careful abstinence from every appearance of evil.[11]

Hall then explained at some length some of these marked characteristics of Ryland before adding, "his whole life was a series of acts of self-denial; his conduct appeared invariably to proceed from the impulse of benevolence and the sense of duty," and that "if the essence of Christian perfection consists in a sole and supreme desire to do the will of God, he probably made as near an approach to it as is attainable in the present state."[12]

Hall and Ryland did not entirely agree in their understanding of Christian doctrine. Hall drew attention to that in his funeral oration. He acknowledged that Ryland adhered to "moderate Calvinism," as modelled and explained by Jonathan Edwards. He

---

[11] Gregory, *Works*, 5:55.
[12] Gregory, *Works*, 5:59.

Piety

continued by explaining that Edwards' writings continued "to exert a powerful influence on his [Ryland] public ministry, as well as his theological inquiries and pursuits."[13] Earlier Hall had affirmed that Ryland:

> though a Calvinist in the strictest sense of the word, and attached to its peculiarities in a higher degree than most of the advocates of that system he extended his affection to all who bore the image of Christ, and was ingenious in discovering reasons for thinking well of many who widely dissented from his religious views. No man was more remarkable for combining a zealous attachment to his own principles with the utmost liberality of mind towards those who differed from him; an abhorrence of error, with the kindest feelings towards the erroneous.[14]

Here is evidence that Hall and Ryland had differing attitudes to piety and friendships. Hall did not share Ryland's Calvinism "in the strictest sense," any more than he shared his own father's stricter Calvinism. Hall had used similar language to describe his father's principles in 1813 in his preface to *Help to Zion's Travellers*. Ryland did not choose the "either/or" path as Hall was inclined to do and to play down doctrinal distinctives in the process. Both piety and doctrinal truth were equally vital to Ryland as they would be to Spurgeon. For that reason neither of them elevated piety above truth and minimised or ignored the differences between Arminianism and Calvinism. To them Arminianism was an erroneous system of theology. Compromising the truth was not an option open to these men. They were fully-persuaded evangelical Calvinists.

Hall held Ryland and also Benjamin Beddome in high esteem. In 1819 Hall penned a brief "Recommendatory Preface to a

---

[13] Gregory, *Works*, 5:65.
[14] Gregory, *Works*, 5:59-60.

Volume of Hymns" by Beddome. He noted among other qualities that "as a preacher he was universally admired for the piety and unction of his sentiments."[15] As a religious poet he highlighted the "poetical beauty ... the simple pathos ... and the piety and justness of thought which pervaded all the compositions."[16] It was also evident that Hall was deeply grieved over the loss of Ryland and Beddome, especially the effects it would have on Particular Baptists. "Our brightest lights have been successively extinguished. In vain do we look around for a Beddome, a Booth, a Fuller, or a Ryland; names which would have given lustre to any denomination, and were long the glory of ours."[17]

Perhaps Hall sensed it was the end of an era. He was now in his sixty-first year. Benjamin Beddome had died in 1795, Abraham Booth in 1806, Andrew Fuller in 1815, and now John Ryland in 1825. All four of these men were committed to Calvinism in the strictest sense of the word. These men had been pillars among the Particular Baptists. The eclipse of Calvinism was already under way and would gather momentum in the following decades of the nineteenth century. To what extent Hall realised this was happening is hard to determine, but he was certainly aware that there were significant differences. However, Hall never appeared to make any observations or critical comments about the theological direction being taken by the Particular Baptists.

Friendships

Hall played a role in these changes because of the particular emphasis he laid on piety at the expense of truth. Ryland could maintain friendships and not compromise his Calvinism. Christopher Crocker draws attention to the wide connections cultivated by Ryland,

---

[15] Gregory, *Works*, 4:381.
[16] Gregory, *Works*, 4:381.
[17] Gregory, *Works*, 5:68.

Piety

a survey of Ryland's connections reveals a "who's who" of eighteenth-century Baptists and to a lesser, but still valid extent, wider evangelicalism ... Ryland enjoyed relationships with evangelical Episcopalians, members of the Kirk, "Orthodox" Methodists together with British Dissenters and American divines. In Bristol the evangelical Dissenters even held a fortnightly breakfast. Indeed, very few of his own denomination "have ever had more of my affection and esteem, than several of the ministers of the establishment, I have felt the same disposition towards many in the church of Scotland. Much friendship, generous friendship towards our Mission ... shown by many in both these communities ... and our dissenting brethren."[18]

Ryland's catholicity of spirit and warm friendship was clearly in evidence. He cultivated a close relationship with the Anglican Calvinist, John Newton (1725-1807), reflected in the eighty-three letters Newton wrote to between 1771 and 1803.[19] He was also close to other Anglicans like Thomas Scott (1747-1821) and William Wilberforce (1759-1833), the Scottish Presbyterian John Erskine (1721-1803), and maintained correspondence with New England Congregationalists like Samuel Hopkins (1731-1803), Jonathan Edwards, Jr. (1745-1801), and Timothy Dwight (1752-1817).[20] Erskine, in particular was devoted to the work of Scottish evangelical missionary endeavour. Such endeavour was close to the heart of the Particular Baptists.

Fuller had followed a similar practice. There were even occasions when he preached for Dan Taylor of the New Connexion

---

[18] Christopher W. Crocker, "The Life and Legacy of John Ryland Jr. (1753-1825): A Man of Considerable Usefulness—An Historical Biography" (PhD thesis, Bristol Baptist College, 2018), 336. This catholicity of Ryland is more fully explained and endorsed by Lon Graham, *All Who Love the Redeemer: The Catholicity of John Ryland Jr.* (Eugene, OR: Pickwick Publications, 2022).

[19] Grant Gordon, *Wise Counsel John Newton's Letters to John Ryland Jr.* (Edinburgh: The Banner of Truth Trust, 2009).

[20] Haykin, "The Sum of All Good."

The Theology of Robert Hall Jr.

Baptists. For his part, Hall deliberately cultivated friendships with, for example, General Baptists, but on a different basis from that of Ryland and Fuller. He soft-pedalled any theological differences.

In his funeral sermon for Ryland, Hall had spoken in the first part at some length on the importance of friendship. He understood friendship to be deeply rooted in the gospel. While Christ did not formally prescribe the cultivation of friendship, "he prescribed the virtues out of which it will naturally grow."[21] Hall drew attention to Christ's own conduct, "his humility, forbearance, gentleness, kindness, and the most tender sympathy with all the infirmities and distresses of our fellow-creatures; and his whole life was a perfect transcript of these virtues."[22] Friendship in virtuous minds was, Hall urged,

> but the concentration of benevolent emotions, heightened by respect and increased by exercise, on one or more objects. Friendship is not a state of feeling, whose elements are specifically different from those which compose every other. The emotions we feel towards a friend are the same in kind with those we experience on other occasions; but they are more complex and more exalted. It is the general sensibility to kind and social affections, more immediately directed to one or more individuals, and in consequence of its particular direction, giving birth to an order of feeling more vivid and intense than usual, which constitutes friendship.[23]

Hall stressed the value and importance of such friendships. "Next to the immediate guidance of God, by his Spirit, the

---

[21] Gregory, *Works*, 5:42.
[22] Gregory, *Works*, 5:42.
[23] Gregory, *Works*, 5:42.

Piety

counsel and encouragement of virtuous and enlightened friends afford the most powerful aid, in the encounter of temptation and in the career of duty."[24]

Therefore, it is not surprising to find Hall cultivating a wide circle of friends. He cultivated warm friendships with men whose piety he found attractive. That would have included his three biographers, all long-standing friends—Olinthus Gregory, John Morris and John Greene. While he was in Leicester he enjoyed a significant friendship with Joseph Goadby, who was a New Connexion Baptist in Ashby, and Joseph Freeston, pastor of a General Baptist congregation in Hinckley. He was in the habit of exchanging pulpits with Goadby. In addition Hall's family would stay there for two weeks and Hall would join them during their stay to take his tea and smoke his pipe.[25]

Hall's support for Bible societies and missions

While he was in Leicester he also enjoyed a close friendship with the Rev. Thomas Robinson, the Anglican vicar of the parish of St. Mary-de-Castro.[26] It was an age when missionary societies, bible societies, and Sunday schools were being actively and zealously promoted. Hall and Robinson were involved in promoting a local branch of the Bible Society and on occasions could be seen walking arm in arm to the meetings.[27] Robinson had taken the initiative, and despite the fact that he was a strict Churchman, had sought out Hall to work with him in this venture. When Robinson

---

[24] Gregory, *Works*, 5:46.

[25] Bertha and Lilian Goadby, *Not Saints but Men: Or the Story of the Goadby Ministers* (London: Kingsgate Press, n.d.), 63.

[26] For a survey of the life and work of Robinson see Gerald T. Rimmington, "Thomas Robinson: Evangelical Clergyman in Leicester 1774-1813. (https://www.le.ac.uk/lahs/downloads/2001/GRimmingtonTLAHS2001.pdf).

[27] J.W. Morris, *Biographical Reflections of the Rev. Robert Hall, A.M.* (India, New Delhi: Isha Books, 2013), 238-239.

died in 1813 Hall took the opportunity to speak of his friend at the next annual meeting of the Bible Society. Hall represented him, "as the great focus of piety and benevolence, as the sum and centre of the moral system, in the town and neighbourhood."[28]

Zeal and enthusiasm for mission endeavour also characterised Hall. He fully supported Carey and the work which Carey, William Ward, and Joshua Marshman spearheaded in Serampore. It made no difference that Carey was one of the "moderate Calvinists," along with Fuller and Ryland and one who owed much to Hall's own father. That was not the issue for Hall. "The venerable Carey" received a significant tribute from Hall in the funeral sermon for Ryland. In Hall's estimation, Carey was "a man who unites, with the most profound and varied attainments, the fervour of an evangelist, the piety of a saint, and the simplicity of a child."[29]

He also befriended Carey's nephew Eustace, and it was no surprise that Hall preached *An Address to the Rev. Eustace Carey*, when he was set apart as a missionary to India, on January 19, 1814. In the course of his sermon Hall reasoned with the younger Carey. It was a word of caution, but in so doing Hall seemed to be recommending a version of Christianity that avoided advocating any particular system of theology. He urged him:

> It is above all things necessary for you to acquaint yourself with the general doctrines of Christianity in their full extent; but it will be neither necessary nor expedient to initiate your converts into those controversies which, through a long course of time, have grown up among Christians.[30]

He continued in a manner that probably reflected his own

---

[28] Morris, *Biographical Reflections*, 272.
[29] Gregory, *Works*, 5:69.
[30] Gregory, *Works*, 2:224.

Piety

convictions and practices in dealing with truth and error. Always anxious to avoid theological controversy he exhorted Eustace: "Endeavour to acquire as extensive and perfect a knowledge as possible of the dictates of inspiration, and by establishing your hearers in these, preclude the entrance of error, rather than confute it."[31] Behind his exhortations to Carey were his fears of introducing theological subtleties and disputes that he thought had plagued European Christianity for too long. He told him if he wanted to follow that path then he should abandon his New Testament and instead imitate the church of Rome and return to the schoolmen. A few sentences further on Hall revealed his fears. He doubted whether any of the denominations of Christianity were following the "more pure, simple apostolical mode of presenting the gospel."[32] He maintained:

> Few or none of them have derived their sentiments purely from the sacred oracles, as the result of independent inquiry; but almost universally from some distinguished leader, who at the commencement of the Reformation formed his faith, and planned his discipline, amidst the heat and fury of theological combat. Terms have been invented for the purpose of excluding error, or more accurately defining the truth, to which the New Testament is a stranger, and on those terms associations and impressions ingrafted, which in some instances, perhaps little correspond with the divine simplicity of the gospel.[33]

Hall immediately qualified what he meant. He was not suggesting that those who had followed such a pattern were in error themselves. He was simply enquiring, "Whether we have not all in our turn receded somewhat from the standard, if not by the

---

[31] Gregory, *Works*, 5:225.
[32] Gregory, *Works*, 5:225.
[33] Gregory, *Works*, 5:225.

adoption of positive error, yet by a disproportionate attention to some parts of revelation, to the neglect of others equally important, in consequence of an undue partiality to our respective peculiarities."[34]

The consequences of Hall's emphasis

The concerns that Hall expressed have some validity. There is always the danger of losing the clarity of the gospel of Jesus Christ. Yet at the same time it is impossible to read the New Testament—the book of Acts, and especially the Epistles—without being faced with the appearance of error and wrong practices in the church and the actions needed to deal firmly with them. Hall did not want to promote any particular party and believed that the best way to proceed was to establish the hearers of the gospel in the "dictates of inspiration." That meant he did not want to see the distinctives of Calvinism or any doctrinal system promoted. Such matters can hardly be pushed to one side as if they were not important and of no consequence. As has already been noted, for Spurgeon, Calvinism was a mere nickname for what he believed to be the biblical gospel. Holding firmly to that Calvinism, which for a long time had been characteristic of Particular Baptists, was absent in Hall's exhortations to Eustace Carey.

By this process of establishing hearers in the "dictates of inspiration" Hall claimed he was returning to apostolic preaching and practice. The priority he placed on piety and the thrust of his exhortations to Eustace Carey, together with some of the friendships he formed during his life suggest that in practice he was toning down the distinctives of Calvinism. This was not the path Ryland had followed. He had said in 1817, "Most assuredly ... I fully subscribe to the position of the Assembly of Divines at

---

[34] Gregory, *Works*, 5:226.

Piety

Westminster."[35] For Ryland, Calvinism was synonymous with evangelical truth and genuine Christianity. "At the heart of his identity Ryland considered himself a Particular (or Calvinistic) Baptist in the vein of English Puritanism."[36] "In Ryland's own view nothing novel was discovered; rather he and his friends acted as reformers recalling their denomination back to its Calvinistic roots, and so recapturing a biblical piety and urgent sense of mission that eventually radiated throughout Baptist and evangelical ranks."[37]

This was not the path Hall mapped out for himself and for others to follow. As has already been pointed out Hall's own sympathies with Baxter would have led him in a different direction. Richard Baxter was renowned for his piety expressed in many of his practical works but not for his Calvinistic orthodoxy. We have already mentioned that Hall shared Baxter's antipathy for detailed creeds and confessions of faith and he may have shared, at least for a significant number of years, Baxter's view of justification.

Hall was right to emphasise the importance of piety. It is always a much-needed, healthy emphasis, one which reflects the teaching of Christ and the apostles. However, piety cannot be divorced from doctrinal truth and integrity. They belong together, like twins from the same womb. Yet as the nineteenth century advanced so the emphasis he had placed on piety, tending to pare down doctrine, drifting into forms of sentimentalism and subjectivism divorced from the Scriptures. Spurgeon strenuously resisted such tendencies:

> Oh, for a church of believers in Jesus who know why they believe in Him; persons who believe the Bible, and know

---

[35] Quoted Crocker, "The Life and Legacy of John Ryland Jr.," 247.
[36] Crocker, "The Life and Legacy of John Ryland Jr.," 12.
[37] Quoted Crocker, "The Life and Legacy of John Ryland Jr.," 251.

what it contains; who believe the doctrines of grace [Calvinism], and know the bearings of those truths; who know where they are, and what they are, and who therefore dwell in the light, and cannot be deceived by the prince of darkness![38]

E.J. Poole-Connor in his small work *The Apostasy of English Nonconformity* recorded the words of the liberal, philosophically-inclined Congregationalist, James Baldwin Brown (1820–1884). At a meeting of the Congregational Union a proposal was made that a more definite statement of doctrinal belief should be drawn up. Baldwin's rejection of that proposal expressed the prevailing mentality of the day, "What need had they of sign-posts when they enjoyed the presence of the Living Guide?"[39]

Poole-Connor also drew attention to the original constitution of the Baptist Union, formed in 1832. It had no doctrinal basis other than a statement on baptism by immersion as the only Christian baptism. William Young Fullerton (1857–1932), served as President of the Baptist Union in 1917, following five years (1912-1917) as the Home Secretary of the Baptist Missionary Society. Yet despite a close relationship with Spurgeon in his youth, he could declare with emphatic approval, "that this institution [Baptist Missionary Society] had not, never has had, and never will have, any creedal basis."[40] By the time Baldwin and Fullerton made these statements it was very evident that the leaven had done its work and effectively leavened the whole loaf.

The observation of Andrew Fuller cuts both ways. A sound faith does not always produce all-round Christian character. All true gospel churches of the present day would benefit from an

---

[38] Spurgeon, *An All-Round Ministry: Addresses to Ministers and Students* (London: The Banner of Truth Trust, 1965), 172.

[39] Cited E. J. Poole-Connor, *Apostasy of English Nonconformity* (London: Thynne and Co., Ltd. 1933), 16.

[40] Poole-Connor, *The Apostasy of English Nonconformity*, 18.

Piety

injection of the same kind of piety and zeal that marked Hall's life. We are not for one moment criticising Hall's zeal, or calling into question his sincerity and his devotion to serving God. However, it is never appropriate to promote piety while, at the same time, encouraging a lukewarm approach towards doctrine and theology. Hall would have been horrified by the doctrinal decline that assumed such prominence in the latter decades of the nineteenth century. Sadly, by pruning evangelical Calvinism and downplaying its importance Hall contributed to the undermining not only of evangelical Calvinism but also of evangelicalism in its wider horizons in the years following his death.

10
Baptism and the Lord's Supper

Robert Hall became an ardent advocate of open communion. Gregory devoted a whole volume to Hall's views on the subject and the practice he vigorously promoted in contrast to the practice of men like Abraham Booth, Andrew Fuller, and Joseph Kinghorn (1766-1832).[1] Particular Baptists had never been of one mind on the subject of the terms of communion. There were those, like Booth, Fuller, and Kinghorn, who defended the practice of strict communion, that is, the restriction of the Lord's Table to those baptized on profession of their faith. On the other hand there had been those like John Bunyan who have argued for open communion. The prominent London pastor William Kiffen had strenuously defended strict communion over against Bunyan's views.

Strict communion was the practice of the majority of Particular Baptists at the end of the eighteenth and the beginning of the nineteenth century. That view had been challenged by John Ryland's father, John Collett Ryland, and by Daniel Turner (1709-1798), the pastor of a Particular Baptist church in Abingdon.[2] However, the issue was bigger than baptism and the Lord's Supper. It was a matter of church order and church discipline. When Hall took up the cause of open communion in 1815 he was the pastor of Carey's former congregation in Leicester. He was in his prime as a preacher and as an influential thinker and writer. People would listen to what he had to say. His passionate promotion of open communion eventually made a huge impact on

---

[1] Gregory, *Works on Terms of Communion* in *Works*, volume 3.
[2] For a fuller discussion of Ryland and Turner and the debate generated by their views see Robert W. Oliver, *History of the English Calvinistic Baptists, 1771-1892: From John Gill to C. H. Spurgeon* (Edinburgh: The Banner of Truth Trust, 2006), 58-88.

Particular Baptist churches. Many eventually abandoned strict communion because Hall's arguments for open communion held sway after his death. It was only then that open communion gradually became the principal practice. What is often overlooked, however, is the effect this practice had on the ecclesiology of Particular Baptist churches.

Hall on Baptism

When Hall resigned from the Academy and the church in Broadmead in 1790 he included in his letter an explanation of his convictions about baptism. Suspicions were rife that Hall was not really a Baptist. He was quick to point out that he was "both in respect to the subject and to the mode of this institution, a Baptist."[3] The seeds of his views expressed twenty-five years later though had already been sown. He would not re-baptize someone who had been sprinkled as an adult believer, even though he was firmly convinced that immersion was the ancient mode of baptism. He affirmed that "sprinkling, though an innovation, does not deprive Baptism of its essential validity, so as to put the person that has been sprinkled *in adult age* upon a footing with the unbaptized."[4] Then in addition, he said that if that opinion be,

> a sufficient objection to my union with a Baptist congregation, then as all Christendom is composed of Baptists or Paedobaptists, it amounts to my exclusion, as a minister, from every Christian society throughout the whole world: an interdict equally absurd and inhuman, founded upon a conduct merely negative in chimerical [imaginary] situations seldom or never likely to occur.[5]

That note of protest was to become even more prominent in his

---

[3] Gregory, *Works*, 1:32.
[4] Gregory, *Works*, 1:33.
[5] Gregory, *Works*, 1:32.

Baptism and the Lord's Supper

writings after 1815 as he actively took up his pen in the cause of open communion.

Hall was also pastoring a church in Leicester that was effectively made up of two congregations. A similar practice was already in place in Broadmead when Hall first went to Bristol. It had been introduced there by Hugh Evans. There were paedobaptists who had attached themselves to the preaching ministry of the Particular Baptist churches but because those churches practiced strict communion they were excluded from the table. To overcome that obstacle a separate service was held at which those of paedobaptist persuasion celebrated the Lord's Supper. While believer's baptism by immersion remained one of the terms of communion there could be no changes to that pattern of church order. Hall wanted that barrier to be removed. There was an element of pragmatism in his argument, not least because it set aside what others, like Fuller, believed to be the plain teaching of the New Testament. At the same time it was not difficult to see the practical dilemma that Hall wanted to resolve. To him it was a matter of great embarrassment and shame and a contradiction of Christian love to exclude any Christian from the Lord's Supper.

When he was in Cambridge as pastor of St. Andrew's Street Baptist Church, he was more than happy to follow the long-established practice of open communion which existed there. His predecessor in Cambridge, Robert Robinson, had written a defence of open communion but Hall was unable to agree entirely with Robinson because he was willing to open the table to people who held all kinds of different religious convictions. That was a step too far for Hall.

He had the highest regard for both Abraham Booth and Andrew Fuller. In 1778 Booth had published *An Apology for the Baptists*. Booth argued that by insisting on strict communion he was not laying any unwarranted stress on baptism nor was he guilty of bigotry by refusing communion to paedobaptists. Persuaded that loyalty to Christ and to the pattern laid down in the New Testament was of primary importance, he concluded that this required the practice of strict communion. Fuller shared those convictions. They believed that strict communion reflected the biblical church order. Hall was to disagree with them in the strongest terms. In 1815 he set out to reply to Booth's *Apology* and to correct Robinson's loose views.

Hall's tendency to pragmatism

Questions about church government were also among those that Robert Balmer asked Hall in conversation between 1819 and 1823. Balmer was a Scottish Presbyterian and found Hall's views "undecided and somewhat inconsistent."[6] Hall expressed his doubts as to whether any one particular form of church government was prescribed in the Scriptures and added, "that he was disposed to adopt the maxim, 'Whatever is best administered is best.'"[7] That was a somewhat slack, if not pragmatic, line to adopt and one which his Presbyterian enquirer did not share. On another occasion in conversation with Balmer, Hall defended independency as being sanctioned by the word of God. Hall had argued that despite a case of scandalous irregularity on the part of a church and its minister no other church had any claim to interfere and claim jurisdiction. They might remonstrate and advise but nothing more. This was why Balmer thought Hall inconsistent in his views of church government.

The maxim that Hall adopted with regard to church government indicates a clear tendency to expediency and pragmatism. That same tendency to pragmatism is reflected in his arguments for open communion. In his opinion strict communion was totally

---

[6] Gregory, *Works*, 1:161.
[7] Gregory, *Works*, 1:161-162.

inappropriate, so much so that he "fought for his cause with all the fervour of a crusader and the ability of an orator."[8]

Hall and open communion

Hall set out his case in *The Preface* to *On Terms of Communion*. The strength of his convictions is immediately evident. Speaking in general terms first of all he stated, "The practice of incorporating private opinions and human inventions with the constitution of a church, and with the terms of communion, has long appeared to him untenable in its principle, and pernicious in its effects." He continued,

> There is no position in the whole compass of theology, of the truth of which he feels a stronger persuasion, than that no man, or set of men, are entitled to prescribe, as an indispensable condition of communion, what the New Testament has not enjoined as a condition of salvation.[9]

He therefore regarded the convictions of men like Booth and Fuller as belonging to the realm of "private opinions" and "human inventions" and that such could not be substantiated from the New Testament Scriptures. Furthermore, he believed that the practice of strict communion fostered a spirit of separation and seclusion which led to the neglect of some of the most important injunctions of Scripture. Thus, Hall was diametrically opposed to the common practice of many Particular Baptist churches.

Such was the strength of his convictions and his arguments that they eventually came to be the dominant view among Particular Baptists who did not become part of the Strict and Particular Baptist churches in the nineteenth century. There were other Baptists who wanted to develop greater interdenominational

---

[8] Oliver, *History of the English Calvinistic Baptists*, 250.
[9] Gregory, *Works*, 3:3.

relationships and the arguments of Hall were extremely attractive to such men. However, this move was all part of the dumbing-down of doctrinal distinctives that was taking place not only among Baptists but in other denominations as well.

It is not our intention to recount the debate in detail. Others have adequately covered that subject.[10] Our concern is to assess to what extent the advocacy of open communion contributed to the undermining of Calvinism among the Particular Baptists. Hall's basic contention was "that no church has a right to establish terms of communion, which are not terms of salvation."[11]

This view is linked with his conviction that whether someone adopts Calvinistic or Arminian sentiments is not crucial because on either view the hope of salvation is not affected. Hall was concerned with what is often referred to as "primary truth," namely the truths that are essential for salvation. Matters such as the practice of baptism and the Lord's supper, church order and government are regarded as "secondary truths." Such language is misleading, not least because it leaves the door open to thinking that these matters are not of real importance and that Scripture has nothing definitive to say about them. Booth, Fuller, and Kinghorn were persuaded that strict communion was sanctioned by the teaching and practice of the Lord Jesus Christ and the apostles.

Hall dealt with the issue from another angle. He did his utmost to emphasise the fundamental unity of the Christian church. For him it was unthinkable to have a plurality of true local churches, yet for those churches not to enjoy actual communion with each other because of differences over baptism. Amalgamation of the various groups of Christians was Hall's fundamental desire. To exclude paedobaptists was unlawful and destructive of the unity

---

[10] Oliver, *History of the English Calvinistic Baptists*, 235-259, and Michael Taylor, *Baptists at the Table: The Theology of the Lord's Supper among English Baptists In the Nineteenth Century* (Didcot: Baptist Historical Society, 1992), 32-83.

[11] Gregory, *Works*, 3:117.

Baptism and the Lord's Supper

of the church. Hall did not hesitate to use the word schismatic to describe this situation and grieved over the way it came to expression in celebrating the Lord's supper. He deplored what he saw to be a party spirit that deprived a believer of one of the means of grace.

At the same time Hall claimed to be a Particular Baptist, a group of churches whose very existence since the 1630s and 1640s was established on the conviction that the New Testament required believer's baptism by immersion and that any other kind of baptism was therefore invalid. Yet, his method of resolving the difficulty and maintaining the unity of the church and promoting mutual love between Christians was to minimise the importance of baptism.

Not all of Hall's arguments were watertight. To counter the argument that baptism was established before the Lord's supper he maintained there was no Christian baptism until after the resurrection of Jesus Christ. That argument he based on the Great Commission given to the apostles in Matthew 28:18-20. That meant that the baptism administered by John, and baptism administered by the apostles before the death of Christ were not to be regarded as Christian baptism. In fact, Hall went so far as to say those who received these baptisms were not baptized at all. When he considered the evidence of apostolic practice he recognised that baptism invariably preceded admission to the Lord's supper. However, he refused to make that the norm, trying to avoid making participation in the Lord's supper dependent on having been baptized. In his opinion precedents, even apostolic ones, were not to be taken as binding laws.

Kinghorn and others challenged these conclusions.[12] They drew attention to a clear pattern of practice in the New

---

[12] See Joseph Kinghorn, *Baptism a Term of Communion at the Lord's Table* (Norwich: 1816); and also *A Defence of Baptism a Term of Communion In Answer to the Rev. Robert Hall's Reply* (Norwich: 1820).

The Theology of Robert Hall Jr.

Testament, a pattern prescribed by the commandments of the Lord Jesus Christ. For Fuller and also for Kinghorn the matter was one of implementing clear biblical principles and following apostolic practice. They emphasised that in the New Testament whenever a church was planted, it was composed of those who believed in Christ and were baptized in his name. They countered Hall's argument that exclusion was schismatic and a denial of Christian love by saying that such brotherly love "should never induce us to act contrary to the will of Christ."[13]

The effect of Hall's views

The communion debate continued for the rest of Hall's life and after his death. Hall died in 1831 and Kinghorn in 1832. When Hall died strict communion was still the practice of the majority of Particular Baptist churches but open communion was gaining ground. Cornelius Elven (1797-1873) preached in Kinghorn's former church in February 1833. He recalled a conversation with Kinghorn concerning two prevailing deficiencies in the rising ministry of the present day. He explained,

> The first was a very general tendency towards mixed communion, which if it continued to increase, might realize what Robert Hall contemplated with so much complacency, the annihilation of the Baptists as a distinct body of Christians; and secondly, the keeping back of the distinguishing truths of the gospel from a morbid apprehension of approaching too near the confines of Antinomianism.[14]

Shortly before Kinghorn's death the Rev. William Jones wrote to him and expressed similar concerns to those of Elven. His letter concluded,

---

[13] Kinghorn, *Baptism a Term of Communion*, 39.
[14] Martin Hood Wilkin, *Joseph Kinghorn of Norwich* (Norwich: Fletcher and Alexander/London: Arthur Hall and Co., 1860), 412-413.

Baptism and the Lord's Supper

> Well my dear Sir! You see the practice of mixed communion is gaining ground among the English Baptist Churches, after all the labours you have bestowed upon them: and I do heartily wish that this were all; but I much fear that they are rapidly progressing in Arminianism.[15]

The debate over open communion was therefore part of a much larger issue, namely the undermining and perhaps even the disappearance of Calvinism among the Particular Baptists. Elven and Jones were two voices expressing concern.

Some twenty-five years after Hall's death Spurgeon founded the Pastors' College. Reflecting on his reasons for opening another college he expressed his doubts about the doctrines being taught in other institutions. He did not think it was genuine Calvinism. He frankly admitted, "I may have been uncharitable in my judgment, but I thought the Calvinism of the theology then taught to be very doubtful, and the fervour of the generality of students to be far behind their literary attainments."[16]

Following Hall's death his regard for baptism as a non-essential tended to taken up by other Baptists and applied to the Lord's supper. The ordinances of baptism and the Lord's supper were belittled, a dangerous trend for any Christian denomination. Elven may have been overly-pessimistic about "the annihilation of the Baptists" if Hall's arguments prevailed, but his concerns were well-founded. Michael Walker noted a second consequence of Hall's belittling of baptism, namely "the departure of theological rigour. Any movement towards Christian unity must wrestle with doctrinal differences that divide Christians."[17] The drift towards open communion was part of a movement that undermined the Calvinism which characterised the generation of Abraham Booth

---

[15] Wilkin, *Joseph Kinghorn of Norwich*, 431.
[16] Spurgeon, "Concerning the College," *The Sword and Trowel* (April 1, 1870): 146.
[17] Taylor, *Baptists at the Table*, 80.

The Theology of Robert Hall Jr.

and Andrew Fuller. Hall certainly contributed to that undermining by his championing the cause of open communion.

It is significant that following Kinghorn's death in 1832 the church in Norwich invited William Brock (1807–1875) to succeed him. His ministry portrayed the kind of changes being promoted after Hall's death. Brock had been a student in Stepney Academy, having been under the tutelage of William Newman. Newman had upheld strict communion despite student unrest over the issue. Brock already held open communion convictions when he went to Norwich and only became pastor on the understanding that he would not change anything. He was called to Bloomsbury in central London in 1838 and became the president of the Baptist Union in 1869. His successor in Norwich, George Gould, introduced open communion within a decade of Brock's departure.

Brock was one of the three Baptist pastors considered by Russell Campbell.[18] He maintained that these three men, Brock, Charles Stanford, and William Landels, contributed to the decline and eventual loss of Calvinism in the nineteenth century. He was of the opinion that each of them was driven by a spirit of pragmatism, though Brock remained more Calvinistic than the other two. Following the line promoted by Hall, Brock went a step further than Hall. Having been convinced that an open table was the correct practice he became an advocate of open membership. He was more concerned for evangelical unity than he was for Baptist church order and for church purity. The dismantling of Baptist church order and the subsequent undermining of church discipline were all too evident to see by anyone who had sufficient discernment. The loss of a distinctly Baptist church order feared by Cornelius Elven and Joseph Kinghorn moved a step closer to becoming reality.

---

[18] Russell S. Campbell, "The decline of Calvinism among British Baptists in the nineteenth century: a study of three ministers" (DPhil thesis, University of Oxford, 2000).

12
Robert Hall in Perspective

The prominence of Robert Hall

A significant print of an engraving of fifteen men has survived the passage of time. It portrays Baptist leaders of the early nineteenth century together with their signatures. A copy of it may be found in Payne's *The Baptist Union: A Short History*.[1] Barely discernible in the background are faint portraits that appear to represent seventeenth century Baptist forefathers. The seated figures are (from left to right) William Carey, Joseph Kinghorn, John Ryland, Jr., Andrew Fuller, and John Foster. The only man standing in the front row is Robert Hall. The standing men in the back row are Joshua Marshman, William Ward, William Knibb, Thomas Burchell, John Rippon, Dan Taylor, John Gregory Pike, William Steadman and Samuel Pearce.

The portraits are significant for at least two reasons. Firstly,

---

[1] A print in the care of Bristol Baptist College, and copies also in the Angus Library, Oxford.

although the majority of these men were Particular Baptists, Dan Taylor and John Deodatus Gregory Pike were both General Baptists belonging to the New Connexion. Pike was invited to preside over the annual meeting of the Baptist Union in 1842. The drawing is almost certainly intended to convey the decreasing distance between Particular and General Baptists, what was referred to earlier as the "erosion of distinctives."

Secondly, prominent in the front row and standing upright is the unmistakable figure of Robert Hall, whereas the other five men are all seated. The actual date of the drawing remains unknown (the 1850s are a reasonable guess) but it is clearly intended to portray Hall as the main figure among the Baptists of his generation.[2] This persuasion was not an opinion that originated years after his death. It was frequently heard during his life and persisted after his death. Gregory, Morris, Steadman, and Foster were all in agreement. One of the historians of English Dissent echoed their assessment of Robert Hall, that he was regarded by many as "the champion of evangelical truth, both in the pulpit and the press."[3] That statement is an indication of the doctrinal changes that were already in operation in the first three decades of the nineteenth century.

How did Robert Hall come to be regarded as "the champion of evangelical truth?" Was it a valid evaluation of the man? What criteria were used in order to reach this evaluation? Without any

---

[2] I am indebted for this information to Emily Burgoyne, Librarian at the Angus Library in Oxford. In an email, dated March 27, 2019, she noted: In the bottom left hand corner directly below the picture there are the following words "Drawn by L. Huard" and in the bottom right hand corner it says "Engraved by I.H. Baker." The autographs are reproduced on each one and beneath them date is given. it says "Published by J. Heaton & Son, 21 Warwick Lane, Paternoster Row, London." The artist, Louis Alexis Huard (1815-1874) was a French artist, who appears to have lived in London for the last two or three decades of his life.

[3] James Bennett, *The History of Dissenters During the Last Thirty Years, 1808-1838* (London: Hamilton, Adams and Co., 1839), 488.

Robert Hall in Perspective

doubt he was an impressive, eloquent, and impassioned preacher who upheld the cardinal doctrines of evangelicalism.

However, we must ask whether this perception was obscured by his oratorical abilities. Those who heard him were often drawn by what has been referred to as a "mysterious magnetism in the preacher."[4] Most evaluations of Hall are based primarily on his exceptional eloquence and oratorical gifts. There were recorded occasions when the congregation became so absorbed by the preacher that they moved to the edge of their seats and then stood up, leaning forward, hanging on every word that fell from his lips. A few were even found standing on top of the pews yet were not conscious of that fact. Greene recorded one such occasion when Hall had preached in Kettering.[5] He also reported the impact of a sermon Hall preached in Bristol on the text of 1 John 3:2:

> A clergyman who had never heard Mr. Hall before, observed to his friend, at the close of the service, that he had never heard anything like it; and that he could hardly tell whether he was in the body or out of it. Several persons were taken ill from the extraordinary excitement. A physician of my acquaintance told me on the Monday afternoon that he had not got over the impression. Several of the deacons and others declared that they had never heard anything equal to it. I did not recover from the effects before the Wednesday.[6]

Such reports were not isolated events. Taken up with his oratory it is very unlikely that Hall's hearers would have been assessing the content of his sermon. Some obviously came to hear him because he was an oratorical phenomenon second to none in his day. Steadman had recognized the danger but placed the blame

---

[4] Graham W. Hughes, *Robert Hall* (London: The Carey Press, 1943), 14. Hughes provides a vivid description of his preaching and Its effects on his congregation.

[5] John Greene, *Reminiscences of the Rev. Robert Hall*; Gregory and Belcher, *Works*, 4:97, footnote.

[6] Greene, *Reminiscences of the Rev. Robert Hall*; Gregory and Belcher, *Works*, 4:97.

not on Hall but on the folly of his admirers. In every age crowds will still run after excitement and listen to a gifted orator who can capture their ears and sway their emotions.

How was Hall remembered after his death? Much of what has been written about Hall tends to focus on his great oratorical abilities rather than his doctrinal sentiments. Perhaps it is wiser to remember that gifts or a winsome personality can never replace the truth of the gospel. In order to obtain a more accurate estimation of Hall as a preacher has required a careful assessment of his doctrinal convictions. Thus an attempt has been made to compare his opinions with those of his peers among other Particular Baptists, with Spurgeon (born in 1834, three years after Hall's death) as well as those of previous generations.

The declining impact of Calvinism

During the 1820s and 1830s it became increasingly apparent to a number of discerning and concerned leaders of the Particular Baptists that the robust Calvinism of the previous generation was no longer being upheld. Even the numerical growth of the churches could not conceal the changes taking place. There was a notable decline in the doctrinal awareness in many churches. Cornelius Elven and William Jones put their finger on three changes, namely the increasing practice of open communion, the failure to preach the distinguishing truths of the gospel, and the rapid progress of Arminianism.

Joseph Ivimey (1773–1834) was a Baptist historian and pastor of the Eagle Street Church, Red Lion Square, London. Four volumes on the *History of the English Baptists* comprise his *magnum opus*. The research he had undertaken to complete that history provided him with a broad perspective on trends and changes taking place among the Particular Baptists. Preaching in 1828 three years before Hall's death, he recognized the winds of change blowing through the churches. He warned against the dangers of "wavering":

Robert Hall in Perspective

A spirit of laxity is discovering itself in the preaching of some of our ministers, who, if they introduce the doctrines of grace, it is rather by way of implication than by distinct mention of them ... I may certainly be mistaken, but I think I have discovered appearances of "wavering" in regard to some capital truths of the Christian faith, and a spirit of laxity, producing latitudinarian feeling and conduct; and if these things are not checked and counteracted, by our vigorously 'holding fast' the doctrines of evangelical truth in our churches, they will operate as dry rot in a building, weakening the fabric and gradually tending towards its destruction.[7]

It is significant that he drew attention to the lack of distinctive preaching that clearly identified the doctrines of grace, by which he meant Calvinism. He was asking whether preachers really believed in those doctrines any longer. The doctrine of particular redemption had long been one of the identifying marks of Particular Baptists. It was "widely regarded as a test of orthodoxy, and its discussion was a delicate issue."[8] To reject particular redemption was to adopt universal redemption; an Arminian doctrine. The drift away from particular redemption therefore was an indication of a significant undermining of evangelical Calvinism.

Ivimey's concerns were precisely those being expressed by Elven and Jones. He had also been one of the London pastors who attempted, but failed, to set up a General Union of Calvinistic Baptists in 1813. The doctrinal declaration drawn up then had followed a typical Calvinistic pattern. In 1832, when a new union was established, Calvinism was conspicuous by its complete absence. The "dry rot" appeared to have spread quickly.

It would however, be entirely unjust to suggest that Robert

---

[7] George Pritchard, *Memoir of the Life and Writings of the Rev. Joseph Ivimey* (London: George Wightman, 1835), 221-222.

[8] Robert W. Oliver, *History of the English Calvinistic Baptists, 1771-1892: From John Gill to C. H. Spurgeon* (Edinburgh: The Banner of Truth Trust, 2006), 166.

The Theology of Robert Hall Jr.

Hall was the only person responsible for the eclipse of Calvinism among the Particular Baptists during the first three decades of the nineteenth century. For examples, Daniel Turner, pastor in Abingdon, and Robert Robinson, Hall's predecessor in Cambridge had both embraced universal redemption, but neither of them was as prominent or as influential as Hall.

The decline of Calvinism was to become a predominant characteristic of Nonconformity in the British Isles during the nineteenth century. There was a shift away from Calvinism that reflected the "whole ethos of the times."[9] The Welsh preacher John Elias writing in 1831 pointed his finger across the Atlantic Ocean, expressing his amazement at the "confused and carnal" teaching of American divines. He continued, "The truths of the Bible respecting the covenants, the fall of man, original sin, the suretyship of Christ, the substitution in place of his people, the imputation of their sins to Christ and of his righteousness to them, are all darkened by those writers!"[10] Elias had in his mind the New England theologians Joseph Bellamy, Samuel Hopkins, and Jonathan Edwards, Jr., and he seemed aware of the impact these men had on teachers in England, such as the Congregationalist Edward Williams (1750-1813), a theological tutor at Rotherham.

These New England theologians had abandoned particular redemption well before Hall took up his labours in Cambridge and had also adopted the governmental theory of the atonement.[11] They were linking that theory with the doctrine of general redemption and thus effectually doing away with substitution. Hall

---

[9] Kenneth Dix, *Strict and Particular: English Strict and Particular Baptists in the Nineteenth Century* (Didcot: Baptist Historical Society, 2001), 270.

[10] Quoted by John Aaron in "The Translator's Preface," in Owen Thomas, *The Atonement Controversy in Welsh Theological Literature and Debate* (Edinburgh: The Banner of Truth Trust, 2002), xxviii.

[11] For further discussion of the impact of New England theologians, see Oliver, *History of English Calvinistic Baptists*, 166.

did not follow them in everything they taught but when the enquiring young Scotsman, Robert Balmer, asked Hall's advice about what to read on the extent of the atonement, Hall had directed him to Bellamy. Balmer himself became a key figure in the controversy over the extent of the atonement in the United Secession Church from 1841 to 1845. He maintained that the atonement was universal in is extent and his views were called into question.[12]

Arminianism was deemed by many to be more in tune with the age of romanticism than the apparent rigours of Calvinism. Richard Muller describes the change observing, "the 1830s marked the end of the era of Reformed confessionalism and could be called the era of deconfessionalisation."[13] That was certainly true among the Particular Baptists and the trend was already evident long before the 1830s. Caleb Evans was bemoaning the anti-creedal spirit in 1767. Fuller had died in 1815, Ryland in 1825. These men had far more in common with *The Second London Baptist Confession of Faith*. They, and their peers and colleagues in the Northamptonshire Baptist Association, were not responsible for the shift away from the Calvinism of the seventeenth century Particular Baptists.

Hall's role in the undermining of Calvinism

Hall lived at a time when doctrine and theology among the Particular Baptists as well as Nonconformity were changing. In this regard Hall was a transitional figure. Universal redemption became more and more the accepted doctrine but the whole system of confessional Calvinism was being attacked from different directions. Evangelistic work and missions called for a spirit of co-

---

[12] For details of this controversy see Ian Hamilton, *The Erosion of Calvinistic Orthodoxy: Drifting from the Truth in Confessional Scottish Churches* (Fearn, Ross-shire: Christian Focus Publications, 2010), 42–81.

[13] Richard A. Muller, *Calvin and the Reformed Tradition: On the Work of Christ and the Order of Salvation* (Grand Rapids, MI: Baker Academic, 2012), 549.

operation, rather than emphases on differences in doctrine. Winning the masses for Christ and an emphasis on practical Christianity tended to push doctrine to one side as relatively unimportant. In addition, the influence of Wesley and his open avowal of Arminian doctrine, followed by the doctrines and practices of Charles Finney (1792-1875) the American revivalist preacher, made an impact on both General and Particular Baptists. Liberalism from the continent was to make huge inroads into English Nonconformity especially in the second half of the nineteenth century. The latter in particular not only pulled down Calvinism but also seriously undermined evangelicalism. By the time John Clifford was in ascendency in the Baptist Union towards the end of the century, he could assert that in his opinion Calvinism was dead and buried.

Previous chapters have surveyed the views and practices of Robert Hall. At least four of those views and practices made a significant contribution to the undermining of Calvinism among the Particular Baptists.

Firstly, throughout his public ministry Hall preached universal redemption, basing his offers of Christ to sinners on the fact that Christ died for all men. Particular redemption was one of the characteristic doctrines of the Particular Baptists and of evangelical Calvinism, distinguishing them from the General Baptists.

To say that Christ died for all men, as Hall believed and preached, is to actually change the biblical meaning of salvation and redemption. Salvation does not mean that through Christ's death every human being is placed in a position of redeemability. When Christ died on the cross he actually purchased and procured the salvation of particular sinners. By holding to universal redemption Hall was radically changing the nature and purpose of the atonement. Even if he did not realise it, he was effectively diluting and restricting the saving power of Christ atoning work on the cross.

Robert Hall in Perspective

Unlike Hall, Spurgeon stoutly defended and preached particular redemption. Abraham Booth, Andrew Fuller and John Ryland were also firmly persuaded that particular redemption was biblical truth.

While Hall was a teacher at Bristol Academy he had rejected federal theology and the representative headship of Adam. He had denied original sin, positing that sin was an individual matter and that we were guilty only because of our own sins. Rejecting those doctrines had a domino effect leading to the distortion of the truths of Scripture. Whatever his views were in the last years of his life, by separating the atonement from federal theology, the covenant of grace and the representative headship of Adam, Hall made it much easier for himself and others to embrace universal redemption. A contemporary of Spurgeon, Hugh Martin (1822-1885), was not one of those "frosty spirited Calvinists" that Hall had encountered in Aberdeen. Rather he was a staunch defender of evangelical Calvinism. He was firmly persuaded that, "it is suicidal to sever the Atonement of Christ from the Covenant of Grace. The demands alike of theology and faith require a different treatment."[14]

Hall was mistaken to regard the differences between Calvinism and Arminianism as speculative. The rejection of particular redemption strikes at the heart of the biblical gospel because it effectively undermines the work that Christ accomplished on the cross as the all-sufficient redeemer of sinners. Adopting universal redemption disrupts the one plan and purpose of the triune God for the salvation of sinners. It leads to persons in the Trinity having contradictory aims. The electing work the Father and the work of the Holy Spirit are placed in conflict with the purpose of Jesus Christ, the Son of God. Paul Wells concludes that if it is affirmed:

that Christ made satisfaction for all without exception and

---

[14] Hugh Martin, *The Atonement: In Its Relations to the Covenant, the Priesthood, and the Intercession of our Lord* (Edinburgh: James Gemmell, 1887), 171-172.

procured salvation for all, the death of Christ is not in and of itself intrinsically efficacious. The Father chose some, the Spirit applies the work of Christ to some, but Christ died for all and procured salvation for them, albeit hypothetically, as all are not saved. This seems to be a mystery beyond the biblical mystery.[15]

Hugh Martin did not have Robert Hall specifically in mind as he was writing against later nineteenth-century proponents of universal redemption. Nevertheless his comments are pertinent. He asserted:

Piety will always maintain, without an argument, that when our Lord is called our Saviour it is not meant that He is the author of salvability, but the "Author of eternal Salvation" (Heb v. 9). And logic will maintain by an argument the simplest possible, that if the redemption purchased by Christ is merely salvability; and if we are made partakers of the redemption by Christ by the effectual application of *it* to us by His Holy Spirit; then we are made partakers merely of salvability: and so after all that the Father, Son and Holy Ghost have done for us, we are only salvable still![16]

By advocating general redemption Hall removed a key identification marker of Particular Baptists in one stroke and thereby narrowed the distance between Particular and General Baptists. It made the eventual union of the two groups almost inevitable.

Secondly, Hall failed to be distinctive in his preaching. He sincerely believed that he was preaching the whole counsel of God. Yet even at the end of his life, he did not actively and vigorously promote the distinctive tenets of historic evangelical Calvinism upheld by his father, by the Northamptonshire Association, and

---

[15] Paul Wells, "Amyraldianism," in *Sovereign grace o'er sin abounding*. Papers read at the 2018 Westminster Conference, 28.

[16] Martin, *The Atonement*, 171-172.

Robert Hall in Perspective

by Caleb Evans and his predecessors in Bristol Academy, men like Foskett and Beddome. He was also out of step with his Particular Baptist forefathers who had accepted *The Second London Baptist Confession of Faith* at the 1689 National Assembly.

Few could discern whether Hall was distinctly Arminian or Calvinistic in his writing and preaching. That was the assessment of the anonymous contributor to *The Pulpit*: "neither does he present the truth in any decisive character, of Calvinistic or Arminian; so that his sentiments on these points cannot be known from his works."[17] The differences between Arminianism and Calvinism were not crucial. On a number of occasions he expressed his preference for the mind-set of Richard Baxter, and remained very critical of John Owen, who had defended particular redemption.

The convictions of Andrew Fuller stand in marked contrast to Robert Hall. Writing to his friend John Ryland in 1803 regarding the controversy that had arisen between himself and Abraham Booth, Fuller expressed himself in no uncertain terms. He was not thinking about Robert Hall but the point he made is applicable to Hall's lack of distinctiveness.

> Mr. Baxter considers Calvinists and Arminians as reconcilable, making the difference between them of but small amount. *I have no such idea*; and if on account of what I have here and elsewhere avowed, I were disowned by my present connections [by which he meant the Particular Baptists], I should rather choose to go through the world alone than be connected with them [the General Baptists]. Their scheme appears to me to undermine the doctrine of salvation by grace only, and to resolve the difference between one sinner and another into the will of man, which is directly opposite to all my views and experience. Nor could I feel a union of heart with those who are commonly considered in the

---

[17] Anonymous, *The Pulpit* (1831): 287.

present day as *Baxterians*, who hold with the gospel being a new remedial law, and represent sinners as contributing to their own conversion.[18]

Hall regarded Fuller as too narrow and strict in his views, suggesting that Fuller by eyeing matters of doctrine too closely was driving an unwarranted and uncharitable wedge between Christians. For his part Hall made little of these differences of doctrine in the friendships that he maintained during his life, emphasising that piety and practical Christianity were more important than doctrine. Hall's perspective was much more in keeping with the spirit of the age than Fuller's, but it contributed to that "erosion of distinctives" that led to the decline of Calvinism. Truth not clearly preached in one generation is invariably lost in the next.

Thirdly, and closely related to his failure to be distinctive, was his disdain for creeds and confessions. Once again he appears to have been influenced by Richard Baxter and also John Locke. Like them Hall was opposed to the theological systems represented in such confessions as *The Second London Baptist Confession of Faith*. In an age that was intolerant of creeds and confessions nothing Hall said or did arrested or reversed that growing intolerance.

In the Northamptonshire Association and in each of the churches that comprised that association evangelical Calvinism was expressed by statements that embraced the "five points of Calvinism." The church book of Carey's former Leicester congregation had such a statement but there is no indication that Hall expressed agreement with it when he became the pastor. That statement was intended to be a summary, an abstract of the principles that were expressed in *The Second London Confession of Faith*. It was the common practice of the day for pastors to make their own confession of faith before the congregation. However,

---

[18] Andrew Fuller, *The Complete Works of the Rev. Andrew Fuller*, 3 vols. (Harrisonburg VA: Sprinkle Publications, 1988), 2:714. Italics added.

Robert Hall in Perspective

there is nothing on record to show that Robert Hall made such a public confession of his faith when he was appointed as a tutor and a preacher in Bristol, or when he became a pastor in Cambridge and then Leicester. His letter of resignation from Bristol in 1790 is the closest expression of what he believed at that time in his life. (His views, which he expressed in 1809, when he rededicated himself to God were intended for his private use.)

In 1855 when he was in his early twenties Spurgeon nailed his colours to the mast by republishing *The Second London Baptist Confession of Faith*. He was acutely aware of the significance of *The Confession* for the next generation and also had a clear grasp on its historical significance. The truths stated in *The Confession* were not going to be quietly ignored by Spurgeon. He continued,

> Here the younger members of our church will have a body of divinity in small compass, and by means of the Scriptural proofs, will be ready to give a reason for the hope that is in them.
>
> Be not ashamed of your faith; remember it is the ancient gospel of martyrs, confessors, reformers, and saints. Above all it is *the truth of God*, against which the gates of Hell cannot prevail.[19]

Hall when in his twenties displayed very different colours to Spurgeon. He rejected election, particular redemption, the federal headship of Adam and was not prepared to accept original sin, and the imputation of Adam's sin to his descendants. Neither was he consistently clear about justification by faith and Christ's imputed righteousness.

If Hall had held the views he entertained when he left Bristol in 1790, when Bernard Foskett first established the Western

---

[19] C.H. Spurgeon, "Foreword," *The Things Most Surely Believed Among Us.*

The Theology of Robert Hall Jr.

Association and what became Bristol Academy, he would have almost certainly been excluded. No-one ever called Hall to account for his views. Foskett's robust commitment to what he believed were scriptural doctrines clearly identify him as standing in solidarity with those men and churches who signed *The Second London Confession of Faith* at the National Assembly in 1689. He was an evangelical Calvinist. Likewise, Beddome's *Scriptural Catechism* espoused the same doctrines. The same could be said for Hall's father and his contemporaries, among them Fuller, Ryland, and Carey.

In the absence of any recognised doctrinal standards it is not difficult to see how and why a spirit of laxity became a growing tendency among the leaders of the churches and then the churches themselves. While Hall did appear to modify his views in later life it was these doctrines which were less and less believed in Hall's day and in the following generations. The importance of teaching these key doctrines of Scripture and making them clear against error remains. At the beginning of the nineteenth century there was a drift towards a broader evangelicalism. Calvinism slipped out of the picture. One of the reasons was that men like Robert Hall pruned their Calvinism and did not preach it distinctly and vigorously and actively promote or defend it. This pruning process proved a disaster in the long term as the tree almost died.

McNutt, has drawn attention to the fact that Hall was a preacher "who neglected theology in his preaching."[20] The differences between Calvinism and Arminianism were never mapped out in the sermons Hall preached. His hearers did not have the opportunity to evaluate what the scriptures taught nor what he believed on these issues. The differences therefore may

---

[20] Cody Heath McNutt, "The Ministry of Robert Hall Jr., The Preacher as Theological Exemplar and Cultural Celebrity" (PhD dissertation, Southern Baptist Theological Seminary, 2012), 160.

never have appeared to have been of any real importance to them. McNutt acknowledges that Hall was a catalyst for change and suggests that the reason was his neglect of a consistent and vigorous defence of Calvinistic theology rather than his abandoning or his modifying the doctrines of his Particular Baptist forefathers.[21] McNutt may be overstating his case because Hall had not consistently held to distinctive Calvinism throughout his ministerial life. There certainly was a prolonged period when he rejected each one of the "five points of Calvinism."

Finally, Hall contributed to the undermining of Calvinism by his espousal of open communion. He was fully persuaded that a closed table was nothing less that schismatic, creating a sectarian spirit. Hall was not the first Particular Baptist to raise these issues. Attention has already been drawn to the fact that there were both open and closed communion churches among the Particular Baptists. This had been true since their emergence in the seventeenth century.

The practice of open communion became increasingly accepted, especially after his death. This was due in large part to the strident campaign he undertook to promote an open table. He was also writing at a time when his views would find greater sympathy with his readers than perhaps fifty years before. There appeared to be a growing uneasiness about the practice of closed communion. Furthermore, his position as a recognised leader among the Baptists and Dissenters guaranteed a hearing for his book *Terms of Communion*. The desire for evangelical unity was growing and anything that suggested sectarianism was suspect.

The effects that his views had on church order and discipline should not be underestimated. Their impact was not fully felt until after his death when more and more Particular Baptists adopted the practice of open communion, narrowing the gap between

---

[21] McNutt, "The Ministry of Robert Hall," 160.

themselves and the General Baptists. The practice he advocated changed the structure and discipline of the local church, breaking down the pattern of believing, being baptised by immersion as a believer, becoming the member of a local church, and then sitting down as a church at the Lord's table. That was the pattern in the New Testament, which Hall admitted. Nevertheless he did not believe that pattern to be binding. His practice helped pave the way for open membership in subsequent generations which led to even greater changes in the authority and discipline of the local church. It meant, for example, that the decision as to who was to come to the table was taken out of the hands of the pastor or elders of the church and placed in the hands of each individual in the congregation.

Men like Ivimey lived long enough to see what was happening and grieved over the spirit of laxity that replaced the earnest zeal of men like Abraham Booth and Andrew Fuller, men devoted to defending the scriptural standards. Ivimey was not only concerned about maintaining the doctrines of grace but also the discipline of the New Testament that lay behind the practice of closed communion. Ivimey's fears were well-founded. Some men, like William Brock, were to advocate open membership.

Hall had set the ball rolling, even though he was not the only one to promote open communion among the Particular Baptists. He published his convictions in preaching and in print while he was in his prime in Leicester, and at a time when he was widely regarded as the voice of evangelical Dissent. His reputation and wide influence, therefore, were key factors in the promotion and acceptance of his views.

13
Is History Being Repeated?

No one Christian and no one denomination or group of churches is beyond correction or reproach. We have to acknowledge before God and before men that at times we are very inconsistent and the gap between the doctrines we hold and the lives that we lead is sometimes far too wide. The graces of humility, transparency, and sincerity are qualities that should be evident in all Christians in every age.

We must all stand before the judgment seat of Christ and while we live we must seek to maintain a good conscience before God and other men. Despite our differences with Robert Hall, we recognize he aimed to live as a man devoted to God. Yet at the same time we cannot ignore what he believed and preached if we are to learn from his life and work and not make similar mistakes. There were issues over which he was not transparent, issues that he omitted in his preaching.

Could it be that this generation is in danger of falling into the same situation that confronted the eighteenth and early nineteenth century English Particular Baptists? The decline in Calvinism was not restricted to them. It became widespread, wilting before the onslaught of liberal theology and the higher critical theories emerging from Germany. Robert Oliver comments on what happens when Calvinism ceased to be a force in English Nonconformity. Taking his lead from David Kingdon, he suggests that in the earlier part of the nineteenth century it was not so much a question of those doctrines being attacked but of them being

The Theology of Robert Hall Jr.

"quietly ignored."[1] This is akin to Ivimey's concern over the increasing laxity he observed in the churches.

By not distinctly declaring the doctrines of grace Hall was passing over the issues. Inevitably, in that kind of environment what anyone believes becomes relatively unimportant. This weakening of Calvinism which we have identified in Robert Hall opened the door for further decline, leading not only to the loss of Calvinism but to the fatal embracing of liberal theology by many churches. Furthermore, more and more stress was being laid on piety and experience, implying that doctrine was not of primary importance. The impetus for such changes can be traced back to men like Robert Hall.

He was regarded by many as the champion of evangelicalism, but that evangelicalism is not the same as the Protestant orthodoxy stated in the three seventeenth century confessions of English Nonconformity, namely *The Westminster Confession of Faith*, *The Savoy Declaration*, and *The Second London Confession of Faith*.

Does the church of Christ face the same danger today? Are the doctrines of grace, which we call Calvinism, being "quietly ignored?" In the 1960s and 1970s there was a notable resurgence of Calvinism among some Baptists in the United Kingdom and America. It began with the publication in 1958 of *The Things Most Surely Believed Among Us: The Baptist Confession of Faith with Scripture Proof*.[2] A small group of English Baptists published it. They were "convinced that it has a message for this generation, and believe its republication to be long overdue."[3] It was a reprint of Spurgeon's 1855 edition of the 1689 *Confession of Faith*.

---

[1] Robert W. Oliver, *History of the English Calvinistic Baptists, 1771-1892: From John Gill to C. H. Spurgeon* (Edinburgh: The Banner of Truth Trust, 2006), 354. He refers to Kingdon, "C.H. Spurgeon and the Downgrade Controversy" in Erroll Hulse and David Kingdon, eds., *A Marvellous Ministry* (Ligonier, PA, Soli Deo Gloria, 1993).

[2] *The Things Most Surely Believed Among Us* (London: Evangelical Press, 1958).

[3] "Foreword," *The Things Most Surely Believed Among Us*.

Is History Being Repeated?

Subsequently, this same confession of faith has been reprinted on many occasions and translated into different languages. There are now many churches world-wide who have adopted that confession of faith as their own.

However, on the broader evangelical front in the United Kingdom the differences between Arminianism and Calvinism continue to be glossed over because they are absorbed into a kind of "lowest common denominator" Christianity in the interest of Christian unity. Many evangelical churches have statements of faith which are not distinctively Calvinistic. The statements are left open-ended. They do not contain specific Calvinistic statements. Is that because they are being "quietly ignored" by the leaders of these churches or because those truths are no longer believed and preached by them? Sometimes those who insist on stating distinctive Calvinistic doctrine and making that the standard for a church and for fellowship between churches are regarded as being schismatic, because they are seen to be emphasising doctrines that are secondary and not essential for salvation.

However, if Calvinism is relegated and no longer held to be "primary truth" then it will be in grave danger of being "quietly ignored" and then forgotten altogether. Hall believed that the differences between Calvinists and Arminians were secondary. There is a crucial question to be asked. How can biblical Christianity be maintained unless it is clearly stated and vigorously preached? Furthermore, if Calvinism is the purest form of evangelicalism why would churches of the twenty-first century who claim to be evangelical want to confess less truth than their forefathers? How can such an approach possibly strengthen the church of Jesus Christ, or advance the truth of the gospel among the nations of the world and be glorifying to God? The doctrines of Protestant orthodoxy need to be in the forefront or they will be lost.

Preachers and churches therefore, need to be forthrightly and consistently transparent both publicly and privately. Hearers of the preached word need to be able to have the whole counsel of God placed before them. Hall's practice in preaching was to concentrate only on the things he regarded as of central importance, for example the deity of the Lord Jesus Christ, the authority of Scripture, the penal substitutionary atonement of Christ, the necessity of the new birth, and the importance of holiness. He was clear in distinguishing truth from error in such matters. However, in public he did not enter into controversy or distinguish truth from error in matters which he regarded as speculative. That approach could only be detrimental to the cause of evangelical Calvinism in his day. It proved to be the case in the decades after Hall's death.

Therefore, the need to maintain the doctrinal standards of the church of Christ by means of a full confession of faith is paramount. It may be objected that such a document is fallible and cannot replace the Scriptures. Furthermore, it may be objected that such a confession of faith will not guarantee that churches and individuals will not fall into error. Both those assertions are true. However, the confession of faith of a church or a group of churches is only a summary of what they believe to be the teachings of the Bible.

Broadly speaking, the attitude towards creeds and confessions of faith today continues to be largely negative. We are told by some that maintaining confessions of faith destroys liberty of conscience before God. Other voices say we have the Bible and do not need confessions and creeds. However, through the centuries Christianity has produced statements of faith in order to state and clarify the truth of what the Scriptures teach over against error. The church is described in the Bible as "the pillar and ground of the truth," (1 Timothy 3:15). That means that the revelation which God has given for the salvation of men has been entrusted to the church. She is portrayed in the Scriptures as an institution

Is History Being Repeated?

which was designed by God to preserve the truth and to defend it against error and against the attacks of its enemies. Thus by publishing a confession of faith the church is seeking to fulfil her God-given duty. That is what Hall's Particular Baptist forefathers in the seventeenth century did, men like William Kiffen, Hanserd Knollys, and Benjamin Keach, What happened during the nineteenth century among Particular Baptists and more widely among Nonconformists is an eloquent testimony to their costly failure to fulfil this duty and to their short-sightedness that led them increasingly to abandon the truth expressed in these creeds and confessions. Is the church of Christ learning from the past? If not, what happened in Hall's day will be repeated in our own day.

More recently the late Robert Martin has argued for the retaining of creeds and confessions. He gave four reasons for doing so.[4] He affirmed that a confession of faith serves as a useful means for the public affirmation and defence of the truth; it serves as a public standard of fellowship and discipline; it serves as a concise standard by which to evaluate ministers of the Word; it contributes to a sense of historical continuity. If those reasons are valid then there is clearly a significant gap between them and the emphases and practices of Robert Hall. It is scarcely surprising therefore, that the churches of Robert Hall's generation suffered from a decreasing doctrinal awareness.

The obituaries written and sermons preached on Hall's death bear testimony to the fact that he was held in the highest esteem by a wide variety of people. That reputation existed long before he died in 1831. He was regarded as the most eloquent living spokesman for evangelical Christianity. However, the fact remains that few read the works and sermons of Hall today. His works are not in demand whereas there is continued interest in the works of

---

[4] Robert Paul Martin, "The Legitimacy and Use of Confessions," in Samuel E. Waldron, *A Modern Exposition of the 1689 Baptist Confession of Faith* (Welwyn Garden City: Evangelical Press, 2016), 13-29.

The Theology of Robert Hall Jr.

Andrew Fuller and Charles Haddon Spurgeon. Their works continue to be printed in the present century. The shorthand code used by Fuller in his sermons has been cracked and we await the publication of additional sermons from his pen.[5]

The question naturally arises as to why Hall's works are not in demand today. During his life large crowds gathered wherever he preached. His command of the English language, his logical precision, and his overpowering eloquence were gifts that he used to maximum effect. Spurgeon was undoubtedly heard by those who merely wanted to hear a gifted orator, but his sermons and works are being published and read today because of the distinctive biblical gospel that he believed and preached and the lasting impact that they made on his peers and subsequent generations. Spurgeon, like Fuller before him, was an unashamed wholehearted evangelical Calvinist and a Particular Baptist. Sadly, the same cannot be said of Robert Hall.

It is sobering to reflect on the fact that this was the case even though he was orthodox in many of his convictions. He was persuaded of the importance of regeneration and that the necessary consequence of that work of God in the heart was a life of holiness, shaped by the law of God and motivated by the gospel of the Lord Jesus Christ. Hall was a man who preached and defended biblical fundamentals. There were serious questions raised about his evangelicalism while in Bristol and in Cambridge. But in Leicester and then again later in Bristol he showed himself to be an evangelical man. He believed in the inspiration and authority of the Bible. He preached the substitutionary atoning death of Christ and his physical resurrection of Christ. He ably defended other fundamental doctrines which were being challenged during his lifetime. Once he had embraced a full doctrine of the Trinity he maintained

---

[5] https://news.st-andrews.ac.uk/archive/divinity-code-cracked-by-student/ (Accessed 29 January 2019).

Is History Being Repeated?

those convictions throughout the rest of his life. Despite the early fears of Fuller and Ryland, Hall never adopted Socinian views that denied the deity of Christ. Socinianism and Unitarianism had gained a foothold in dissenting churches during the eighteenth century and came to expression in the teachings of Joseph Priestley in particular. Hall took his stand alongside Andrew Fuller, and capably defended the teaching of the Scriptures.

Furthermore, Hall also resisted both hyper-Calvinism and Antinomianism. These errors were to be found among Particular Baptists. Hall was also very committed to the work of missions. He was a very loyal supporter of the labours of William Carey and his colleagues in the Indian sub-continent.

The fact remains that Hall along with others, undermined the evangelical Calvinism of his forefathers and unwittingly contributed to the decline of Calvinism and to the "Downgrade" that confronted Spurgeon. Many could not see that this was the case during his lifetime, nor after his death. Cornelius Elven, William Jones, Joseph Ivimey and John Elias had sounded alarm bells. They might have been regarded as being out of step with the times because of the concerns they raised before and after Hall's death but what subsequently happened shows that their fears and concerns were not groundless. We have the benefit of hindsight and that gives us sharper insights. We are able to make observations and draw out significant lessons for this present day and future generations.

The aim of studying any part of church history is to learn from the men and women of the past. It is invariably a humbling experience. There are always positive things to be commended and imitated as well as mistakes to avoid. In Acts 20:17–38, Luke provided an eyewitness account of Paul's ministry in Ephesus. Biblical truth was paramount and nothing was 'quietly ignored.' The apostle Paul was a man who exercised a faithful preaching-teaching ministry both in public and in private. He carried out this ministry in the midst of trials and difficulties. In order to accomplish it, he "kept back nothing that was helpful, but proclaimed it to you" (v. 20). He went on to testify that he was "innocent of the blood of all men. For I have not shunned to declare to you the whole counsel of God" (vv. 26-27). In the following verse Paul spoke of "the church of God which he [Christ] purchased with his own blood". He testified that the redemptive work of Christ was an accomplished fact. By doing this he was affirming "that when Jesus died, his death actually redeemed, it actually procured everything essential to the deliverance or liberation of those for whom he died."[6]

Paul was a model preacher-teacher in this regard. As an apostle of Christ he was the mouthpiece of the Head of the church, the Lord Jesus Christ. In Scripture we have the whole counsel of God. Paul was committed to delivering the whole counsel of God. Nothing would be 'quietly ignored.' His ministry was exercised in an open and transparent manner both publicly and privately. His exhortation to the church leaders in Ephesus in regard both to themselves and to the church under their care serves as a poignant reminder to church leaders of their calling and duties. Here was man of strong conviction, or resolute courage, totally dedicated to his Lord, and consistently faithful as a preacher of Christ's gospel. The church of the Lord Jesus Christ stands in permanent need of leaders who follow the pattern of the apostle.

---

[6] Robert L. Reymond, *Paul, Missionary Theologian* (Fearn, Ross-shire: Christian Focus Publications, 2000), 401.

14
A Personal Testimony

If you have read this book up to this point it will be apparent to you that the author has not been considering Hall in some dispassionate manner, nor pretending that he is being totally impartial in his judgments. I would acknowledge that I am a wholehearted Calvinist whose sympathies lie with the theology of the great seventeenth century confessions of faith and in particular, because I am a Baptist, with *The Second London Baptist Confession of Faith*. Like Fuller, I am a Calvinist but not because I believe everything Calvin said. Like Spurgeon, I believe Andrew Fuller was one of the greatest Calvinistic Baptist theologians, but I do not agree with everything Fuller said.

Furthermore, I am persuaded with Spurgeon that Calvinism is but a nickname for the full biblical gospel. Yet Calvinism is not to be confined to the five points of Calvinism enunciated by the Synod of Dort to deal with the particular teaching of James Arminius and those who imbibed his teachings. Indeed Packer has pointed out that the five points present the Calvinistic doctrine of salvation in "a negative and polemical form, whereas Calvinism is itself essentially expository, pastoral and constructive."[1]

Calvinism has been defined in different ways by different people. Calvinism is Christianity in its purity. It is evangelicalism in its biblical fullness. The Old Princeton theologian, B.B. Warfield wrote, "Calvinism will not play fast and loose with the free grace of God. It is set upon giving to God, and to God alone, the glory

---

[1] J. I. Packer, "Introductory Essay" to John Owen, *The Death of Death in the Death of Christ* (London: The Banner of Truth Trust, 1959), 5.

and all the glory of salvation."² Calvinism has a very distinctive doctrine of salvation, emphasising with equal force each of the three words in the simple sentence, "God saves sinners."³ At the heart of Calvinism is the conviction that God the Father, through his Son the Lord Jesus Christ, working through the Holy Spirit whom he has also sent, is to be recognized as our one true and only Saviour. The death of Jesus Christ on the cross is not an isolated event in human history but rather the focal point in God's eternal plan to save sinners.

It is principally over the issue of the extent of the atonement that I disagree with Robert Hall. Throughout his life he claimed that general redemption was the only satisfactory basis for urging sinners to turn to Christ and be saved. I believe that he was not being consistent with the Scriptures at this very point. Rather, there is a unity in God's saving purpose. The New Testament writers speak of the death of Christ as the basis for God's offer of the forgiveness of sins. A sinner is forgiven when he or she repents and believes. Hall would have agreed with this. However, the question has already been asked and answered. What did the death of Christ actually achieve—potential or actual salvation? If it was the possibility of salvation, then a sinner must exercise faith to make it effective. If that is true we would in fact be saying it is not Christ whose saves us but rather our faith.

But the gospel proclaims the unity of God's saving purpose and that Christ actually saves "us all." All refers to those whom God predestined, called, justified and glorified, as Romans 8:30 makes clear. Faith is the hand that grasps hold of Christ. It is the means of salvation, yet as far as God is concerned it is also his gift. The death of Christ provides nothing less than the guarantee of

---

² Benjamin B. Warfield, *Calvinism Today*, https://www.the-highway.com/caltoday_Warfield.html

³ This is how J. I. Packer explains Calvinism in his brilliant essay first published in 1959. See Packer, "Introductory Essay," 1-25.

A Personal Testimony

the sinner's salvation, for all those for whom he specifically and personally died. In that way God is glorified, and there is no possibility of human boasting. We do not save ourselves, even by believing on Christ. From first to last it is God who saves sinners.

The wonderful consequences for the Christian who has been taught and humbled by the free grace of God is this—we come to enjoy communion with each person of the Triune God, the Father, the Son and the Holy Spirit in all the freeness of their grace towards us. On our part we are weak, helpless, guilty sinners deserving nothing less than God's wrath and condemnation and eternal punishment in hell. Now we can come into the presence of a holy God because of the blood of Jesus, Hebrews 10:19.

My enjoyment of God the Father, and my fellowship with him, rests in his eternal electing love, set upon me in Christ from before the foundation of the world. It is a love that is almost beyond belief but Scripture assures me that, "nothing shall be able to separate us from the love of God which is in Christ Jesus our Lord" (Rom. 8:39).

Furthermore, my enjoyment of God, the Son, and my fellowship with him, rests in the fact that he is my Redeemer. "He loved me and gave himself for me," said the apostle Paul in Galatians 2:20. When he died on the cross it was for me specifically and personally that he died, to actually save me from my sins, to actually secure my salvation and thousands more like me. My joy in him, and my assurance of salvation would be sadly diminished and undermined if he died only to secure the possibility of my salvation. He is my Prophet to teach me, my Priest who died for me and now constantly to intercede for me, and my King to rule over me and protect me from every danger.

My enjoyment of God the Holy Spirit, and my fellowship with him, rests on the fact that he is the one who effectively teaches me, shows me my Redeemer and applies God's free and saving grace to my heart, by renewing me, working faith and repentance in me, by sanctifying me, by assuring me that I am accepted in the Beloved, and counted as righteous in God's sight because of the obedience and blood of my Saviour Jesus Christ. The Holy Spirit is the Spirit of adoption, and the one who seals me for the day of redemption. He is the guarantee that I will persevere and enjoy that final inheritance with all the saints.

If God the Father had not sent his Son and his Spirit into this sinful world in order to fulfil his eternal purpose no one would be saved. If he had not first chosen fallen sinners in Christ and set his love upon sinners in eternity no one could possibly be saved. It is because of God's eternal electing love that there is a full and free salvation from sin in Christ Jesus.

Soli Deo Gloria

Appendix 1
The Disagreement between Dr Caleb Evans and Mr Robert Hall

John Harris, and Arthur Tozer, A pamphlet issued by them referring to the details of the disagreement of Robert Hall and Caleb Evans noted at length in the Church Meeting book, between November 1790 and January 1791, Bristol, Jan. 31, 1791. The pamphlet consists of an exchange of letters between Caleb Evans and Robert Hall, and three documents numbered I, II, III. It is held in Bristol Baptist College, G99A, 19428. The dilapidated document was copied by Roger Hayden, 5-6 June 2002. The original pamphlet is to be found in Bristol Archives, B Bond Warehouse (via Create Centre), Smeaton Road, Bristol, BS 1 6XN, 30251, *Records of Broadmead Baptist Church—1644-2009*. It is included in this book with the permission of Bristol Baptist College and the trustees of Broadmead Baptist Church.

Roger Hayden's introduction
A small dilapidated pamphlet, issued by John Harris and Arthur Tozer, Bristol, 31 January 1791, refers to the details of the disagreement of Robert Hall and Caleb Evans noted at length in the Church Meeting book, between November 1790 and January 1791. It consists of an exchange of letters between Caleb Evans and Robert Hall, and three documents numbered **1, 11** and **111**.

This document is paper 24 in the documents noted by Essex Lewis, archivist at Broadmead in c. 1920. It is the copy of Isaac Nash, of Redcliffe Street, whose name is one page 1, and inside there is a further "blurred" note from him on page 22 indicating, probably, that he had heard Dr Evans affirm that he would resign if Hall was re-elected. The note in ink has blurred over the years, and a damaged page means part of the note cannot now be known.

Roger Hayden added the following. It is important to note that in the eighteenth and early nineteenth centuries, the Broadmead ministers were pastors of two congregations. [1] the historic Broadmead Baptist Church; and [2] a parallel "Little Church" which comprised Independent members who declined believers' baptism.

Hayden's transcription has been lightly edited for this publication but no changes have been made to the wording. For clarity I have excluded his references to the page numbers in the original pamphlet. There are five places in the transcription which Hayden marked with *. One of those refers to the translation of a Latin phrase. The other four are left without explanation. It is possible that the state of the original pamphlet meant it could not be deciphered. There are breaks in the sentences. It may be that Hayden intended to return to the document and provide relevant notes at these points but for some reason he did not do so. It does not radically affect the reading of the pamphlet however.

Background notes on the document
The following pamphlet does not present Robert Hall in a favourable light. It was written by those who wrote in defence of their pastor Dr Caleb Evans. It is clear that there were two versions of events. The first was that of John Harris, Arthur Tozer, and Caleb Evans, the second was that of John Protheroe, John James and Robert Hall. They could not both be right and Harris and Tozer acknowledge that one or other of the parties was suffering from blindness. They were sure it was not them.

The whole pamphlet makes sad reading. In 1790 Robert Hall was a young man, 26 years of age who had returned to Bristol following his studies in Aberdeen, at the request of Caleb Evans. He became a pastor in the congregation and a tutor in classics at the

Appendix

Academy. Evans was 54 years of age and the much respected pastor of the historic Broadmead Baptist Church and principal of the Bristol Academy. Hall reached the conclusion that there had been a premeditated plan to remove him from Bristol and that outside influences had been brought to bear on Caleb Evans to effect his removal. At the meeting of the two parties at the Bristol Mansion House on Monday 13 December 1790 Hall produced a prepared paper which was seen as a personal attack on the character, conduct, and integrity of Caleb Evans. This paper was, as far as can be discerned, never published by Hall despite requests to do so. Caleb Evans stoutly rejected all the accusations laid against him. The matter was not resolved to anybody's satisfaction and Harris and Tozer decided to go into print for the impartial public to draw their own conclusions.

The matter was never resolved and questions still remain. Hall had been invited to preach in Cambridge for a month in the summer of 1790. He was then asked to return for a longer period. By July 1791 he had accepted the church's invitation to become their pastor. But he was evidently living in Cambridge before that date. He seemed glad to be away from Bristol. On 5 February 1791 just five days after Harris and Tozer had published their pamphlet Hall wrote to a friend Isaiah Birt telling him he was enjoying "the element of peace at least, if not happiness; and indeed after the tumults of strife and din of parties, quiet itself seems happiness." (Gregory, *Works*, 1:267).

On the other hand Caleb Evans died eight months after these events in August 1791. It may be that the stressful events of December 1790 and January 1791 were a contributory factor in his death.

Introduction to the pamphlet by John Harris and Arthur Tozer
The following Papers are printed for the sake of a more extensive and certain circulation that could be easily procured in any other

way. We have no intention of proceeding farther in this unpleasant business, having nothing new to offer that we think essential to the vindication of our characters, or Dr Evans's and being determined to leave the VALIDITY of our testimony, to the judgment of those who are acquainted with us, and who may read what we have written.

We have thought ourselves justified in printing No. 2, of the papers here produced, as our reply to it could not otherwise be perfectly understood, and in that paper itself an appeal is expressly made to AN IMPARTIAL PUBLIC.

The letters prefixed are inserted, the better to explain the nature and design of the meeting which afterwards took place, and to which these letters refer.

JOHN HARRIS
ARTHUR TOZER
Bristol, Jan. 31 1791

[to] Dr EVANS

Dear Sir,

It is now just six o'clock that I have time to write very little, but I would not satisfy myself without just informing you, that there are certain things relating to the affair depending, on which I earnestly wish for some friendly conversation and amicable discussion. Certain considerations have presented themselves to my mind, as if there were something like a premeditated scheme, and perhaps foreign influence exerted in my intended removal from Bristol. I have long resisted such impressions, but they force themselves upon me to a degree I cannot altogether resist. I should be happy to see you, either by yourself, or in company with any other common friend, when I can explain the nature and causes of my apprehensions more at large, and meet I hope with the satisfaction I so earnestly desire.

I am, dear Sir, with sincere respect
Yours &c
R[obert] HALL

Tuesday evening
7th Dec., 90.

[to] Revd Mr HALL

Dear Sir,

When you come to attend the pupils tomorrow, I shall have no objection to converse with you on the subject you mention. As to the *premeditated scheme* and *foreign influence* you speak of, I know nothing at all. I am willing to be examined upon that or any other subject you may think proper to discuss. I was as open as the day with you from first to last, till you thought proper, for so it has appeared to me, to desert me and enlist with those you style your friends against me.

Since that I have withdrawn from the business, and it has been out of my power, as well as my inclination to interfere any further.

Much pains have been taken to alienate your mind from me. I regret the success with which their efforts have in too great a measure been followed, but hope still to continue, what I have always been,

Your faithful, upright and zealous friend
C[aleb] EVANS
Tuesday evening, Dec. 7, 1790.

[to] Dr EVANS

Dec 8, '90 Wed morning

Dear Sir,

As I am well acquainted with the quickness of your temper and the impetuosity of my own, I must beg leave to decline conversing with you upon the subject in hand, without the presence of at least one more. I should prefer two, and have thought of requesting Mr John James to accompany *me* and whomsoever you choose will meet my perfect approbation. I should be glad of early information whether this proposal is satisfactory, and what time you would appoint. The presence of Mrs and Miss Evans will be perfectly agreeable to me or any others.

I am your's &c
R. HALL

Appendix

[to] Revd Mr HALL

Dear Sir,
As you have declined the meeting you proposed, and which I thought was to be an amicable one, I must for the present decline meeting you and Mr James, till I have fixed on some of mine to be with me.

C. EVANS
Wednesday morning
Dec 8, 1790

[to] Revd Mr HALL

Dear Sir,
Mr A. Tozer cannot make it convenient to attend me to a meeting with you and your friend, sooner than Monday evening next. If that time will be agreeable, we will fix the place and the hour of meeting as may be mutually convenient.

In the meantime while I am ready to receive in writing any communication you may think proper to make concerning the premeditated scheme and foreign influence, or any other subject you make think proper to introduce, and to return a written, explicit answer,

I am, Sir, your's &c
Wednesday afternoon, Dec. 8
C. EVANS

The Theology of Robert Hall Jr.

[to] Dr EVANS

Dear Sir,

I beg leave still to decline any discussion till the time you mention, which meets my perfect approbation. Particulars of the nature I shall bring forward are in my humble opinion better agitated in conversation, for *litera scripta manet* *

I am, your's &c
R. HALL
Wednesday evening
Gloucester Street
* *What is written remains*

[to] Dr EVANS

Dear Sir,

Upon my application to Mr James this evening to accompany me in our intended interview, he seems reluctant to engage in a business of this nature, except in conjunction with some other person; I have therefore by his earnest request, solicited the favour of Mr Protheroe's company on the occasion, which he has been so kind as to promise if it meets your approbation, hoping at the same time you will bring with you what number of friends you please. I should be happy to know the place and time of meeting.

I am, your's &c.
R. HALL
10th Dec. 90

Appendix

[to] Revd Mr HALL

You first proposed meeting me alone, unless I chose another person to be present. I agreed to meet and converse with you the next day. You then declined it, and made a second proposal of bringing Mr James with you. I agreed to it, and fixed on Mr Tozer to be with me. You said it met your perfect approbation. I proposed in the mean time exchanging our thoughts by writing. You declined it, and for the very reason for which I wished it, because *litera scripta manet*; a reason that would have equally applied to me as to you. Last night you sent me a third proposal; Mr James not chusing to be alone in the business, you tell me you have engaged Mr Protheroe, to whom I am sure I have no manner of objection. But upon my stepping out last night after supper to consult a friend upon the subject, I was advised to refuse this third proposal, because it was a third, and I was trifled with. But, fearing no man, and having a consciousness of my own integrity I accept it. And this evening having called upon the Mayor, am authorized to request you to bring your friends with you to the Mansion-house, Monday evening a quarter before eight precisely, to meet the Mayor, Mr Tozer and myself. Or should the Mansion-house be objected to, the Mayor will give us the Vestry at the above hour. If I should hear nothing from you to the contrary, I shall expect you at the Mansion-house, at the time mentioned.

I am, your's &c.
C. EVANS
Saturday, Dec 11, 1790

The Theology of Robert Hall Jr.

[No. I]

Mr Hall having proposed by letter a meeting with Dr Evans, and mentioned Messrs Protheroe and James as the gentlemen he had chosen to attend him; we at the request of Dr Evans attended the said meeting, which was held at the Mansion-house last Monday evening.

The design of this interview as expressed by Mr Hall was to have *an amicable discussion* of some particular points relative to a *premeditated scheme* which he apprehended had been formed, and *foreign influence*, which he supposed to have been exerted, respecting his intended removal to [from?] Bristol. The business was opened by Dr Evans, who desired the letters which had passed betwixt him and Mr Hall relative to this meeting might be read. This being done, Mr Hall produced a letter which he said he had the Saturday before and had intended sending Dr Evans. After *repeatedly* insisting that he would not be interrupted whilst reading it, he went through the whole without the least interruption whatever. The letter contained, in our opinion, many gross insults and bitter invectives against Dr Evans as well as misrepresentations of his conduct. We think it is our duty to add, that not a single fact appeared to us to be substantiated by Mr Hall that in the least reflected on Dr Evans's character or conduct. Through the whole evening's conversation which lasted nearly four hours, Dr Evans preserved a calmness of temper worthy the Christian and the Gentleman, notwithstanding Mr Hall was greatly irritating and reprehensible. In the course of the conversation Mr Hall insinuated that the resolution proposed by the Chairman at the Church Meeting, Lord's Day evening, the 5th instant was dictated by Dr Evans, the Chairman declared that *that* resolution originated with himself. Mr Hall answered to this effect, "*That* declaration implies that other parts of your conduct *did not.*" An insinuation as unhandsome as it was unfounded. Having stated nothing but facts, we

Appendix

leave those who may see this narrative to draw their own conclusions respecting them.

Mansion-house
Dec 17, 1790
JOHN HARRIS
ARTHUR TOZER

[No. II]

Having seen a paper signed by John Harris and Arthur Tozer, in which the conference betwixt the Revd Dr Evans and the Revd Mr Hall, at the Mansion-house, Dec 13, 1790, is, in our opinion very partially and improperly stated. We waited on J Harris, Esq: to satisfy ourselves whether that paper bore their signature, who acknowledging it did, we expressed our sensibility of the affront offered us, in circulating a writing of this nature without our concurrence or knowledge. We conceive it as a duty incumbent upon us as friends of Mr Hall. Thus publicly to point out the particulars wherein we imagine the statement of the above paper partial; and after representing some of the leading features of the conversation that took place, we shall leave the decision to the judgment of the impartial public.

In the paper to which we refer, it is stated that the purpose of the meeting as expressed by Mr Hall, was "to have an amicable discussion" of the points in question. We do not deny that Mr Hall used this expression, but it ought not to be forgotten that the note which contained it was conveyed to Dr Evans on the Tuesday evening, and that, betwixt that, and the conference on Monday, the conduct of Dr Evans in exerting his influence to obtain the decision of Thursday was so openly hostile as to render any idea of an amicable discussion chimerical; and it was to that meeting, held

215

the Lord's Day before as stated in the above paper, to which Mr Hall referred, when asked, if the resolutions did not come from Dr Evans; this mistake we think it proper to rectify.

It is declared, that the letter Mr Hall read at the Mansion-house, contained, "Many gross insults and bitter invectives against Dr Evans as well as misrepresentations of his conduct." To which we can only reply, that in our opinion it did not. That Mr Hall has found it necessary in his own vindication to read this letter in several places, in none of which it has been understood to contain either, and we apprehend, that its severity consists chiefly in its truth; a conviction is some measure strengthened by Dr Evans declaring he was not prepared to answer it.

It is declared that "that not a single fact appeared to us to be substantiated by Mr Hall that in the least reflected on Dr Evans's character or conduct." We are sorry to be obliged in this point to differ from the gentlemen who made this declaration; but must in conscience affirm, that there was not one charge of importance advanced by Mr Hall, to which Dr Evans gave a satisfactory answer. The charge of most consequence, which stated, that the resolutions of the last church meeting were occasioned by the personal influence of Dr Evans, appeared to us to be established upon the most indubitable evidence; for one of the Gentlemen acknowledged, that he had written letters and personally requested the attendance of members to vote against Mr Hall, and Dr Evans confessed he had come to a resolution to resign if Mr Hall should be re-chosen. It is declared, that, "Through the whole evening's conversation which lasted nearly four hours, Dr Evans preserved a calmness of temper worthy the Christian and the Gentleman, notwithstanding Mr Hall was greatly irritating and reprehensible." That Mr Hall was pointed and severe we readily acknowledge, the natural and perhaps proper expression of resentment for ungenerous treatment; but can by no means admit that his behaviour was incompatible with the character of the

Appendix

gentleman or Christian, which we must maintain he supported equally with Dr Evans.

Far from courting the approbation, or dreading the displeasure of any, we have given our opinion with the utmost freedom and impartiality, but we do not intend to prolong this disagreeable controversy, whatever remarks may be made on what we have written.

Bristol, Jan 12, 1791
JOHN PROTHEROE
JOHN JAMES

[No. III]

Having received a paper, by post, Saturday the 15th inst. Dated January 12th, and singed *John Protheroe* and *John James,* in which there is the most direct contradiction of the facts we have attested, in a paper signed by us at the Mansion-house the 17th December last, and which they say they have seen; we think ourselves obliged, in justice to our own characters as well as that of Dr Evans to make the following reply.

In this paper Messrs. Protheroe and James express, "their sensibility of the affront offered us, in circulating a writing of such a nature as that signed by us at the Mansion-house, without their concurrence or knowledge."

We answer. — That paper was occasioned *solely* by the reports which were circulated at the time, giving, what we *knew* to be a mistaken representation of the meeting at the Mansion-house; and by the indecent manner in which, it was well known Mr Hall had expressed himself respecting it. We had no idea of offering any affront to Messrs Protheroe and James, but merely to attest the truth, as far as we could judge of it, in vindication of the injured character of Dr Evans, on whose part, and by whose desire we attended the meeting. We still abide by everything in that paper, as *truth* to the best of our knowledge and belief, and nothing *but truth*, leaving aside every individual to receive or reject our testimony as their conscience may direct.

This paper further states, that Mr Hall's letter, proposing an "amicable discussion," was prior to the decision of the Thursday, after which "every idea of an amicable discussion was rendered (they say) chimerical, Dr Evan's conduct had been so *openly* hostile in exerting his influence to obtain the decision of the meeting."

We answer. — Mr Hall, previous to his reading at the Mansion-house the paper, which we state to have contained many gross insults and bitter invectives against Dr Evans, *desired it might be observed*, that he had written what he was going to read, the *Saturday week preceding*, (as we noted in our first paper) *that we might not imagine* any severe things which might be contained in it, proceeded from the disappointment, which it might be supposed had arisen since. The paper we complained of, had been drawn up *before* Mr Hall's *first* letter to Dr Evans desiring an *amicable discussion*, which in our opinion, *wholly* sets the explanation given by Messrs Protheroe and James, in their paper.

In reply to what we stated, that Mr Hall's paper contained many gross insults and bitter invectives Messrs Protheroe and James declare, *"that in their opinion it did not."* That Mr Hall had found it necessary in his own vindication to read that letter in several places, in *none of which*, had it been understood to contain either, and that they apprehended its severity consists chiefly in its TRUTH, a conviction (they add) in some measure strengthened by Dr Evan's declaring he was not prepared to answer it." To the first part of this charge, which fixes on us the most direct falsehood, we have no other answer, than a renewal of our former assertion; leaving all whom it may concern to judge for themselves

Appendix

our competency and credibility. We accordingly *re-assert*, that Mr Hall's paper DID contain many gross insults and bitter invectives against Dr Evans, as well as misrepresentations of his conduct; and further, that we know some whom told Mr Hall, that it contained such things, as no Gentleman would chuse to address to another, or words to that effect.

To the next assertion, "That its severity consisted chiefly in its *truth*, and that Dr Evans declared he was not prepared to answer it." We thus *publicly and solemnly* aver, that of its *truth no evidence* was produced at the Mansion-house; and, that whether *prepared* or not, Dr Evans *did answer it*, in our opinion, in the most candid and satisfactory manner.

We well remember, that when Mr Hall had read his paper through, Dr Evans asked the Gentlemen present, whether he was to be considered as a man of veracity, and worthy of belief in what he might say in answer to the charges brought against him; if not, he said, he had nothing to do but to take his hat and wish the company a good evening, as he certainly disdained to hold conversation with those who impeached his veracity. If they considered him as *a man of veracity*, he was ready to meet every *charge* that had been exhibited: (or words to that effect). This being assented to, Dr Evans addressed Mr Hall, upon the *impropriety and unfairness* of meeting him with an elaborate *written paper*, saying that he ought to have given him a copy of it, that he *might have been prepared to answer it*, that is, as we apprehend with a *written answer:* Dr Evans added, that every criminal (and such that paper made him) had a right to a copy of his indictment: Mr Hall replied, that Dr Evans *should* have a copy of it, to which Dr Evans answered, he should be obliged to him for it; and added, I do not shrink from any one of the charges you have advanced, nor from a *tittle* of them, but am ready to answer them in a most explicit manner. Here a long discussion began, which continued several hours; the details of which, could we recollect it with the most perfect accuracy, would be tedious to relate. At the opening of it, Dr Evans read a paper which he had drawn up November the 29th, with an intent, as he observed, to have read it at the Church Meeting, December the 5th, but *did not read it,* that it might not be said he had done anything to inflame the minds of the members at that Church Meeting, before he withdrew from it. This paper contains in our opinion, a full confutation of the invidious charges which had been brought against him, on account of his conduct at two former Church Meetings, the only ones held on this business at which he presided; and to every other charge, Dr Evans appeared to us to return a *cool* and *candid* answer.

Messrs Protheroe and James say, "They must in conscience affirm, that there was not one charge of importance advanced by Mr Hall, to which Dr Evans gave a SATISFACTORY answer." The two *grand* charges brought forward by Mr Hall, in his written paper were a *premeditated Scheme,* formed by Dr Evans to effect his removal, and his acting probably under *foreign influence.* Each of these charges were founded entirely on suspicion, and as appeared to us, had no other foundation than misconceptions and misrepresentations of circumstances to support them. As to the *first*, these gentlemen will themselves recollect, that Dr Evans, after it had long been canvassed, stood up and expressed himself to this effect. "I stand in the presence of God, and as far as I know what passes in my own heart, I solemnly declare there is no foundation for it whatever." This declaration might not be *satisfactory* to these Gentlemen, but it was entirely so to us. Mr Hall's reply they cannot have forgotten - "I do not believe it - your making use of such solemn appeals does not at all add to your credibility;" and then, or soon after added, "I would not believe it if you were to swear it at the altar." [at this point Hayden added an * with no explanation.]

These Gentlemen allow, that Dr Evans was "pointed and severe, but they stile his severity a natural, and perhaps proper

Appendix

expression of resentment for ungenerous treatment, " and add, "they can by no means admit, that his behaviour was incompatible with the character of the Gentlemen or Christian, which they maintain he supported "equally with Dr Evans." Let the public judge. We will only say that [a second *. It appears part of the text is missing.] We have been informed that Mr Hall, and one at least of his friends who were present with him at the Mansion-house, positively deny that he made use of the last expression here. Though he allows that he did at another time and upon another occasion, in the presence of A. Tozer. But these Gentlemen must certainly have forgotten themselves, as there is no one fact we are more certain of, and have in more perfect recollection, than that he did make use of these expressions, or expressions of the same import, in the conversation that passed at the Mansion-house the evening referred to. Had Dr Evans expressed himself in the manner Mr Hall did (as we have just mentioned) we should have judged it an unhappy illustration of the character of wither the *Gentleman* or the *Christian*. And of the ungenerous treatment given Mr Hall, and complained of by these Gentlemen we are ignorant.

Dr Evan's reply to Mr Hall, was to this effect. "Really, Sir, I am reduced to a most humiliating situation. You advance charges against me which no one can answer by [but?] myself, and which you will receive no answer to from me. Take away what you call my solemn appeals. All I mean is simply and absolutely to deny that there is any foundation for what you have advanced, I mean to deny it Root and Branch."

As to the charge of *foreign influence* Dr Evan's declared, that it had not the smallest foundation in truth: that so far from having employed the Rev. T. Dunscombe, as an emissary by artful methods, to effect Mr Hall's removal from hence, and to excite what Mr Hall called his *Gypsy Prophecies* of his removal; he had not wrote a word to him, nor to the Tomkins's of Abingdon, (whose names were introduced by Mr Hall), nor to any of his friends in London, or elsewhere, on the subject; and yet *this* part of the narrative has been read by Mr Hall to his friends *to our certain knowledge*, as late as the Saturday before he left Bristol.

Upon this charge we are happy to be able to refer to the following Letter, from Mr Dunscombe, dated 29th December 1790, in answer to a Letter from Dr Evans, giving an account of the Meeting at the Mansion-house. In this Letter are the following passages. "A thousand thanks to my dear friend, for his favour of the 21st instant – never did a letter so electrify me with astonishment and grief. I was astonished to find that you had been treated so cruelly and so unjustly, and I was astonished to find Mr Hall had been capable of acting so foolish, so infatuated a part. You have been a father to the man who now treats you with insult. He *knows* that you have been so, and he many times spoken to me in the strongest terms of his consciousness thereof, nor can I account for the strange revolution in his views and feelings respecting you. To *prove* the allegations brought against you, my testimony I perceive is necessary, and if proved, I become a criminal, and must be condemned with you. Poor man, little does he know of either of us, if he thinks us capable of uniting to form a plan, which would not stand the investigation of any tribunal that he could summon, or even a tribunal higher than that of mortals. I never mentioned his name to an individual of the Cambridge people, till I met him there. I was happy *to* meet him there, but it was *perfectly accidental*. My visit was purely that of friendship to the afflicted family, nor did I know that Mr Hall was expected there, when I sent the family word what day I intended being with them."

But these Gentlemen further say, and we confess we could not read it without astonishment, "The charge of the most consequence, which stated that the resolutions of the last Church Meeting were occasioned by the *personal influence* of Dr Evans, appeared to us to be established on the most indubitable evidence;

Appendix

for one of the Gentlemen present acknowledged he had written letters, and personally requested the attendance of members to vote against Mr Hall, and Dr Evans himself confessed he had come to a resolution to resign if Mr Hall should be re-chosen."

Whatever the opinion of these Gentlemen may be of our veracity, we have no inclination to dispute theirs – we are willing to persuade ourselves, that they believe what they here assert, to be true; but this we must declare in justice to ourselves, as well as the character of Dr Evans, that either *their* minds or *ours* must have been totally blinded by prejudice, as we find ourselves, according to our best recollection obliged to affirm the very reverse. So far was the principal charge as they call it, against Dr Evans, from being *proved* upon indubitable evidence, that it appeared to us upon *indubitable evidence disproved*. – And so far was Dr Evans from confessing he had come to a resolution to resign if Mr Hall was re-chosen, that he declared the contrary; and particularly, that he had *not* said it, whatever he might have thought: Upon which we perfectly remember Mr Hall replied, "If you thought it, I'll answer for it you said it." A reply which we considered as highly unbecoming and impertinent; and at the same time altogether inconsistent with the charge he had brought against Dr Evans as a man of art, duplicity and design. But upon this charge we have further to observe, that to our *certain knowledge* Dr Evans, for the sake of peace *actually advised the passing of the motion*, intended to be made for a re-invitation of Mr Hall, and to have presided at the Church Meeting, to be held for that purpose, – that his *not* being present was at the instance of his friends who advised him against it; and that of the *forming* and *determining* upon the resolutions which were proposed and carried at each of the two last Church Meetings, Dr Evans had not the least knowledge directly nor indirectly. Of the truth of this Arthur Tozer for himself declares, that he offered to make an oath before the Mayor, at the Mansion-house, if they would not believe him, without. – This he is still ready to do, and should this not be deemed sufficient, he offers to bring forward several Gentlemen equally acquainted with the business with himself to join him in the deposition. He further adds, that upon Mr Hall's charging Dr Evans with having used all his influence amongst his friends at Downend, which he, Dr Evans, positively denied, saying he had not been among his friends there, nor wrote to one of them – nor attempted to influence any single member of the Church; then, he, A Tozer, replied, that Dr Evans had nothing at all to do with the matter – that it was *he* who had wrote to Downend; and he was about giving his reason for so doing, but Mr Hall ungenteely interrupted him, by saying, "then I suppose you was Secretary, with several other candid observations." A Tozer denies having said he wrote to invite them, or personally requested any one member to come and *vote against Mr Hall*, as the paper of Messrs Protheroe and James affirms.

We beg leave to add, that with respect to the determination of the last two Church Meetings, we cannot help judging it impossible for any impartial person to censure them. The fact stands simply thus – Mr Hall sends a Letter to the church, expressing his determination to leave them, giving as his "reason for it, his differing with them in sentiment, and that he wished to be connected with a people of sentiments more congenial to his own, and where he should not be in danger of falling into the arts of collusion or incurring the vexations of honesty."

Upon some of the members calling for a re-invitation of Mr Hall (though he had uniformly professed his determination to go) the Church determines, that *before* they could judge the propriety of a re-invitation of Mr Hall they ought to know wherein that difference of sentiment consisted which he had urged as the reason for leaving them, and accordingly they desire three Gentlemen to wait on him, and request him to inform them. He does so in a written letter produced at the last Church meeting, December 9th, in the close of which he informs the Church that it was not in his

Appendix

power at present to accept any invitation to continue, as he held himself engaged in honour *as a probationer*, for six months to a respectable society in Cambridge. Upon this the Church agreed (without at all taking his sentiments into consideration) to thank him for his candour in the account he had given of them, and to resolve that, as Mr Hall had given notice to the Church in his first letter to leave them, and in his second, that he was a *probationer to another Church*; he was disengaged from all connection with us, and we were at full liberty to look out for another Minister as a successor. What there was ungenerous in all this we know not, but we *do* know and affirm that it was entirely without the knowledge, privity or consent of Dr Evans, that the resolutions of these Church Meetings were formed and agreed upon.

Mr Hall we remember, at the meeting at the Mansion-house, gave as a reason for his amazing alteration of sentiment respecting Dr Evans, that "recent events often threw a great light on past transactions;" and we think it is equally true that *past transactions often throw a light upon recent events*.

In a letter of Mr Hall's to Dr Evans, March 19.1790, are these words; " An expression you let fall to me in your letter struck me a good deal, you say, You hope you will be permitted to die in peace. Am I to understand this as intimating a suspicion of my having a design to make a party in the congregation? If this is your meaning you must think me the *meanest* and most *ungenerous* of men. No, were my talents for popularity as great as they are small, and could I draw the *whole* Meeting after me, I should blush at the idea of such conduct." If it be asked what then could have effected such a change in Mr Hall's views and conduct, as late recent events have manifested? Let the following extract of a Letter to Dr Evans from a particular friend of Mr Hall's and *with* whom Mr Hall conversed so late as November 25th last, answer. And let it be remembered that this conversation was long since a meeting with Dr Evans and Mr Hall had with a few friends at Mr James's

(November 8) and at which meeting (Mr Hall declared at the Mansion-house) his eyes began to be opened with respect to Dr Evan's conduct. [a third * suggests words that cannot be recovered] and further it should be [a fourth * presumably the same as the third] Mr Hall it has been privately affirmed denies having said at the Mansion-house, that his eyes began to be opened at the meeting he had with Dr Evans and a few friends at Mr John James's, Monday Nov. 8. But we cannot fail to recollect it, we remind him, that he assigned as the reason for it, the stress laid at that meeting on what he himself had mentioned to him in the morning of the day of *one person* only having made use of the term "Dr Evan's Party." Mr Hall then turned to the Mayor and mentioned the person's name he referred to. And further, Dr Evans stood up with surprize and said, – "Mr Hall, surely you forget that the meeting at Mr James's was on the Monday preceding the Thursday, on which you gave me so full a justification?" Upon which Mr Hall made some slight reply, saying, he did not give way to the impression, but resisted it, or words to that effect. [Again, some words missing] remembered that it was more than *ten days* after the last two Church Meetings, of which, and of Dr Evans's conduct at them Mr Hall so severely complains in his written paper which he read at the Mansion-house.

This letter is dated January 12th, 1791.

"Mr Hall when I saw him last, spoke of his obligations to your friendship – he told me he greatly respected and honoured you; indeed I never heard him speak more highly of you, and he said it would ever be his concern and happiness to have an interest in your respect. He spoke to me with the GREATEST ABHORRENCE, of some person or persons WISHING HIM TO QUARREL WITH YOU."

We could add much more; but we have no greater desire to prolong this disagreeable controversy that Messrs Protheroe and

Appendix

James can have; at the same time we could not be silent under the unprovoked attack they have made on our characters, as well as that of our worthy Pastor. If Mr Hall would fairly publish his paper, word for word as he read it at the Mansion-house, the public will then judge for themselves which account of it is the most just and accurate, that of Messrs Protheroe and James, or that of

JOHN HARRIS
ARTHUR TOZER

Bristol, Mansion House
Jan 25, 1791

Bibliography

Anonymous. "Obituary for Robert Hall." *The Evangelical Magazine and Missionary Chronicle*, 9. n.s. (1831): 158–159.

Anonymous, "A Critical Analysis of the Writings of the late Rev. Robert Hall, A.M.," *The Pulpit* (Thursday March 24, 1831): 430.

Anonymous, *The Things Most Surely Believed Among us: The Baptist Confession of Faith with Scripture Proofs, Adopted by the Ministers and Messengers of the General Assembly which met in London in 1689,* London: Evangelical Press, 1970.

Bebbington, D. W. *Evangelicalism in Modern Britain: A History from the 1730s to the 1980s.* London: Unwin Hyman Ltd., 1989.

Beddome, Benjamin. *A Scriptural Exposition of the Baptist Confession.* Birmingham, AL: Solid Ground Christian Books, 2006.

Bennett, James, *The History of Dissenters during the Last Thirty Years, 1808-1838.* London: Hamilton, Adams and Co., 1839.

Booth, Abraham. *An Apology For The Baptists: In Which They Are Vindicated From The Imputation of Laying Unwarrantable Stress on The Ordinance of Baptism. And The Charge of Bigotry in Refusing The Lord's Table to Paedobaptists.* London, 1778.

Brewster, Paul. *Andrew Fuller: Model Pastor-Theologian.* Nashville, TN: B&H Publishing Group, 2010.

Briggs, J. H. Y. *English Baptists of the Nineteenth Century.* Didcot, Oxon: Baptist Historical Society, 1994.

Bristol City Council, Port Cities, Bristol. http://discoveringbristol.org.uk/slavery/routes/bristol-to-africa/bristol-trading-port/slave-trade-entry/

Brown, Raymond. *English Baptists of the Eighteenth Century (1689-1815).* London: Baptist Historical Society, 1986.

Brown, Stewart J. "Protestant Dissent in Scotland," in Andrew C. Thompson, ed. *The Oxford History of Protestant Dissenting Traditions, Volume II: The Long Eighteenth Century c.1689-c.1828.* Oxford: Oxford University Press, 2018.

Carey, Eustace. *Memoir of William Carey, D.D. late missionary to Bengal; Professor of Oriental Language in the College of Fort William, Calcutta*. London: Jackson and Walford, 1836.

Copson, Stephen and Morden, Peter J. *Challenge and Change: English Baptist Life in the Eighteenth Century*. Didcot, Oxon: Baptist Historical Society, 2017.

De Yong, Peter Y. *Crisis in the Reformed Churches*. Grand Rapids: Reformed Fellowship, Inc., 1968.

Dix, Kenneth. *Strict and Particular: English Strict and Particular Baptists in the nineteenth century*. Didcot, Oxon: Baptist Historical Society, 2001.

Elwyn, T. S. H. *The Northamptonshire Baptist Association: A Short History*. London: The Carey Kingsgate Press Limited, 1964.

Evans, Hugh and Caleb. *A charge and a sermon together with an introductory discourse and confession of faith delivered at the ordination of Rev. Mr. Caleb Evans, August 18, 1767 in Broadmead, Bristol*. Bristol: 1767.

Finlay, Christopher J. "Mackintosh, Sir James, of Kyllachy, (1765–1832)," *Oxford Dictionary of National Biography*. Oxford: Oxford University Press, 2004, Vol. 35.

Finn, Nathan. *Help to Zion's Travellers*. Dallas, TX, Memphis, TN: Borderstone Press, LLC., 2011.

Fuller, Andrew. *The Complete Works of the Rev. Andrew Fuller*. 3 vols. Harrisonburg, VA: Sprinkle Publications, 1988.

Gibson, David & Gibson, Jonathan, eds. *From Heaven He Came and Sought Her: Definite Atonement in Historical, Biblical, Theological and Pastoral Perspective*. Wheaton, IL: Crossway, 2013.

Goadby, Bertha and Lilian. *Not Saints but Men: Or the Story of the Goadby Ministers*. London: Kingsgate Press, n.d.

Godfrey, W. Robert. *Saving the Reformation: The Pastoral Theology of the Canons of Dort*. Sanford, FL: Reformation Trust Publishing, 2019.

Gordon, Grant. *Wise Counsel: John Newton's letters to John Ryland, Jr.* Edinburgh: Banner of Truth Trust, 2009.

Gordon, James M. *Evangelical Spirituality: from the Wesleys to John Stott*. London: SPCK, 1991.

Bibliography

Graham, Lon. *All Who Love the Redeemer: The Catholicity of John Ryland Jr.* Eugene: Pickwick Publications, 2022.

Greene, John. *Reminiscences of the Rev. Robert Hall, A. M. Late of Bristol, and sketches of his sermons preached at Cambridge prior to 1806.* London: Frederick Westley, and A. H. Davis, 1832.

Gregory, Olinthus, ed. *The Works of Robert Hall, A. M. with a memoir of his life, and a critical estimate of his character and writings.* 6 vols. London: Henry G. Bohn, 1851.

Gregory, Olinthus and Belcher, Joseph, eds. *The Works of the Rev. Robert Hall. A.M.* 4 vols., New York: Harper and Brothers, 1849.

Hall, Robert, [Senior] *Mercy manifested: a letter to a friend, relating the dying consolations of Mrs. Jane Hall.* London: 1777.

Hall, Robert, [Senior], *Help to Zion's Travellers*, London: 1814.

Hall, Robert, Letter to Dr. John Ryland, 25 March 1792, Bristol Baptist College.

Hall, Robert, Two hundred and nineteen unpublished sermons preached at Leicester 1812–1823, 8 vols. Taken down in shorthand and transcribed by G. W. Riley. Donated by Dr. E. B. Underhill to the Angus Library, Oxford in 1886. (Angus Library Catalogue Nos. 35.g.16–23).

Hamilton, Ian, *The Erosion of Calvinist Orthodoxy: Drifting from the Truth in Confessional Scottish Churches.* Fearn, Ross-shire: Mentor Imprint for Christian Focus Publications, 2010.

Harris, John and Tozer, Arthur, A pamphlet issued by them referring to the details of the disagreement of Robert Hall and Caleb Evans noted at length in the Church Meeting book, between November 1790 and January 1791, Bristol, Jan. 31 1791. The pamphlet consists of an exchange of letters between Caleb Evans and Robert Hall, and three documents numbered I, II, III. It is held in Bristol Baptist College, G99A, 19428. The dilapidated document was copied by Roger Hayden, 5–6 June 2002. The original pamphlet is to be found in Bristol Archives, 30251, *Records of Broadmead Baptist Church—1644-2009*.

Hayden, Roger, ed. *Church Book: St. Andrew's Street Baptist Church Cambridge, 1720-1832, English Baptist Records 2.* Baptist Historical Society, 1991.

_____.*Continuity and Change: Evangelical Calvinism among eighteenth-century Baptist ministers trained at Bristol Academy, 1690-1791*. Chipping Norton, Oxfordshire: Nigel Lynn Publishing and Marketing Ltd., 2006.

Haykin, Michael A. G., "'The Sum of All Good,' John Ryland, Jr. and the Doctrine of the Holy Spirit." Churchman 103/104, 1989, 332-353.

_____. "The Elder Robert Hall and his *Help to Zion's Travellers*," The Banner of Truth, No. 343, April 1992.

_____. One *Heart and One Soul: John Sutcliff of Olney, His Friends and His Times*. Darlington: Evangelical Press, 1995.

_____. "Particular Redemption in the Writings of Andrew Fuller (1754-1815)" in David Bebbington, ed., *The Gospel in the World: International Baptist Studies in Baptist History and Thought*. vol.1, Carlisle, Cumbria/Waynesboro, GA: Paternoster Press, 2002, 107–128.

Haykin, Michael A.G., Paul, Roy M., Yoo, Jeongmo, eds., *Glory to the Three Eternal, Tercentenniel Essays on the Life and Writings of Benjamin Beddome (1718-1795)*. Eugene, Oregon: Pickwick Publications, 2019.

Hood, E. Paxton. *Robert Hall*. New York: A. C. Armstrong, 1881.

Hughes, Graham W. *Robert Hall*. London: The Carey Press, 1943.

Hughes, Graham W. *Robert Hall (1764-1831)*. London: Independent Press, 1961.

Hughes, Joseph. *The Believer's Prospect and Preparation described in a discourse delivered in Broadmead Meeting Houser, Bristol on Sunday morning, March 6, 1831, on the occasion of the death of Robert Hall, A. M*. London: Holdsworth and Ball, 1831.

Kingdon, David. "C. H. Spurgeon and the Downgrade Controversy," in Erroll Hulse, David Kingdon, eds. *A Marvellous Ministry*. Ligonier, PA: Soli Deo Gloria, 1993.

Kinghorn, Joseph. *Baptism a Term of Communion at the Lord's Table*. Norwich, 1816.

_____. *A Defence of Baptism a Term of Communion in Answer to the Rev Robert Hall's reply*. Norwich, 1820.

Bibliography

_____. *Arguments Against the Practice of Mixed Communion, and in Support of Communion on the Plan of the Apostolic Church; With Preliminary Observations on Rev. R. Hall's Reasons for Christian, in Opposition to Party Communion.* London: 1827.

Laws, Gilbert. Andrew *Fuller: Pastor, Theologian, Ropeholder.* London: Carey Press, 1942.

Lloyd-Jones, D. M. *Romans: An Exposition of Chapter 1, The Gospel of God.* Edinburgh: The Banner of Truth Trust, 1985.

Martin, Hugh. *The Atonement: in its Relations to the Covenant, the Priesthood, the Intercession of our Lord.* Edinburgh: James Gemmell, 1887.

Martin, Robert Paul. "The Legitimacy and Use of Confessions," in Samuel E. Waldron, *A Modern Exposition of the 1689 Baptist Confession of Faith.* Welwyn Garden City: Evangelical Press, 5th edition, 2016.

Morris, J. W. *Biographical Recollections of the Rev. Robert Hall. A.M.* First published 1833, reprinted in India, New Delhi: Isha Books, 2013.

Muller, Richard A. *Calvin and the Reformed Tradition: On the Work of Christ and the Order of Salvation.* Grand Rapids, MI: Baker Academic, 2012.

Mursell, J. P. *A sermon occasioned by the death of the Rev. Robert Hall, A.M., preached at Harvey Lane, Leicester, March 6, 1831 by J. P. Mursell.* London: Hamilton, Adam and Co., n.d.

Nettles, Thomas J. *The Baptists: Key People Involved in Forming the Baptist Identity.* 3 vols., Fearn, Ross-shire: Mentor Imprint for Christian Focus Publications, 2007.

Newlands, William. "Character of the Rev. Robert Hall, A.M." *The Manchester Times* (March 10, 1831): 510. www.britishnewspaperarchive.co.uk/viewer/print/bl/0000083/18310319/013/0006.

Oliver, Robert W. *History of the English Calvinistic Baptists, 1771-1892: From John Gill to C.H. Spurgeon.* Edinburgh: The Banner of Truth Trust, 2006.

Packer, J. I. "Introductory Essay," to John Owen, *The Death of Death in the Death of Christ.* London: The Banner of Truth Trust, 1959.

_____. *Knowing God.* London: Hodder and Stoughton, 1973.

Payne, Ernest A. *The Baptist Union: a short history.* London: The Carey Kingsgate Press Limited, 1959.
Pollard, Richard T. *Dan Taylor (1738-1816), Baptist leader and Pioneering Evangelical.* Monographs in Baptist History, vol.9. Eugene, OR: Pickwick Publications, 2018.
Poole-Connor, E. J. *The Apostasy of English Nonconformity.* London: Thynne & Co. Ltd, 1933.
Pritchard, George. *Memoir of the Life and Writings of the Rev. Joseph Ivimey.* London: George Wightman, 1835.
Reymond, Robert L. *Paul Missionary Theologian.* Fearn, Ross-shire: Christian Focus Publications, 2000.
Rimmington, Gerald T. *Thomas Robinson: Evangelical Clergyman in Leicester 1774-1813.* https://www.le.ac.uk/lahs/downloads/2001/GRimmingtonTLAHS2001.pdf
Rinaldi, Frank W. *The Tribe of Dan: The New Connexion of General Baptists 1770-1891: A study in the transition from revival movement to established denomination, Studies in Baptist History and Thought,* Vol. 10. Milton Keynes: Paternoster, 2008.
Ryland, John. *The Work of Faith, the Labour of Love, and the Patience of Hope Illustrated: In the Life and Death of the Reverend Andrew Fuller, late Pastor of the Baptist Church at Kettering, and Secretary to the Baptist Missionary Society, from its commencement in 1792.* London: Button and Son, 1816.
Sell, Alan P. F. *John Locke and the Eighteenth-Century Divines.* Cardiff: University of Wales Press, 1997.
Sellars, Ian. *Nineteenth-Century Nonconformity.* London: Edward Arnold Ltd., 1977.
Spurgeon, C. H. "Particular Redemption." *The New Park Street Pulpit.* Vol. 4. London: Passmore and Alabaster, 1892.
_____. "Concerning the College." *The Sword and Trowel* (1 April 1870): 146.
_____. *C. H. Spurgeon's Autobiography.* 4 vols., London: Passmore and Alabaster, 1899.
_____. *An All-Round Ministry: Addresses to Ministers and Students.* London: The Banner of Truth Trust, 1965.
Steadman, Thomas. *Memoir of the Rev. William Steadman, D. D.* London: Thomas Ward and Co., 1838.

Bibliography

Swann, Thomas. *A sermon occasioned by the death of the Rev. Robert Hall, A.M. of Bristol. Preached in Birmingham, on the Lord's Day, March 6, 1831, by Thomas Swann, Pastor of the Baptist Church, Cannon Street.* London: Hamilton, Adam and Co., 1831.

Sweeney, Douglas A. and Guezlo, Allen C., eds. *The New England Theology: From Jonathan Edwards to Edwards Amasa Park.* Grand Rapids, MI: Baker Academic, 2006.

Taylor, Michael. *Baptists at the Table: The Theology of the Lord's Supper among English Baptists in the Nineteenth Century.* Didcot, Oxon: Baptist Historical Society, 1992.

Thomas, Owen. *The Atonement Controversy in Welsh Theological Literature and Debate.* Edinburgh, The Banner of Truth Trust, 2002.

Trestrail, Frederick. *Reminiscences of College Life in Bristol during the ministry of the Rev Robert Hall, A.M.* London: E. Marlborough and Co., 1879.

Underwood, A. C. *A History of the English Baptists.* London: The Baptist Union Publication Dept., Kingsgate Press, 1947.

W. [Warren], R. [Robert] H. [Hall]. *The Hall Family.* Bristol: J. W. Arrowsmith, 1910.

Walker, Austin. *The Excellent Benjamin Keach*, Kitchener, ON: Joshua Press, 2015.

Warfield, Benjamin Breckenridge. "Edwards and the New England Theology," *Studies in Theology, Vol. IX, The Works of Benjamin B. Warfield.* Grand Rapids: Baker Book House, 1981.

_____. *Calvinism Today.* https://www.the-highway.com/caltoday_Warfield.html

Watts, Michael R. *The Dissenters, II: The expansion of evangelical nonconformity, 1791-1859.* Oxford: Clarendon Press, 1995.

Wells, Paul. "Amyraldianism," in *Sovereign Grace o'er sin abounding.* Papers read at the 2018 Westminster Conference.

Whelan, Timothy. "Robert Hall and the Bristol Slave-trade Debate of 1787-1788," *The Baptist Quarterly.* XXXVIII, No. 5, 2000, 212-24.

_____. "'I have confessed myself a devil': Crabb Robinson's Confrontation with Robert Hall, 1798-1800." *Charles Lamb Bulletin.* New Series 121, 2003.

———. "I am the greatest of the prophets: a new look at Robert Hall's mental breakdown, November 1804," *Baptist Quarterly*, 42, 2007.

———. *Nonconformist Women Writers 1720–1840*. London: Pickering & Chatto, 2011, 8 volumes.

Wilkin, Martin Hood. *Joseph Kinghorn of Norwich*. Norwich: Fletcher and Alexander, London: Arthur Hall and Co, 1860.

Minute Books

Arnesby Baptist Church, Minute Book, 1752–1819, Leicester Records Office, Wigston, Leicester. Catalogued as N/B/7/3.

Church Book for Harvey Lane Particular Baptist Church, Leicester, Leicester Records Office, Wigston, Leicester, I, 1760–1794. Catalogued as 24D71.

Particular Baptist Fund Minutes, 6 vols., Volume 5, 1774–1802, Angus Library, Regent's Park College, Oxford.

Unpublished theses

Campbell, Russell S. "The decline of Calvinism among British Baptists in the nineteenth century: a study of three ministers." D. Phil. thesis, University of Oxford, 2000. Referred to and quoted from with permission of the Modern History Faculty Board, University of Oxford.

Crocker, Christopher W. "The Life and Legacy of John Ryland Jr. (1753–1825): A Man of Considerable Usefulness—An Historical Biography." PhD thesis, Bristol Baptist College, 2018.

MacLeod, Angus Hamilton. "The Life and Teaching of Robert Hall, 1764–1831," Master of Letters thesis, University of Durham, 1957.

McNutt, Cody Heath. "The Ministry of Robert Hall, Jr.: The Preacher as Theological Exemplar and Cultural Celebrity," PhD dissertation, Southern Baptist Theological Seminary, 2012.

Robison, Olin C. "The Particular Baptists in England, 1760–1820," PhD dissertation, Oxford University, 1963.

Acknowledgements

During the research for and writing of this book a considerable number of people and institutions have contributed to its final version. In the first place I am indebted to two American friends for making available to me both the English and American editions of Robert Hall's works. Lenny Byerly is pastor of Grace Baptist Church of Dolgeville, New York State, and George McDearmon (now retired) was pastor of Ballston Lake Baptist Church, New York State. Those volumes became my essential working tools.

I have received constant encouragement from Robert Oliver (now retired) but formerly pastor of Bradford on Avon Baptist Church, Wiltshire. He was also kind enough to read through the first draft, to suggest grammatical corrections and to assess the actual content of each chapter. Michael Haykin, the Chair and Professor of Church History and Director of The Andrew Fuller Center for Baptist Studies at the Southern Baptist Theological Seminary, Louisville, Kentucky, urged me to research the life and doctrinal views of Robert Hall and was kind enough to invite me to lecture on Hall at Southern Baptist Theological Seminary in 2010. The content of those lectures has now been refined in the light of further research, but the opportunity to present that material was certainly an impetus to continue researching Hall. I am also indebted to him for reading through the manuscript and making a number of valuable comments which I believe have sharpened the arguments being presented. I would also like to express my heartfelt thanks to Dr Roy Paul, who edited an earlier version of my manuscript and to Dr Ryan Griffiths who suggested a number of changes in the earlier chapters which improved the flow of the book.

Dr. Cody McNutt was also involved in lecturing on Hall on the same occasion at Southern Seminary in 2010. He was then a pastor in Louisville and undertaking a PhD on Hall. He is now Senior Pastor at First Baptist Church, Covington, Georgia, having completed his studies in 2012. The interaction we enjoyed as we both grappled with Hall was mutually stimulating.

I first met Tim Whelan, Professor of English at Georgia Southern University, when we were both working in the Angus Library in Oxford. He provided details relating to Hall's days as a tutor in Bristol Academy and links with Caleb Evans and the Steele family, and has always been a source of encouragement. Paul Helm (now retired) but formerly a Professor of Theology at Regent College, Vancouver, and more recently Professor of Theology at Highland Theological College, Scotland, provided help in defining the influence of John Locke on English Dissent during the eighteenth century.

Michael Brealey, Librarian and Archivist at Bristol Baptist College very kindly made available to me photocopies, and placed on CD material held in the archives of the College. He also kindly allowed me to photograph other material relevant to Robert Hall. Revd. Emma Walsh and the staff at the Angus Library, Oxford were, as always, extremely helpful, especially in rediscovering the sermon notes taken down by G. W. Riley while Hall was preaching in Leicester. The staff of Dr. Williams's Library also helped me acquire background information for the life and ministry of Hall. The Bodleian Library, Oxford, kindly provided access to Russell S. Campbell's thesis on the decline of Calvinism in the nineteenth century. The staff at the Record Office for Leicestershire, Leicester & Rutland, in Wigston, provided me with help in deciphering diaries and church books relating to Hall. The staff at the Arnos Vale Cemetery, Bristol, proved very friendly and helpful in locating the Hall family graves in that cemetery.

Thanks are also due to Johnny Hutton, pastor of Arnesby

Acknowledgements

Baptist Church, Leicestershire, for giving me access to the church graveyard where Hall first learned to read from the grave inscriptions. My son, Jeremy, pastor of Maidenbower Baptist Church also gave me very helpful suggestions in finalising the last chapter of the book.

Other friends have encouraged me and urged me to complete the work. While I was a pastor at Maidenbower Baptist Church, Crawley, the church was happy for me to undertake research by spending days in libraries and visiting sites relating to Hall. However, completion of the book had to await my retirement in 2018, and then recovery from cancer and subsequent treatment, as well as the upheaval of downsizing and moving to Derby in 2020.

Finally, I want to thank Chance Faulkner, Editor and Co-Founder of H&E Publishing for his encouragement and editorial work that went into producing my book on Robert Hall.

Above all, I want to acknowledge the constant support and encouragement of my wife, Mai. As a young Christian she was introduced to The Westminster Confession of Faith by her Welsh Calvinistic Methodist pastor, Rev. H. H. Williams. She was familiar with the doctrines of evangelical Calvinism before we met. She has often joined me in my travels and notably was a great help in battling against briars and nettles in Arnos Grove cemetery as we endeavoured to gain close access to Hall's tombstone! She was very patient and understanding while I spent the first few months after my retirement in the study completing this book. I owe her more than words can tell.

Index

A

Antinomianism, viii, 20, 24, 52, 69, 115, 128, 135, 138, 139, 146, 151, 174, 199
Arianism, 20
Arminianism, vi, vii, 12, 18, 20, 27, 30, 49, 51, 54, 55, 59, 60, 65, 68, 83, 113, 114, 115, 116, 127, 128, 140, 149, 150, 155, 172, 175, 180, 181, 183, 184, 185, 187, 190, 195
Arminius, James, 201
Arnold, Thomas, 95
Ash, John, 66
Atheism, 36, 37, 41
Attwater, Jane, 81

B

Balmer, Robert, 26, 120, 133, 170, 183
Baptist Missionary Society, 5, 22, 164, 234
Baptist Union, 47, 48, 61, 129, 130, 164, 176, 177, 178, 184, 234, 235
Baxter, Richard, vii, 16, 25, 28, 68, 70, 115, 127, 135, 139, 163, 187, 188
Bean, James, 139
Beattie, James, 72
Beddome, Benjamin, 21, 66, 129, 155, 156, 187, 190, 229, 232
Belcher, Joseph, 4
Bellamy, Joseph, 26, 133, 135, 182, 183
Bennett, David, 103
Bennett, W., 25
Birt, Isaiah, 66, 207
Bogue, David, 103

Booth, Abraham, 20, 29, 156, 167, 169, 172, 175, 185, 187, 192
Bristol Baptist Academy, vi, vii, 5, 11, 20, 21, 33, 56, 129, 185, 187, 190, 207, 232, 238
Brock, William, 46, 176, 192
Brougham, Henry, 38
Brown, Archibald, 61
Brown, James Baldwin, 164
Brown, John, 26
Bunyan, John, 20, 146, 167
Burchell, Thomas, 177

C

Calvin, John, 16, 20, 61, 115, 136, 201, 233
Campbell, George, 71, 74
Carey, Eustace, 160, 162
Carey, William, vi, 2, 19, 22, 23, 38, 42, 45, 46, 52, 53, 99, 100, 115, 129, 160, 161, 162, 167, 177, 188, 190, 199, 230, 232, 233, 234
Chalmers, Thomas, 42, 109
Church of England, v, 38, 129, 139
Clifford, John, 60, 130, 184
Closed communion, 191, 192
Coleridge, Samuel Taylor, 99
Creeds, 16, 54, 59, 60, 67, 68, 70, 79, 151, 163, 188, 196, 197

D

Depression, 42, 59, 93, 94, 95
Doddridge, Philip, 67
Downgrade Controversy, 47, 129, 130, 194, 232
Dwight, Timothy, 157

E

Ecclesiology, viii, 168

Edmonds, Thomas, 101
Edwards Jr., Jonathan, 182
Edwards, Jonathan, 11, 18, 23, 25, 72, 154, 157, 235
Elias, John, 182, 199
Elven, Cornelius, 174, 175, 176, 180, 181, 199
Erskine, Ebenezer, 72
Erskine, John, 157
Erskine, Ralph, 72
Evangelical Calvinism, 9, 20, 21, 23, 24, 30, 43, 45, 46, 48, 52, 66, 113, 115, 116, 130, 147, 165, 181, 184, 185, 186, 188, 196, 199, 239
Evans, Caleb, vi, 11, 14, 20, 21, 54, 63, 65, 66, 67, 69, 70, 71, 77, 81, 82, 83, 84, 85, 89, 90, 92, 99, 111, 113, 129, 153, 183, 187, 205, 206, 207, 230, 231, 238
Evans, Christmas, 68
Evans, Hugh, vi, 20, 66, 169

F

Federal theology, 185
Finney, Charles, 184
Flower, Benjamin, 37, 40
Foskett, Bernard, vii, 20, 21, 66, 129, 187, 189, 190
Foster, John, 4, 55, 56, 98, 177
Francis, Benjamin, 66
Freeston, Joseph, 150, 152, 159
French Revolution, 35, 36, 38, 41
Frend, William, 35
Friendship, 4, 7, 11, 71, 72, 82, 97, 149, 151, 155, 156, 157, 158, 159, 162, 188, 222, 226
Fuller, Andrew, vi, viii, 7, 9, 13, 17, 22, 23, 24, 27, 45, 46, 47, 52, 56, 69, 77, 81, 100, 113, 118, 129, 138, 147, 151, 156, 164, 167, 169, 176, 177, 185, 187, 190, 192, 198, 199, 201, 229, 230, 232, 233, 234, 237
Fuller, Andrew Gunton, 147
Fullerton, William Young, 164

G

General Baptists, vi, 3, 20, 27, 47, 150, 158, 159, 178, 184, 186, 187, 192, 234
Gifford, Andrew, 66
Gill, John, 68, 70, 233
Goadby, Joseph, 159
Gould, George, 176
Great Awakening, 45
Greene, John, 5, 53, 96, 136, 137, 143, 149, 159
Gregory, Olinthus, 3, 4, 159

H

Hall (neé Smith), Eliza, 99, 101
Hall Jr., Robert
    as a preacher, v, vi, 1, 2, 5, 11, 13, 14, 34, 40, 50, 56, 58, 59, 78, 116, 146
    baptised, 11
    baptism, 110
    concern for the poor, 7
    death, v, viii, 1, 2, 38, 44, 176, 180
    Early theological sentiments, 11
    his catholicity, 7
    his conversion, 102, 103
    his orthodoxy, 11, 13, 14, 16, 92
    his statue, 6, 8
    his writings, 3, 8
    marriage, 101
    materialism, 14, 17, 65, 82
    mental breakdown, vii, 29, 42, 63
    mental breakdowns, 93, 97
    on open communion, viii, 5, 68
    on particular atonement, viii, 12, 25

Index

training at Aberdeen, v, 34
Hall Sr., Robert, v, 9, 11, 17, 18, 21
Hall, Eliza, 4
Hall, Jane, 11
Harris, John, 87
Henry, Matthew, 21
Hill, Rowland, 42
Hinton, John Howard, 48, 60
Hollick, William, 95, 102
Holy Spirit, 12, 16, 17, 24, 45, 50, 82, 108, 120, 121, 185, 186, 202, 203, 232
Hopkins, Samuel, 157, 182
Howe, John, 68
Hughes, Joseph, 2
Hyper-Calvinism, viii, 18, 20, 23, 24, 65, 115, 128, 138, 199

I

Irving, Edward, 42
Ivimey, Joseph, 180, 192, 194, 199, 234

J

Jay, William, 7
Jones, William, 174, 180, 199

K

Keach, Benjamin, 20, 146, 235
Kiffen, William, 20, 167, 197
Kinghorn, Joseph, 66, 167, 172, 173, 174, 176, 177, 232, 236
Knibb, William, 177
Knollys, Hanserd, 20, 197

L

Landels, William, 46, 176
Liberalism, 184
Lloyd-Jones, Martyn, 137
Locke, John, vii, 67, 68, 70, 188, 234, 238
Luther, Martin, 20

M

Mackintosh, James, 34, 37, 71, 97
Marshman, Joshua, 160, 177
Martin, Hugh, 185, 186

Morris, John Webster, 4, 30, 159
Mursell, J.P., 2, 6, 7, 8, 233

N

Napoleon, 39, 41
Nelson, Horatio, 39
New Connexion, vi, 27, 47, 158, 159, 178, 234
New Connexion Baptists, 27, 158
Newlands, William, 1, 2, 3, 48, 49, 51
Newman, William, 176
Newton, James, 71
Newton, John, 157, 230
Noon, John, 64
Northamptonshire Association, vi, 9, 19, 21, 22, 23, 29, 45, 52, 113, 115, 183, 186, 188, 230

O

Open communion, 5, 130, 167, 168, 169, 170, 171, 172, 174, 175, 176, 180, 191, 192
Open membership, 176, 192
Opium, 97, 98
Owen, John, 68, 69, 75, 187, 201, 233

P

Packer, J.I., 137
Parr, Samuel, 7
Particular Baptist Fund, 29, 236
Peace of Amiens, 39
Pearce, Samuel, vi, 66, 177
Pelagianism, 139
Perseverance of the saints, 19, 22, 114, 126
Philip, Binnie, 6
Phillip, James, 102
Phillips, James, 102
Pike, John Gregory, 177
Pitt, William, 38, 40
Politics, v, 6, 33, 34, 35, 36, 71
Porteous, Beilby, 38
Pragmatism, 169, 170, 176

Prayer, vii, 17, 23, 39, 52, 63, 64, 96, 110
Priestley, Joseph, viii, 15, 72, 81, 153, 199
Princess Charlotte, 7, 42

R

Rationalism, 67
Rippon, John, 66, 177
Robinson, Henry Crabb, 37
Robinson, Robert, 82, 84, 159, 169, 182
Robinson, Thomas, 7, 159, 234
Roman Catholicism, viii
Ryland Jr., John, vi, 7, 13, 15, 16, 21, 22, 45, 52, 56, 63, 65, 72, 73, 74, 77, 81, 102, 105, 115, 128, 129, 152, 153, 156, 163, 167, 177, 185, 187, 190, 230, 231, 232, 236
Ryland, John Collett, vi, 11, 19, 63, 167

S

Savoy Declaration, 46, 194
Scott, Thomas, 157
Second London Baptist Confession of Faith, 188
Second London Confession of Faith, viii, ix, 20, 29, 46, 66, 116, 117, 122, 123, 126, 127, 131, 147, 183, 187, 188, 189, 190, 194, 201
Separatist Independency, 20
Slavery, 33, 34
Smalley, John, 23
Socinianism, viii, 13, 15, 16, 24, 34, 35, 81, 82, 128, 146, 153, 199
Spurgeon, C.H., viii, 8, 60, 61, 65, 129, 130, 131, 147, 148, 152, 155, 162, 163, 164, 175, 180, 185, 189, 194, 198, 199, 201, 232, 233, 234

Stanford, Charles, 46, 176
Steadman, William, 55, 56, 66, 104, 177, 234
Steele, Anne, 90, 92
Steele, Mary, 90
Stennett, Samuel, 29
Stepney Academy, 176
Strict communion, 167
Strong, Nathan, 133
Suicide, 93
Sutcliff, John, vi, 22, 23, 45, 66, 153, 232
Swann, Thomas, 2, 235
Synod of Dort, 28, 114, 121, 126, 201

T

Taylor, Dan, 27, 158, 177, 178, 234
Thomas, Joshua, 66
Timms, Joseph, 101
Toleration Act, 139
Toller, Thomas, 7, 69
Tomkins, Joseph, 91
Tozer, Arthur, 87
Traill, Robert, 146
Trestrail, Frederick, 5
Turner, Daniel, 167, 182

U

Unitarianism, 199

W

Warburton, William, 72
Ward, William, 160, 177
Warfield, B.B., 201
Watts, Isaac, 67
Wesley, John, 27, 28, 109
Westminster Confession of Faith, 46, 72, 194, 239
Whitefield, George, 42
Wilberforce, William, 97, 157
Williams, Edward, 182

Other books by Austin Walker

www.hesedandemet.com

www.ingramcontent.com/pod-product-compliance
Lightning Source LLC
Chambersburg PA
CBHW021057080526
44587CB00010B/276